VARIETIES

AN ANTHOLOGY

my writings

ESSAYS, HISTORY, POLITICS, HUMANITARIAN, ACTIVISM, EDITORIALS,

SPEECHES, COMMENTARIES, AND MY LIFE

CESAR D. CANDARI, M.D.
FCAP EMERITUS

The book cover was designed by
my nephew Benjamin C. Candari IV,
an architect, AIA Principal
of FSC of Honolulu, Hawaii

This book was printed in the United States of America

To order the book, call/email
(702) 269-6490
drcdcmd@cox.net

Author/Publisher
Cesar D. Candari, M.D., FCAP Emeritus

Library of Congress Control Number: 2012910747

ISBN   1477534741

EAN   9781477534748

FOREWORD

"VARIETIES An Anthology" were my previous writings, editorials, speeches, opinions and commentaries. In it I emphasized the values that played a very important role in my life. I have nurtured, labored, and ultimately reaped the fruits of that seed to the heart's glorious delight. If these writings of my journey will touch or influence the course of someone's life, then I will have the boldness to say that the mission of this book has been accomplished.

These collections are my own, a selected writings of variety of subjects expressing my voice to be valued and learned from the principles I have religiously followed. Some writers are 'struggling to be heard above the conformist din of modern existence.' I wish to share my views and opinions on issues of daily events with no hesitation. To choose what printed words to go with, I go for first-person most of the time.

How I selected my subjects were simple. I am a people observer.

They say every writer is original. I am a medical doctor, but I don't write only medicines. I believe in being a writer that goes to the general public's interest in my desire to inform and to share. There are many dreams and thoughts to explore. The skyline springs with thoughts and ideas. Freshen them with effusive luster.

Am I within journalistic norm? Every time I decide and tackle a title, I confine myself to "get the cream" and survey with concerns, albeit with confidence that it is an 'apropos of absolutely nothing but amazement.' A subject is always an inspiration; it spurs me to dig over the theme realize the interest lies within the limits of reason. To offer the readers in terms of my viewpoint, I analyze how to provide a source of motivation for one to be successful in life and in their relationship with others! They are inspirational topics and stories that enlighten the heart, mind and soul.

I firmly believe in what you impressed you expressed!

On my graduation in high school as valedictorian, I wrote my valedictory address. I had my experience as an orator, however, writing was not my forte. Foremost, the theme in the valedictory speech was "A Dream Comes True". After delivering the speech to my classmates, I remembered feeling like I had accomplished a small piece of writing, which was my own. That was how my flavor for writing begun.

I take pride in my articles, which were a big challenge to write. I frequently get stuck. I struggle to get unstuck so I can continue to churn out pages of brilliant phrases. I realize that a simple and straightforward manner of writing is best.

In an introspective analysis of what I had gone through in my life, I have to reprint my memoirs from my first book "Success is a Journey". Reprinting of one's autobiography in a second book is proper. Benjamin Franklin has done it. I wish to share these memories with the young, growing Filipinos to guide their personal growth on having dreams, goals and desires. I wish my words to spur the future generations of Filipino Americans to make great achievements and emulate others with good works.

Mundane as one may say - for there are more refined and intellectually written publications, more authoritative than "VARIETIES An Anthology" - but I take an author's pride. Whatever the ultimate assessment of this book will be, it is an accurate glimpse of my life on this earth and is truly my own collections of articles and writings.

ACKNOWLEDGEMENT

FIRSTLY, I WISH TO thank my dear wife Cely and life partner for fifty years. You have been an inspirational guiding force and have helped me tremendously both mentally and spiritually. I would never have been what I am today without my dear wife. I was so lucky that from the time I came to the United States; you have helped keep track of every event in my life - letters, speeches, articles - so that this book was completed quickly and efficiently.

It is with great joy and pride to have my children who inspired me. Thank you very much.

I would also like to thank my friend Steven Vendeland, a writer, editor, founder and president of Ambassador's Ink.

I am very grateful to those of you, my friends and colleagues who has read my writings for your support and appreciation of what I have expressed over the years.

DEDICATION

*To my dear wife Cely. Without her, this
Book would not have been possible.*

CONTENTS

CHAPTER ONE ★

PHILIPPINES MY NATIVELAND

I hope to stand firm enough to not go backward, and yet not go forward fast enough to wreck the country's cause.

- ABRAHAM LINCOLN

BRIEF PHILIPPINE HISTORY- PAST AND PRESENT

Dateline, July 2011

THE 1980s HISTORY of the Philippines is of extreme interest to all Filipinos. I am writing this essay after my strong anti-Marcos involvement starting in 1985. I became a devoted supporter of Movement For Free Philippines (MFP).

The following is a summary of interesting tidbits of history of the Philippines for every Filipino American to know. These are extracts taken from glimpses of Philippine conditions from Spain's colonization to the present democratic Philippines. Although it may appear to be a late story to tell, I hope this information will educate many Filipinos.

Today, the country is being subjected by oddity of events that it is a less-attractive place to live in permanently. As a retired physician, I thought of our country as my favorite place of retirement; many other Filipinos working abroad have similar plans. We all now know that it is a politically beleaguered homeland that several are having second thoughts about it.

The overwhelming events in the Philippines today...the civic, social, political and economic pictures...convey a sad story. From the beginning of the Spanish rule up to the present time, the disparity between the rich and the poor is estimated at thirty percent middle-class and rich and seventy percent economically disadvantaged class and poor. The People-Power Revolution in 1986 was a historical event that could never be forgotten by all Filipinos no matter where they were in those days.

Under Spanish Rule: In 1521, when Magellan used fire in burning the homes of our forefathers in Mactan off Cebu Island, Lapu-Lapu rose and took up arms. He and his warriors killed Magellan and several of his European soldiers along the shores of Mactan Island. Lapu-Lapu was a hero and could be considered the forerunner of a nationalist – even if the archipelago at that time was bogged down in tribal wars. Interestingly, the Filipino nation was not born despite the defeat of Magellan. We were under Spanish rule for more than three centuries (1565-1898). The intolerable abuses of the Spanish regime resulted into the formation of a group of reformist movement that later paved the way for the Philippine Revolution. Native firebrands launched revolutions in many parts of the archipelago. Not one succeeded. A young doctor-writer, Jose Rizal, used his pen to expose the brutalizing, depressive and inhumane treatment of the Spanish colonizers. Dr. Rizal was arrested and then executed by a firing squad at Bagumbayan on December 30, 1896. This spurred the Katipunan that was organized by our heroes Andres Bonifacio and Emilio Aguinaldo. Bonifacio and Aguinaldo engaged in an ugly infighting resulting in the execution of Bonifacio. They failed to coalesce their forces and fight side by side against the enemy, and the leaders lost their souls to greed and thirst for power.

In 1898 The American-Spanish War ensued. Commodore George Dewey invaded Manila Bay and overpowered the dull Spanish Navy. The Spaniards eventually surrendered to the Americans.

American Time: On June 12, 1898, in Cavite el Viejo (now Kawit), Cavite, Philippines, the KKK (Katipunan) patriots of General Aguinaldo proclaimed the Philippine Declaration of Independence. With the public reading of the Act of the Declaration of Independence, Filipino revolutionary forces under Gen. Emilio

Aguinaldo proclaimed the sovereignty and independence of the Philippine Islands from the colonial rule of Spain. However, on December 10, 1898, the Americans annexed the Philippines with Spain by the Treaty of Paris. This brought about the Filipino-American war in February 1899 that lasted for three years; 4,000 American soldiers lost their lives. Filipinos were outgunned, with 250,000 to 1,000,000 were killed in the fighting. This led to the capture of Aguinaldo by U.S. forces on March 23, 1901. On July 4, 1902, U.S. President Theodore Roosevelt proclaimed a full and complete pardon and amnesty to all people in the Philippine archipelago that had participated in the conflict, effectively ending the war. The Philippines remained an American colony from 1902; in 1935, a semiautonomous Philippine Commonwealth was inaugurated in Manila with Manuel L. Quezon as president and Sergio Osmeña as vice-president. This became the United States-based Philippine government-in-exile during the Japanese occupation. Much learning took place on democratic principles, structure and governance.

Japanese Occupation: The Philippines came under the Japanese empire from 1941-1945, which produced disaster, devastation and annihilation of the Filipino people from the Japanese imperialist forces. You all remember the Death March in Bataan. General Douglas McArthur fled to Australia with a promise: "I SHALL RETURN!" The American forces returned in October 1944 to liberate the country. Manila City was the second most-devastated city (after Warsaw, Poland) in the world during World War II.

Our country celebrated the independence of the Philippines from the Americans on July 4, 1946. Hukbalahap (Hukbong Bayan Laban sa Hapon) led by Luis Taruc waged bloody war against the government in a communist rebellion. From 1947 to 1972, six presidents were elected under the democratic system, namely Roxas, Quirino, Magsaysay, Garcia, Diosdadao Macapagal, and Marcos. Our politicians and bureaucrats learned to engage in graft and corruption. A common slogan from politicians was "What are we in power for?" The Philippine economy in the 50s and 60s was said to be good, surpassing Asian countries. However, the gap between the rich and the poor remained the same.

Dictatorship: Proclamation No. 1081 (Proclaiming a State of Martial Law in the Philippines) was signed on September 21, 1972, by Mr. Marcos. It was invested with dictatorial powers and hundreds of presidential decrees, many of which were never published before they took effect.

With the stroke of a pen, President Marcos closed the Philippine Congress and assumed its legislative responsibilities.

Under the command of the president, the military arrested opposition figures, including Benigno Aquino, Jr., journalists, student-and-labor activists and criminal elements. Approximately 30,000 detainees were kept at compounds run by the Philippine Army or the Constabulary. Weapons were confiscated, and "private armies" connected with prominent politicians and other figures broke up. Newspapers were shut down; the mass media was brought under tight control.

Years of dictatorial abuse followed, as crony capitalism shackled free enterprise. There was near economic collapse, and the middle class was slowly demoralized. The gap between the rich (30%) and poor (70%) widened, as the people remained in a quagmire. Mr. Marcos claimed that martial law was the prelude to creating a "New Society" based on new social and political values.

President Marcos, his wife and a small circle of close associates, the crony group, felt free to practice corruption on an awe-inspiring scale. During this time, Mr. Marcos called for self-sacrifice and an end to the old society. However, in the "New Society" Marcos' cronies and his wife, former beauty queen Imelda Romualdez-Marcos, were alleged to willfully engage in rampant corruption. Although always influential, Imelda Marcos built her own power base with her husband's support during these years. As governor of Metro Manila and Minister of Human Settlements (a post created for her), she exercised significant powers. When martial law was lifted in 1981 and a "New Republic" was proclaimed, very little had actually changed. Marcos easily won re-election.

The beginning of the end of the Marcos era occurred when his chief political rival, Liberal Party leader Benigno "Ninoy" Aquino, Jr., was assassinated on August 21, 1983. Mr. Aquino had just disembarked from an airplane at the Manila International Airport when an assassin shot him to death at the tarmac. Before that, Mr. Marcos had jailed the opposition leader for eight years, then sent to the United States for medical treatment and was subsequently exiled in Boston, Massachusetts. Several Marcos cronies were charged with the crime but later acquitted; however, the court convicted some of the soldiers who had escorted him out of the plane and into the tarmac. Ninoy Aquino became a martyr and his murder became the proximate cause of popular indignation against a corrupt regime.

Mr. Marcos claimed that martial law was the prelude to creating a "New Society" based on new social and political values. Marcos was considered the quintessential plutocrat, having looted billions of dollars from the Filipino treasury.

Ninoy Aquino became a martyr, and his murder led to popular indignation against a corrupt regime of Marcos.

Edsa Revolution: The Catholic Church, a coalition of old political opposition groups, the business elite, the left wing, and even factions of the armed forces began to exert pressure on the regime. Feeling confident with the support given by the Reagan White House, Marcos called for a quick presidential election on February 7, 1986.

When the Marcos-dominated National Assembly proclaimed Marcos the winner, Cardinal Jaime Sin and key military leaders - Minister of Defense Juan Ponce Enrile and acting Chief of Staff of the Armed Forces Lieutenant General Fidel V. Ramos - rallied around the apparent majority vote winner, Corazon Cojuangco Aquino, Ninoy Aquino's widow.

The People-Power Movement – a popular uprising of priest, nuns, ordinary citizens, children, and supported by military units – ousted

Marcos eventually. The dictator fled on the supposed day of his inauguration on February 25, 1986. It brought Corazon Aquino to power in an almost-bloodless revolution. People Power was our shining glory! The whole world applauded our saintly courage, our dignified defiance, and our bloodless solution to expel a dictator. We were the toast of all freedom-loving countries, the envy of all oppressed people. These made news headlines as "the revolution that surprised the world." The majority of the demonstrations took place at Epifanio de los Santos Avenue, known more commonly by its acronym EDSA, in Quezon City, Metropolitan Manila. It involved more than 2 million Filipino civilians along with political, military and religious figures.

The Philippines after the Revolution: After the 1986 EDSA revolution, Cory Aquino became president. During the Aquino presidency, Manila witnessed six unsuccessful coup attempts, the most serious occurring in December 1989. Coup attempts by Greg Honasan and his fellow Reform-the Armed-Forces Movement leaders harassed the amateur Aquino presidency. The unbelievable and ignorant voters elected Honasan as a senator later. Is it not a crime to be a leader of a coup? It certainly should be.

She was virtuous, full of probity, sincere and with good intentions for the country. But what happened under Cory? Power struggles, political squabbles, and the infighting for juicy deals harassed her presidency. The real murderer of her husband was never found. Sad to say, after the indomitable EDSA revolution, the Filipino resolve didn't happen. The Land Reform of Cory was never perfect. Hacienda Luisita remained untouched. People Power was **"ningas kugon"** power. Since 1986, what has improved? I say nothing. There is that historic continuum of growing socio-economic inequality, rampant political corruption and a host of other intractable problems and *numero-uno* - massive levels of poverty. Cory did not leave a shining legacy. Her presidency was considered a disaster. She announced a revolutionary government but did nothing revolutionary. A writer Jose Sionil stated, "she transformed the EDSA I revolution into a restoration of the oligarchy."

The poor suffered terribly. Democracy may have returned, but the economic growth was additionally hampered by a series of natural disasters, including the 1991 eruption of Mount Pinatubo that left 700 dead and 200,000 homeless.

The alleged billions of dollars that the dictator Marcos stashed away abroad were never recovered.

After Cory Aquino, Fidel Ramos was elected as president. He was a proponent of privatization, less government, more private sectors! The economy went on a roll. But all of Ramos' gains during his presidency faded away into thin air. The poor became poorer than ever.

Because he was a popular movie actor, Joseph 'Erap' Estrada was elected president. He enjoyed widespread popularity, particularly among the poor moviegoers. In October 2000, however, Mr. Estrada was accused of having accepted millions of pesos in payoffs from illegal gambling businesses. The House of Representatives impeached him, and he was forced from office on January 20, 2001.

Politically, it is a despicable country. To win an election you must be filthy rich. Filipinos in general have to be responsible; however, they are noted to be openly immature in our politics. Between a handsome movie star and an honest-and-brilliant political scientist, many people will vote for the "reel" celebrity.

Vice President Gloria Macapagal-Arroyo (the daughter of the late President Diosdado Macapagal) was sworn in as Estrada's successor on the day of Erap's departure. We thought effulgent, eternal splendor finally arrived. We were inspired that Malacañang regained its honor and dignity. But more total failure happened instead!

More catastrophes happened. The peso plummeted to a horrifying US$1 to P51. Graft and corruption ruled the country. Estrada was pardoned and now running again for president of the Archipelago. Despite a number of policy reforms by the administration of Arroyo, the Philippines continued to face an endless number of challenges. Businesses were continued closing shop. Thousands of workers were being retrenched. Prices of food and gasoline were very high. The streets had become permanent garbage dumps creating stench throughout the neighborhood. Maggots multiplied leading to the spread of diseases, thereby creating a health epidemic multiply to spread diseases. The whole nation was witnessing sickening crimes attributed to the inept people in the government.

The whole nation was witnessing sickening crimes attributed to the inept people in the government. Gloria Arroyo's accession to power was further legitimized by the mid-term congressional and local elections held four months later when her coalition won an overwhelming victory. Her initial term in office was marked by fractious coalition politics as well as a military mutiny in Manila in July 2003, after which she declared a month-long nationwide state of rebellion.

Gloria Arroyo in her Machiavellian maneuver declared in December 2002 that she would not run in the May 2004 presidential election but she reversed herself in October 2003 and decided to join the race. She was re-elected and sworn in for her own six-year term as president on June 30, 2004.

Electoral sabotage was alleged in years 2004 and 2007 elections. Graft and corruption, plunder and thievery ruled the country.

In 2005, a tape of a wiretapped conversation surfaced bearing the voice of Arroyo asking an election official (the famous "Garci" manipulator) if her margin of victory could be maintained. She was caught on tape talking to then Comelec Commissioner Virgilio Garcillano, seeking assurances from the poll official of a one million-vote margin over the late Fernando Poe Jr. in the 2004 elections. The tape sparked protests calling for Arroyo's resignation. Arroyo admitted to inappropriately speaking to an election official, but denied allegations of fraud and refused to step down. This election was perceived to be the dirtiest and most tainted election in the country's history.

Arroyo unsuccessfully attempted a controversial plan for an overhaul of the constitution to transform the present presidential-bicameral republic into a federal parliamentary-unicameral form of government.

More impeachment cases were filed against her up to the last days of her nine-year reign, but she survived them all. For instance, in 2006, disillusioned soldiers staged another uprising. Her husband and her son Mikey were both in trouble for alleged corruption scandals.

If the assumed multi-millions of dollars in the banks of the Arroyos are true, clearly she perpetuated an atrocious regime of mass fraud and thievery during her presidency. Another one in question was the $503-million North-rail project. This is only a microcosm of a presidential plunder that must face justice.

To the Filipinos, these alleged colossal corrupt deals and questionable justice system are sickening to the stomach. How I wish Noynoy could wake up and exercise his righteous power, that corrupt officials must face justice, that the guilty must be put to jail! I truly hope and pray that the present government of Noynoy shall not lose the battle against corruption and poverty. We must find the momentum to move forward.

What we need are economic, civility, justice and accountability. Most of all, we must end the poverty in our country. The dispensation of the latter rests with the rich and the government. What is needed is the sacrifice on the part of the affluent to share their wealth and the intelligent planning and vision on the part of the government to spur economic development. Doing so will go a long way in alleviating the economic plight of our people.

Because of the hard life and endemic abject poverty, the people learned to make sarcastic jokes about those in government. A common joke I heard was that while there was only one Marcos who stole the people's money, there were hundreds of Marcoses in the Aquino administration.

We know that Mrs. Aquino was honest, admired for her probity, but the people around her were not, as evident from a lack of dramatic changes from the Marcos regime. If 'under the table,' was the order of the day during Marcos' time, it was 'under the table, 'over the table' and even the 'table itself' in the present administration.

There was respect for civil liberties, but pundits as feeble and fractious also were associated with Aquino's administration. Several attempted coups staged by disaffected members of the Philippine military hampered a return to full political stability and economic development.

All these reflect the desperation of Filipinos during their perpetual war against poverty, inefficiencies in general, and problems of civility and social order. I pray that the present government is not losing the battle.

PHILIPPINE POLITICS
WITH BUMBLED VERSION

Dateline, March 2012

WE CELEBRATED THE independence of the Philippines from the Americans on July 4, 1946. During the two decades and a half that followed as a democratic country, six presidents were elected and served one after the other in peaceful transition. On September 21, 1972, Marcos issued Proclamation 1081, which declared martial law over the entire country. Under the command of the president, the military arrested opposition figures, including Benigno Aquino, Jr., journalists, student-and-labor activists and criminal elements. Approximately 30,000 detainees were kept at compounds ran by the Philippine Army or the Constabulary. Weapons were confiscated, and "private armies" connected with prominent politicians and other figures broke up. Newspapers were shut down; the mass media were brought under tight control. With the stroke of a pen, President Marcos closed the Philippine Congress and assumed its legislative responsibilities.

During the 1972-1981 martial law period, invested with dictatorial powers, Mr. Marcos issued hundreds of presidential decrees, many of which were never published before they took effect Years of dictatorial abuse followed, as crony capitalism shackled free enterprise. There was near economic collapse, and the middle class was slowly demoralized. The dictator destroyed the economy of our country.

The beginning of the end of the Marcos era occurred when his chief political rival, Liberal Party leader Benigno "Ninoy" Aquino, Jr., was assassinated on August 21, 1983. Mr. Aquino had just disembarked from an airplane at the Manila International Airport when an alleged assassin shot him to death at the tarmac. The People-Power Revolution in 1986 was a historical event that could never be forgotten by all Filipinos no matter where they were in those days. The People-Power Movement – a popular uprising of priest, nuns, ordinary citizens, children, and supported by military units – ousted Marcos eventually.

The dictator fled on the supposed day of his inauguration on February 25, 1986.

It brought Corazon Aquino to power in an almost-bloodless revolution. People Power was our shining glory. I am one of the critics who would censure Cory for wasting the chance of a new beginning and not doing enough during her administration to uplift the Filipino people. From Cory Aquino, FVR, Joseph "Erap" Estrada and Gloria Macapagal Arrroyo, the Philippines were marred by hopeless civic, social, political, and economic problems. The poor gets poorer. We are jubilant Filipinos with Noynoy Aquino III, as the 15th President of the Philippines. We are, however, faced still with an array of problems. There is so much to be desired about the Philippines that we know today. It is not free from the ravage of economic bondage. There is so much greed, dishonesty, opportunism, frustration, and unfathomable graft and corruption in the government. Do you know what *Buwaya* means? These are crocodiles in our government now, young and old officials of the country gnawing the government that devour our wealth. Nobody stops them. How Noynoy Aquino can correct this is beyond my imagination. How I wish he could. The current hullabaloo in the Philippines, the problem of the former President and now congresswoman Gloria Macapagal Arroyo is looming constitutional crisis resulting from the DOJ's disregard of the SC TRO allowing the Arroyos to leave Manila in a rush to have medical treatment. Or is it an escape from being prosecuted? There is indeed now a constitutional crisis between the Executive and Judicial branch of government. Recently, GMA was arrested (hospital arrest) for electoral sabotage in 2007 – a non-bailable case. The present debacle in the Philippine Supreme Court is declared by many as unlawful to allow the "escape of GMA" at daylight, of going out of the country in the guise of medical treatment. Arroyo is alleged to have committed a wide range of corrupt acts during the nine years she was in power, including bribery and cheating to win the 2004 presidential elections; the plunder case against Arroyo over the scuttled $329-million National Broadband Network (NBN) deal.

The allegations were all denied. The former president is also facing six or more plunder charges... as Filipinos we have to do our share on defending our country.

It is alleged multi-millions of Arroyo's dollars are stashed in unknown places abroad. According to news releases, GMA had planned these escape months before she became a congresswoman. Will she be on house arrest or in government hospital arrest? Will justice be served? ... As Filipinos we have to do our share on defending our country.

To backtrack in a nutshell this was what transpired: GMA took over the Presidency following the impeachment of former President Joseph "Erap" Estrada in 2001. In spite of a number of policy reforms by the then administration of Gloria Arroyo, the Philippines continued to face important challenges. Again, the whole nation was witnessing sickening crimes attributed to the inept people in the government. Gloria Arroyo's accession to power was further legitimized by the mid-term congressional and local elections held four months later when her coalition won an overwhelming victory. Her initial term in office was marked by fractious coalition politics as well as a military mutiny in Manila in July 2003 led by Lt. Antonio Trillanes IV, to expose corruption in the government and in the military, was subsequently quelled. She declared a month-long nationwide state of rebellion.

As I stated earlier "Gloria Arroyo in her Machiavellian maneuver declared in December 2002 that she would not run in the May 2004 presidential election but she reversed herself in October 2003 and decided to join the race."

She was re-elected and sworn in for her own six-year term as president on June 30, 2004. In 2005, a tape of a wiretapped conversation surfaced bearing the voice of Arroyo apparently asking an election official (the famous "Garci" manipulator) if her margin of victory could be maintained. She was caught in tape talking to then Comelec Commissioner Virgilio Garcillano seeking assurances from the poll official of a one million-vote margin over the late Fernando Poe Jr. in the 2004 elections. The tape sparked protests calling for Arroyo's resignation. Arroyo admitted to inappropriately speaking to an election official, but denied allegations of fraud and refused to step down. This election was perceived to be the dirtiest and most tainted election in the country's history. Attempts to impeach her failed later that year. More impeachment cases were filed against her up to the last days of her nine-year reign, but she survived them all. For instance, in 2006, disillusioned soldiers staged another uprising. Her husband and her son Mikey are both in trouble for alleged corruption scandals. If the multi-millions of dollars in the banks of the Arroyos are true, no question she perpetuated an atrocious regime of mass fraud and thievery committed during her presidency.

Another one in question was the $503-million North-rail project. This is only a microcosm of a presidential plunder that must face justice. GMA is facing 6 more additional alleged plunder.

With all these problems, Arroyo probably thought nothing could go wrong. But Newton's Law, or "karma" if you will, is finally catching up on her. Of all people Erap Estrada just proclaimed recently that this is the Karma for Arroyo. Many people use the term without knowing the meaning of karma.   " If one sows goodness, one will reap goodness; if one sows evil, one will reap evil. In Hinduism, karma refers to the "totality of our actions and their concomitant reactions in this and previous lives, all of which determines our future." Thus, if you do something bad to some people, something bad will also befall you later.

Using all resources at her disposal, including the liberal disbursements of the people's money, she finished her term in full. She even managed to win a seat in the House of Representatives, representing her province of Pampanga after her presidential term was over.

Because she survived them all, Arroyo probably thought nothing could go wrong. But again Newton's Law, or "karma" is catching up on her. For every action, there is a corresponding equal and opposite reaction. The time of reckoning has come.

However, this is not over yet. The SC led by Chief Justice Renato Corona Arroyo's midnight appointee and GMA's lawyers are fighting back to declare the arrest of GMA to be unlawful and can be reversed.

There is nothing to be said for the Arroyo presidency something categorically optimistic. Her presidency has been nine long years of incompetency, plunder, waste, misconduct, and fractiousness.

To the Filipinos, these colossal corrupt deals; the questionable justice system is sickening to the stomach. How I wish Noynoy could wake up and exercise his righteous power- that corrupt officials must face justice and if proven guilty must be put to jail! Stop impunity. All these, of course, reflect the desperation with which the Philippines were fighting its seemingly perpetual war against poverty and governmental inefficiency in general and the problems of civility and social order in particular. I really hope and pray that the present government of Noynoy shall continue to fight and win the battle. Noynoy Aquino must have the responsibility to lead the country and propel it to an industrialized nation in the years to come; no more graft and corruption, and those who erred must face justice.

Every statement and action in this writings is factual. Every bumble is a matter of record and completely verifiable.

ECONOMIC FREEDOM FOR OUR COUNTRY
THE PHILIPPINES

Dateline, January 2011

MANKIND DISCOVERED DEMOCRACY not once but many times. Filipinos fought the *guardia civil* of the Spanish regime; we had skirmishes with the *Americanos* in the 1900s; and we were guerillas during the Japanese occupation. We finally rediscovered democracy at the indomitable EDSA revolution; however, although we have regained our freedom, we are faced with an array of problems. We are burdened with vast economic, social and political conflicts, and so we are not completely free. As one Philippine government official stated, the cry is as much for justice as it is for economic freedom, law and order, and rice and fish. Virtually 70% of the Philippine population is trapped in the vicious cycle of poverty and exploitation. There is much to be desired about the Philippines that we know today; it is not free from the ravages of economic bondage. Filipinos continue to wallow in sordid living conditions and unimaginable poverty complicated by insurgencies, unresolved civil strife and army coups. There is a sense of hopelessness in the business community, with so much greed, dishonesty, opportunism and frustration in the government.

The poor and the oppressed masses in the Philippine society have always gotten the worst of both worlds. With greater propensity, their political leaders have been unresponsive to their economic plight, a dismal crisis that has been encumbered by the deficiency of the country's democratic process.

While Filipinos now enjoy democracy, life is still difficult. Unemployment is endemic; the price of food and other commodities is continually rising. The devastation brought by the recent earthquake and typhoons has compounded the miseries of the people. There is an expression of despair in their eyes: what can we do? We ask if there will be deliverance from these crippling maladies.

We cannot live by love of democracy and freedom alone--we also need economic justice and power, of which the dispensation rests with the rich and the government. The affluent need to make sacrifices by sharing their wealth and intelligent planning; in addition, the government must have the vision to spur economic development. Doing so will go a long way in alleviating the economic plight of our people.

The Philippines needs to rebuild itself by infusing capital and mobilizing its natural resources. It is a potentially rich country with a lot of natural resources. Its deposits of nickel, iron, copper, manganese, high-grade chromium, gold, and other base metals remain unexplored. Oil deposits have been discovered in Palawan. The country must develop a way to harness these vast assets of moneymaking resources and export them to the industrialized countries of the world.

The fertile lands in the provinces must be cultivated and utilized for the benefit of the people. The leaders in government have responsibilities for leading the country as an industrialized nation in the years to come.

THE ABJECT POVERTY IN OUR HOMELAND

Dateline, 2001

BACKGROUND: IT WAS a time for helping our countrymen. Medical missions were in abundance, with medical, civic, and social organizations in America participating. My wife and I joined these humanitarian projects. After participating a number of years in these medical missions, I had seen enough of the poorest of the poor. Yet, there were places in the Philippines that dramatically contrasted the life of the poor.

Accesses to medical care for millions of very poor Filipinos were almost non-existent. The costs of medicines were expensive, if not prohibitive. Things were not going to be better, especially with the Philippine currency crisis during those years of 2001. And whenever a crisis of this magnitude occurred, the price of every basic commodity went up, including the "*galunggong*," a small mackerel-like fish. Could I see the currency crisis in the faces of these poor families? I'd say no--they couldn't care less. If one were to wait for the government and the rich politicians who ran the country to improve the lot of the poor, he would have to wait a very long time. The specter of poverty continued to linger. They had been suffering the effects of economic injustice for decades.

I took a 1976 Toyota taxi from Manila hotel to Ermita. The taxi was so rundown that noxious fumes seeped through the holes in the corroded chassis to the back seats and floor. It shuddered to the grinding halt for traffic at the corner near the once opulent Philippine Cultural Center. While the taxi was stopped, a grimy-faced woman holding a worn-out handkerchief over her nose with one and a baby on the other came over and tapped at the car window. I took such pity on her I gave her 50 pesos.

The scene was similar along Roxas Boulevard near the US Embassy, places heavily visited by tourists. As I got out of the foul smelling taxi I was immediately surrounded by a swarm of small children wit outreached hands, begging for money.

As I walked towards the American Express Office on United Nations Street, I noticed the badly cracked and filthy sidewalks wit garbage strewn everywhere. As I walked, I ad no respite from the pleading faces and grasping hands and yet there was not much I could do. My thoughts were on the piles of uncollected garbage along the streets because of the possible epidemic they might bring.

As I walked further, I come across a crowd of people of all ages covering their noses with handkerchiefs presumably to protect themselves from the gasoline fumes and the garbage smell. The narrow street was jammed with jeepneys and cars honking their horns and filling whatever space there was in or outside the lanes. There was no traffic order and no sense of courtesy on the part of the drivers. Undisciplined was the right word to describe the madness.

These scenes I described are pretty common in Manila and suburbs and they are not very pretty to think or write about. I am at a loss on what to do with all these things I observed.

Poverty in the Philippines is a major obstacle to the success of future generations of the Filipino. According to the most recent data collected by international sources concerning poverty in the Philippines, 44% of the population survives on less that $2 US per day!

It is not all bad news, however. The situation is improving with each passing decade. Filipinos are a people of hope, work ethic, and resourcefulness, and the onslaught of poverty will slowly begin to be repelled and the victory won.

Together we can all work to break the cycle of poverty in the Philippines and we pray PNoy will be successful in his dream to abolish abject poverty in the Filipino people. I hope and pray it is not hopeless.

THE PHILIPPINES TODAY

Dateline, March 2012

PRESENTLY THE MARCOS family is back into the high road of power. We have the appalling amnesia. Yes, Filipinos easily forget. Filipinos elected them again and they are gloating and mocking at our gullibility. Would you believe political dynasties run our country? Many politicians today monopolize the politics on their respective provinces, like the Marcoses, Arroyos, Roman and Garcia of Bataan, Singson of Ilocos Sur, Garcia and Osmena of Cebu, and Zubiri of Bukidnon. They are all in their comfortable and privileged cocoon.

The Philippines today looked more like a conglomerate of repetitious widespread corruption and criminality, specter of poverty, bold inequality, and callous and irresponsible economic and political leaders.

What, then, does the future hold for Filipinos? President Noynoy Aquino stated: *"My first task is to lift the country from poverty... Kung walang corrupt walang mahirap... matuwid na daan.. kayo ang aking boss."* Reforms are needed in the Judiciary branch of the Supreme Court. Former President Arroyo is still in hospital arrest. Corona is facing impeachment. As I write this book, the case of Chief Justice Corona is still in limbo.

We have a fractured country, a fractured culture developing due to the gross neglect of our leaders. It might be corrected in generations to come, but we must start now to make such repairs.

Sadly, the awful social ills are deeply ingrained in our culture. They are so ingrained that I honestly think that any serious attempt to banish them will likely fail. But that's just my own humble take. Hopefully others would prove me otherwise.

We are jubilant Filipinos with Noynoy Aquino III, as the 15th President of the Philippines. We are, however, faced with an array of problems. There is so much to be desired about the Philippines that we know today. It is not free from the ravages of economic bondage. There is so much greed, dishonesty, opportunism, frustration, and unfathomable graft and corruption in the government. Do you know what Buwaya means? These are crocodiles in our government now, young and old officials of the country gnawing the government that devour our wealth. Nobody stops them. How Noynoy Aquino can correct this is beyond my imagination.

There is a looming constitutional crisis resulting from the DOJ's disregard of the SC TRO allowing the Arroyos to leave Manila for medical treatment. Or was it an escape from being prosecuted? There is now a constitutional crisis between the executive and judicial branch of government. Recently, GMA was arrested (hospital arrest) for electoral sabotage in 2007 – a non-bailable offense.

Many said it was unlawful to allow the "escape of GMA" at daylight by going out of the country for medical treatment. A debacle in the Philippine Supreme Court followed. Arroyo is alleged to have committed a wide range of corrupt acts during the nine years she was in power, with all allegations were all denied. The former president is also facing six or more plunder charges. As Filipinos we have to do our share on defending our country. It is alleged that millions of Arroyo's dollars are stashed in unknown places abroad.

According to news releases, GMA had planned these escape months before she became a congresswoman. Will she be on house arrest or in government hospital arrest? Will justice be served? As Filipinos we have to do our share on defending our country. What a shame if we just say *wala tayong magawa- bahala na*. Let's move on... and where do we go? Watching the same history to repeat itself?

Noynoy Aquino must lead the country and propel it to an industrialized nation in the years to come, with no more graft and corruption. There must be an effective and visionary leadership with priority in economic initiatives.

The political system is what destroys the Philippine society. It requires reform. It needs to be torn down completely and rebuilt anew. The graft and corruption, the sordid picture of stealing people's money, plunder by almost every politician is no more a shock to Filipinos. It is the now the Filipino psyches of – the cynical frame of mind that are now deeply-ingrained in everyone – *wala tayong magawa- bahala na.* (Nothing we can do. So be it)

There are twenty million of Filipinos that are confronted with the possibility of hunger everyday.

The enormity of problems facing the Filipinos particularly in its deliverance from economic injustice demands heroic sacrifices from everyone. Democracy restored is not all that we need; we must also be free from hunger and want. Only then can Filipinos declare themselves free at last.

THE PHILIPPINES TOMORROW

Dateline, June 2012

AS I WRITE this article today, the Corona Impeachment Trial ended and the Scarborough Shoal conflict still covered incessantly the media as a major significant issue, a crisis in the South China Sea that to me is frightening of what is going to happen. The Philippines is locked in a territorial dispute with China. Wrong ideas are still in the minds of our intellectuals in the Philippines.

The sad situation still exists in the Philippines. Are Filipinos capable of living by the "rule of law"? Filipinos in general tend to put their own interest first before other people. Government is a kleptocracy and a family dynasty. The nepotism and cronyism that infest the Philippines public life will stay. Corruption will persist for the upper economic and political classes in the Philippines. It is rampant in these socio-economic and political strata. The oligarchic classes are a status quo in Philippine Society-- based on a monopolistic access to material resources and political power. Those are the hubris. **Quo Vadis Philippines?**

As the case of election sabotage against GM Arroyo shall be on trial soon (when is soon?), a huge question is whether justice will prevail. The darkest hour in our judicial history apparently was resolved. We have been dragged to the opposite side of delicadeza, of honor, of integrity. I pray we can cross this bridge and rebuild our dignity from the debris. A positive point may be, is the fact that we have seen its ugliness, its nauseating effect, and everything else that doesn't nurture life. It was as though what people suspected were affirmed beyond the shadow of a doubt – that Rene Corona was dirty.

The territorial squabbles with China are a problem. American bases were kicked out and see what is happening now - the Spratleys-Chinese's recent incursion in the Scarborough Shoal - surely to be taken over by China. The U.S. doesn't care. Why? Filipino nationalists kicked out the American bases. Did we improve in many things because we kicked them out? Absolutely no!

On a positive note, President Aquino is determined to turn the corner by instituting genuine, wide-ranging, meaningful reform, and acting on its belief that good governance is the bedrock of equitable progress.

The President Noynoy Aquino said he is now tackling the problem of graft and corruption. He said, "It is with this principle in mind that we have allocated unprecedented sums to alleviate extreme poverty and are concentrating on providing more opportunities for employment."

There are some signs that the country – with its young population of nearly 100 millions people, the world's 12th largest – has turned a corner. There are three reasons to be hopeful, if not yet exactly cheerful:

- First, the Philippines, after years of indebtedness, is a net creditor. Overseas remittances from the roughly 8 millions Filipinos working abroad have steadily added to foreign exchange reserves. At nearly $80 billions, these are higher than the external debt. Revenues from back office businesses have quintupled over six years from $2.00 to $11 Billions.
- Second, the country is getting its fiscal house in order. The deficit has narrowed from a worrying 5-6 per cent a decade ago to a manageable 2 per cent.
- Third, the political situation is vastly improved. Benigno "Noynoy" Aquino, elected president in 2010, has made a creditable start. For one, his government has sent out a strong message that it will not tolerate corruption. "Thy will be done?"

The Philippines in my view is not a hopeless case. The perennial question - Will it degenerate into a greater social, political, and economic tragedy?

As the final phase of this book was ready for publication, the impeachment of Corona - a TV telenovela, a moro-moro ended. He was found guilty.

Justice, has indeed, prevailed. This is a resounding impact to all Filipinos sending a message loud and clear that there must be accountability and transparency in our leaders in government.

AQUINO'S SUCCESSFUL CRUSADE, THEN WHAT'S NEXT?

Dateline, June 4, 2012

WOW! THIS CORONA impeachment case, which ended in a guilty verdict, is the best declaration of how President Simeon Aquino III can pave the way to the imperative change that has never occurred with recent Filipino presidents.

We post commentaries after the passing of a historical event, the conviction of Chief Justice Renato Corona by the Senate Impeachment Court. It was an event with a dramatic ending of a political telenovela. Not so much of justice, it was morality theatrical production of good against evil.

To backtrack, here's what my prediction: that no matter how we desired the right principle, a guilty judgment would be doubtful. I also questioned whether the media have an effective posting of enormous negative views about JC Corona. The answer is no. Nothing can achieve positively in our country governance; instead, it is ingrained into a totally corrupt officials. My prediction was that Corona would be set free. You might not agree with me, but I have to say it anyway because of my loss of confidence and respect for our officials and leaders. No matter how we sweeten the news and predictions that Corona will be eventually convicted, this is an utter false hope and I don't put my faith or trust in anyone anymore. After a while you just get tired of being disappointed constantly. Friedrich Von Schiller stated, "Disappointments are to the soul what the thunder-storm is to the air."

The 23 Senator judges, which Senate President Juan Ponce Enrile presided, made a right decision. 20 senators voted guilty. 3

considered Corona innocent. I have a very high regard for Enrile who is absolutely sensible and a great leader. I was totally wrong of the outcome of the impeachment of Chief Justice Corona. I was overtly pessimistic. The truth, indeed, prevailed. Justice in action. Is the "Wind of Change" emminent? More questions. No definite answers.

The out bursting demeanor of a lady Senator Miriam Santiago, one of the three stooges, is a disgrace to the Filipino people. She, a hypertensive lady with a semblance of an incredible cheekiness, remains smug, an obnoxious virtual chanticleer blinded by her narrow agenda of personal image building. She branded the prosecutors " mga gago" (morons). She admitted the Philippines is one of the most corrupt nations in the world and concluded Corona should not face justice. That's her inanity.

It simply tells us that those plutocrats and gluttonous oligarch with the shame of dishonesty, liars, and thievery must face justice during President Noynoy Aquinos's administration. There are those involved in the scam of millions of dollars that hurt our country. This shameless audacity of these government officials must stop and never again happen.

The three stooges, the senator judges who voted not guilty in the impeachment of Chief Justice Corona, belong to the dungeon of mindless misfits. Those who defended Corona were selfish stooges who wanted to trample on the law of the land. Yes, the three stooges, the triumvirate who declared Corona innocent are blinded by their shallow principles. This is the day of shame, disgrace to Corona and those three Senator Judges.

Corrupt officials, if proven guilty, must be in jail! Noynoy must fight for the reclusion perpetua to any corrupt government official. The midnight appointments of former president Arroyo are to be revoked if proven illegal. This is a political chutzpah of a corrupt president.

After Corona's impeachment and guilty finding, we must ask if Filipinos are in the doorsill of a new Philippines? This may be the start of getting rid of those corrupt politicos? It will take time, decades. But away with those plutocratic oligarchy that would transform the government into the exclusive domain of kleptocrats and greedy oligarchs. Yes, *Da-an Matuwid*, we must have. A "Crusade for Change"; this is Noynoy's burning desire. Let us help him set forth on a new direction from hereon, a Renaissance, a resolve as never before that our beloved country—that the Philippines "under God, shall have a new birth of governance and shall not perish from the earth."

Noynoy shall be the president who will save the Filipino people from relentless poverty.

C J Corona in his trickery and dishonesty, greed, a liar in his SALN, his Machiavellian was a self-destructive manner.

One of the three stooges, Senator Bongbong Marcos, is vying for president of the Philippines in a few years because of ambition to follow the footsteps of his dictator father, Ferdinand Marcos. In the Roman Empire where Julius Caesar became the dictator, he was slain by Brutus at age 55 because of his ambition. If Bongbong becomes elected, is Brutus, the murderer of Caesar, ready for him?

I hope we get rid of the filthy politics. Noynoy Aquino MUST SAVE the Filipinos. The people and nation had fallen before the shame of dishonesty and thievery.

At the last hour of her presidency in 2010, 250 political appointments were made that included Corona for Chief Justice of the Supreme Court, 302 military promotions, all in midnight salvo. GMA is absolutely out of her mind. What a shame. She has all the erratic and faux mentality as she undresses for the presidency of the Philippines. Do Filipinos feel sorry for GMA? She is now in hospital arrest facing a number of charges - election sabotage, thievery, plunder, and more. GMA is next to face justice. From President for 9 years to a congresswoman is a disconcerting scenario. She has the ambition to do what? For what reason? She must have a plan to save her life. She already knew what is going to happen to her. All the bad things you do in life come back to you.

Humorous things are prevalent in our Congress. If GMA were a man, "we must laugh at a man to avoid crying for him", a quote from Napoleon Bonaparte.

I am a US citizen; however, my persona is still Filipino. Every Filipino is hurt badly by the graft and corruption pervading relentlessly in our country from Marcos presidency to GMA at the present. The stolen money must be returned; the perpetuator must be prosecuted and justice be done.

All these reflect the desperation with which the Philippines are fighting its seemingly perpetual war against poverty and inefficiency in government in general and the problems of blatant graft and corruption, civility and social order in particular. President PNoy must win the battle. The Senate's guilty verdict of Corona serves as a strong warning to the perceived untouchables in Philippine government.

Mr. President, are we in the right track? *Walang mahirap kung walang Corrupt. Matuwid na landas.* The people are your boss. These are your ultimate crusades. The Filipino people support you.

The country is in your hands in the next 4 more years.

"OCCUPY" MOVEMENT FOR THE PHILIPPINES?

Dateline, November 18, 2011

PHILIPPINE COLUMNIST JOSE Ma. Montelibano recently wrote his glimpses of his homeland in "How Will We Survive?" He discussed the United States Wall Street Occupation movement, a dramatic moment of unknown long-term effects. His point reminded me of our native land, the Philippines. During the tenure of six Philippine presidents since the 1946 Independence, over 17 million Filipinos have populated the country. Sad to say, there has been no change in the gap between the rich and the poor: 30% rich and 70% poor.

Today the populations of 102 million Filipinos are represented by 70%-80% trapped in the vicious cycle of poverty and exploitation. For more than five decades people have grown poorer and poorer, with a growing number living in abject poverty. Perhaps the greatest consequence is the lack of food and resulting hunger afflicting so many. Today, the Philippines' economy is smaller than Pakistan's; a quarter of our 102 million people live on less than $1.25 a day. And our reaction seems to be one of defeat: *wala tayong magawa, bahala na* (we can't do anything, so be it).

As a physician, I had participated in a number of medical missions in the Philippines. I had seen enough of the poorest of the poor. Access to medical care for millions of very poor Filipinos is virtually non-existent.

THE POOR: Before the medical mission to Pampanga, I joined a tour of Manila observing the slums of the metropolis where six million poor survive — barely. The faces on the city streets told many sad tales. We witnessed the travesty of 30,000 helpless, impoverished squatters living around the waste dump in Payatas, the Manila's main waste dump; garbage is piled seven stories high. Twenty-five percent of the inhabitants live in informal settlements, often in places unsuitable for living. Urban poverty is caused by low household incomes and the internal migration of poor rural families to urban areas.

I saw a large slum area near the outlet of Pasig River with shanty houses; it was a heart-breaking sight to view the scores of gloomy shantytowns along the banks of the river, some precariously constructed on stilts. Somehow 800,000 people live there. Pasig River flows right through the heart of Manila. Tons of sewage, including human excrements was conveniently dumped into the Pasig River. Little wonder why the river stinks to high heavens. The abject poverty lingers as poverty rapes and kills the spirit of the poor.

We all too often underestimate poverty's complexity and cruelty, how it kills, maims and aborts life. But once you see it first hand, you can never forget. I have to look at facts that are, like the sun, too painful for my direct gaze; instinctively, I look away. "The unreported deaths of the poor by reason of their lack of food, shelter, clothes, medicine and simple hope are underestimated" according to a Philippine columnist Montelibano.

In the encyclopedia of nations, the following are very clear. Rural areas mostly remained underdeveloped, thereby leaving most of the peasant communities to subsist on a hand-to-mouth existence. Meanwhile urban areas, especially Metro Manila, cornered major infrastructure and social projects, thereby attracting most of the investments and jobs in the manufacturing and industrial sectors. Among the poorest Filipinos, most family income is derived from entrepreneurial activities such as selling food on street corners or collecting recyclable materials to sell at the junkyards. Most of the poor are lowland landless agricultural workers, lowland small farm owners and cultivators, industrial wage laborers, hawkers, micro-entrepreneurs, and scavengers.

Due to inadequate access to community health centers, members of poor households are not able to maximize health services benefits, such as family planning, resulting in larger families with malnourished and uneducated children. The condition of the poor is made worse by a lack of housing, clean water and electricity, especially in the urban areas.

THE AFFLUENCE: For no other reason than to demonstrate the stark contrast in the Filipinos' strata of life, the wealthy make grand overtures to demonstrate their good fortune. Only a few miles away from barrio San Jose, a venue for our medical mission, and a completely contrasting haven of affluence exist. Once the U.S. Clark Air Base's 250-hectare lahar-covered landscape, the place has since been transformed into a Mimosa resort.

There, one can see the glamorous Mimosa Regency Casino, with 200 slot machines and card tables of all sorts. Entertainment and revue dancers from Las Vegas come here. For luxurious resort accommodations, a Holiday Inn Hotel stands with 337 air-conditioned rooms. The former Chamber's Hall of the American GI in Clark field is replete with gourmet restaurants, duty-free shops, boutiques and luxurious accommodations. We were in the midst of a 36 all-weather golf course, which acclaimed Honolulu-based team of Nelson, Wright and Haworth had designed. Newly built two-car garage homes and tile-roofed villas were clustered within the premises for long-term vacationers with spacious bedrooms, modern kitchens, tasteful fixtures and furnishings.

The rich Filipinos used this as a nearby gateway from the hustle and bustle of urban life. The scenery, the aura, the landscape, the ambiance, and the bright neon lights sprouting from tree branches were like the brightest of day. If I were to compare the beauty and lavishness of Mimosa with the depressed areas of Santo Nino and San Jose, I would find no greater contrast. I was in limbo as to how our government could solve this problem of poverty in our homeland.

SOLUTIONS: President Noynoy Aquino has stated he wants to end corruption and solve our crippling poverty. Yet what must be done? I say stop oligarchy, a huge impediment to the progress of the country, and bring back the billions of plundered dollars stashed abroad. Remove thievery and plunder in government officials and cronies. Arrest the crooks, smugglers and tax cheats. Develop infrastructure, fund education, and create employment. The agricultural and fisheries sectors must be revitalized to halt the migration of poor farmers to urban areas.

As writer Wallace stated: "If tax effort is brought up to the 17-18 percent as elsewhere in Asia, if tax changes are pushed through could add about P95 billion, that could be put into education and health." The money is there – now we just need the boldness.

There needs to be a serious reconsideration of a political culture that serves itself, not the tens of millions toiling in poverty. We need to combat financial greed, opportunism, and the corruption, scam, plunder, and thievery of politicians. "Occupy Manila" and all cities in the Philippines for the economic recovery and moral reformation of our nation. We must encourage the use of nonviolence to maximize the safety of all participants. Can this be done? Do our countrymen have what it takes to make the necessary sacrifices to build a real future for our homeland? Or are we willing to accept the status quo and watch future generations suffer through the unacceptable conditions that haunt the Philippines today? Are we not concerned of global recession that will sweep across the globe?

Well, we have seen the unthinkable happen during the spring revolutions in Northern Africa, resulting in significant political upheaval in brutal dictatorships. We are witnessing different kinds of revolutions at different stages in nations like the United States, Greece and Syria today. The world is changing, and it is time our country and countrymen change with it. I say we can seek true and everlasting reform, that we occupy our cities in a nonviolent manner and demand true, dramatic economic and political changes. A new Philippines begins today!

"KABIT" – CONCUBINE

Dateline, March 14, 2012

LATELY THE SENATORS of the Philippines serving as judges, and whose prosecutors are the members of congress in the impeachment process inundated us with the immoral cataclysmic demeanor of Chief Justice Renato Corona under prosecution. Journalist Macasaet after the 16th day of impeachment hearing stated, "The unfitness of Mr. Corona to lead the Court is not just in the evidence of his guilt. His demeanor disqualifies him from the post." You can call him a pusillanimous human being not worth to be Chief Justice of the Supreme of the Island - the Republic of the Philippines.

A veteran journalist of Manila, William Esposo wrote: "If the Chief Justice Corona is man enough he should admit the fact that he has a long-standing romantic relationship with a gentle lady named EVA with whom the Chief Justice has two (2) illegitimate sons."

The impeachment is a Moro Moro. I have enough of it. Now, I will spend my time to share with the readers the enigmatic qualities maintained by Filipinos; why concubines are accepted, matter- of-fact constant, shrug their shoulders and seemed not really an issue of immorality in our country, the Philippines. A Filipino would likely say, *walang bali 'yan* (that is nothing to interest me). This relationship between a man with a legal wife and with another woman- a *KABIT-* is relationships not frowned upon by the community. Am I right? I have to say it anyway. It is a formidable nature of a man with a KABIT- the concubinage that is customarily, if not, a standard flaunt of Filipinos even in lower class, albeit more common in the high echelon of society- including former Presidents of the Philippines. Police and Jeepney Drivers in the Philippines have their own concubines, and nobody pays any attention.

Indeed it is un-catholic obedience of the Bible by the Chief Justice of the land of roughly a million of Filipinos, 80% of which are *Catolicos* (catholics).

Can you imagine a senator is publicly known as a horny father, fathered 72 children by 16 different women? He has to support everyone, one million pesos a month to these concubines who bore his children. Where do this politico dig up the resources of moolah, is a vital question. They have to be a corrupt official, steal moneys, and become plunderers. Not rare in our country! It is a fact in the landscape of our filthy politics. This is the fealty they have to be.

What makes it so popular practices of Filipino men or even some women in the Philippines? Did Filipinos follow the Islamic practice? In Muslim, "Slave women were required mainly as concubines and menials. A Muslim slaveholder was entitled by law to the sexual enjoyment of his slave women."

In our country, when someone has the Affluence Means Richness, have the spondulicks, they make it sure that a *kabit* is built-in in their daily lives. It is even accepted by some Filipinos or by the doer as one with prestige and one with identity and fame, bravado, a macho- man, and takes great joy and pride to be called a *babaero*-womanizer, albeit Casanova is more appealing to them. Having many women is a sign of luxury and power over others who could not.

While Don Juan is a legend, the word Casanova originates from the name of the man Gian Giacomo Girolamo Casanova, and is nowadays used to refer to a man who is a woebegone- a womanizer. In the Philippines, he buys a nice expensive car, and considers it as his second home where his legal wife cooks in the kitchen, however, used the Mercedes- (Benz) as a romantic setting where his concubine builds a fire.

Blair and Robertson, historians, author of fascinating and marvelous volumes of books - very informative history and culture of people in the Philippines, made their take about Filipinos or native Indios in pre-colonial Spanish times. Both are pioneers in looking specifically for how the Indios take slave women and keep them as concubines - in our lingo KABIT. Why were polygamy, concubinage and abortion practiced 300+ years of Spanish rule in the Philippines? By research of Blair and Robertson, Filipinos were converted in the Catholic faith. These observations stated, "indeed there were changes in the norms of the pre-colonial natives. During those times, most of the native Indios daily practices and rituals were conceived sinful. The marital practices of the natives mostly belonging to the chief class of the Philippines prior to their conversion from the pagan beliefs were allowed to have as many concubines as they want as long as they could support these women. The Western colonizers based on the Catholic religion condemned these carnal sins – adultery, polygamy and fornication all of which were parts of the traditions. And gradually, the Philippines and its people reinvented its practices and culture as well, in accordance to the preaching of the oppressors. Do we still have in the Philippines, concubine as norm?

Do we still have Maria Clara (ang dalagang Pilipina) in our country?
Many questions now with no real answers.

To fast forward, what is happening now with regards to concubine in the country? Most recent, an ex-Philippine Ambassador was arrested for keeping a concubine. Similarly rich man in Manila was charged with "concubinage" for allegedly conducting the affair with his wife's best friend in a family-owned Manila apartment.

To quote a wife, "my husband is an abuser, a scrooge, an incorrigible philanderer, and worse, a pervert." And I'd say her husband has the art of infidelity.

Now, back to Chief Justice Corona. Isn't he an infidel? Is he adulterous -a crime and therefore, a criminal, if indeed he has another woman with two other children? Esposo continued to say, "For Chief Justice Renato C. Corona not to mention his children with EVA as if they do not exist at all, is the highest form of ignominy and immorality that he can commit not only against his legitimate wife and family but against his oath as the highest magistrate of the land." No one is above the law and more so if you're the "Chief Justice of the Republic of the Philippines." He is wantonly wrong but believes the powers of his office, as Chief Justice will right that wrong.

You be the judge. Obviously, he cannot judge himself- a Chief Justice of the Supreme Court of the Philippines. The Chief Justice is Machiavellian in a self-destructive manner.

CHAPTER TWO ★

THE METROPOLIS
12,000,000 PEOPLE

What is the city but the people?

- WILLIAM SHAKESPEARE

TRAFFIC IN MANILA

Dateline, February 2011

TRAFFIC IN MANILA is crazy. It is horrendous, hellish!

I visited Manila several times; I was there last January 2011. The traffic in this city is simply a nightmare, with bottlenecks everywhere, chaotic and senseless traffic jams. Every road is clogged in the metro complex. The EDSA highway from Quezon City to Makati is a horrible gridlock with different types of transportations fighting to move a little more.

It would take two hours from Cubao to the Buendia intersection, a mere distance of approximately fifteen miles.

As of 2011, the greater urban area of Manila has a population at around 21,295,000. There are 600 thousand motor vehicles (per 1997 data) using the inadequate road system. There are too many jeepneys, private cars, trailers, passenger buses, junky trucks and delivery vans plying their way in every thoroughfare in the city. The streets are narrow, with many in bad condition. There is little order, and the proper use of primary and secondary routes are unregulated.

Jeepney passengers are jammed and suffocated in clouds of dust and pollution, yet the government has not done anything to correct the tragedy of the local public transportation system. Do the public officials even care?

Government intervention is needed to correct this problem. The president must take notice and send directives to the local governments and the Department of Public Works and Highways to upgrade the roads and install more new light rail transit lines.

There are now "overpasses or fly-overs" in many major thoroughfares, but it seems they are not able to ease the traffic anarchy. The major cities in many European countries, as well as in the U.S. and Japan, use subway trains. I don't see why the Philippines could not start thinking of subway lines. Some have speculated that subways are not possible in Manila because the soil is too muddy and soft, and the water level is too high.

According to writer Bernardo Villegas, "Solving the traffic and transport problem in the Metro Manila area has taken and will take a long time. There are no quick-fix solutions. At least three major agencies of the government — the Metropolitan Manila Development Authority (MMDA), the Department of Public Works and Highways (DPWH), and the Department of Transportation and Communications (DoTC) — will have to closely collaborate to find creative solutions to this long-standing problem."

After the Skyway, MMDA recently proposed a plan for the construction of the so-called sky bridge that will connect Makati and Quezon cities. This is a good start, but it is not enough.

The public must have an alternative transportation other than the thousands of jeepneys driven by undisciplined kamikaze Filipino drivers. These jeepneys pick up passengers and unload them in the middle of the road, a practice that significantly contributes to the traffic tyranny.

There is a blatant indiscriminate and unregulated use of sirens by vehicles on the road. It obviously disturbs further an already jam-packed traffic in the metropolis. My question is will this decree improve the traffic in Manila?

The sirens' effectiveness is unquestioned in solving traffic jams, and the politicos are making a popular scheme out of them. Because they can afford a few thousands of pesos for installing a quick traffic-dispersal device, the politicians and allies take advantage of the device. Fortunately, decree (No. 96) abolished this abuse, hitting the illegal use of the *wang-wang* by unauthorized people.

Buses were the most popular means of transportation by the poor and daily commuters. The passengers were packed like sardines in these buses suffering to a point of near suffocation by the constant assault of dust, gasoline fumes and other forms of pollution in their system. Do you know that there are seven thousand buses plying back and forth in EDSA, a 26-kilometer freeway? Records show there are about hundreds different owners of these buses of different colors and names. Practically anyone with money can buy a bus and become a "franchised" bus operator. A good number of these vehicles are colorum buses. It was total nonsense the way Metro Manila Development Authority regulated and managed the traffic operation. The Department of Transportation and Communication must do something to confront this horrible problem, and Malacanang Palace must lead the effort!

THE WANG-WANG USE ABUSED

Dateline, September 2011

IN HIS INAGAURAL speech last June 30, 2010, President Noynoy Aquino had spoken out against the *wang-wang*, (sirens) which he said has become "a symbol of inequality." Indeed, he is right.

Following that, he proclaimed a Decree (No. 96) that abolished the abuse and hit hard the illegal use of the wang-wang by unauthorized people that want to use it in pulling over other motorists in Metro Manila's traffic, so that they could travel faster. The traffic situation is simply a nightmare. There are bottlenecks everywhere, if not chaotic-and-senseless traffic jams. The EDSA highway from Quezon City to Makati is a horrible gridlock with different types of transportation fighting inch by inch each other and not respecting lanes in order to move on. Horns are blasting. It now takes two hours from Cubao (Quezon City) to the Buendia intersection (Makati City), a mere distance of approximately 15 miles. There is a blatant indiscriminate and unregulated use of sirens by vehicles on the road. It obviously disturbs further an already jam-packed traffic in the metropolis. My question is: Will this decree improve the traffic in Manila?

The sirens' effectiveness is unquestioned in perkily solving traffic jams and the politicos are making a popular scheme out of it. Because they can afford a few thousands of pesos for installing a quick traffic-dispersal device, the politicians, their families and also civilians who have connections in government take advantage of the device for sale in several stores in Manila. To quote one writer, "the worst kind is an ambulance (usually from distant towns or provinces) navigating main streets, curtains drawn literally in a veiled attempt to simply beat traffic. It is not unheard such ambulances, blinkers and all, run errands for the local mayor or on local-government business, aside from life-and-death situations." The National Capital Region Police Office (NCRPO) has confiscated some 148 sirens and blinkers in its anti "wang-wang" campaign following the order of President Benigno "Noynoy" Aquino, III. Imagine 148 cars (it should be more than that) with sirens used to travel all over Manila. Just 50% of those cars traveling on the road would surely sidetrack the heavy traffic in the city.

I have witnessed many times a high-ranking official with escorts blasting their wang-wang and car horns to part the solid sea of traffic in front of them. (Can you imagine Moses parting the Red Sea?)It was in 1997 when I started writing about traffic problems in Manila every time I went home for a vacation. It may have changed. It was total nonsense the way Metro Manila Development Authority regulated and managed the traffic operation. The Department of Transportation and Communications must do something to confront this horrible problem. I emphatically said then that Malacañang Palace must lead the effort! Consider this one. These traffic delays in Manila affect everyone, the common people and the executives alike. You may lose an appointment, get exhausted, or just stay away from it all. Jeepney passengers are jammed and suffocated in clouds of dust and pollution. Yet the government has not done anything to correct the tragedy of the public transportation system in Manila. Do the public officials care?

CHAOTIC PUBLIC TRANSPORTATION
A TRAGEDY

Dateline, 2011

MANPOWER LOST TO traffic jams: Consider this. These traffic delays in Manila affect everyone: the common people and executives alike. You may lose an appointment, get exhausted, or just stay away from it all.

There is significant loss of time and productivity encountered by every office worker in Manila due to delays in traffic. I sat down and with my calculator, I figured out the hours lost in this traffic. If a worker spends two hours delay in commuting, a 5-day work week and a 12-hour work day would amount to his wasting away 480 hours, or 40 working days, or two working months a year trying to get to his workplace. And if he spends two hours one-way or four hours a day, he would be spending twice as much time, or four working months a year, on the road. This is the tragedy of a chaotic public transportation system in Manila---a gigantic waste of time, money and energy, not to mention hard on one's health and peace of mind.

These traffic delays in Manila affect everyone. You may lose an appointment, get exhausted, or just stay away from it all. There is significant loss of time and productivity encountered by every office worker in Manila due to delays in traffic. I sat down and with my calculator I figured out the hours lost in this traffic. If a worker spends two hours delay in commuting, a 5-day workweek and a 12-hour workday would amount to his wasting away 480 hours/year trying to get to his workplace. And if he spends two hours one-way or four hours a day, he would be spending twice as much time, or four working months a year, on the road. This is the tragedy of a chaotic public transportation system in Manila. It is a gigantic waste of time, money and energy!

In a 2009 study by the MMDA, it was reported that the average vehicle speed on EDSA is 10 KPH on a normal day. The air pollution that emits from road transportations is particularly deadly and is a perfect formula for an environmental disaster. It is hazardous to the environment and the people.

The Department of Environment and Natural Resources and other concerned government agencies like the Land Transportation Authority and Metro Manila Development Authority (DENR) planned to initiate a move to decongest traffic in EDSA and ultimately reduce air pollution. DENR is proposing the removal of bus terminals in major thoroughfares and their relocation to the northern and southern parts of Metro Manila. DENR supported the idea that only motorists with adequate parking spaces in their residences should be allowed to register their vehicles - those who park at sidewalks will no longer be allowed to do so.

Why are there thousands of privately owned cars? The answer is the Filipino psyche. Although cars are classified as luxury items, Filipinos dream to own a car before anything else. Additionally, most private car owners consider their vehicles as an extension of their home--but with one difference: a home is where his wife cooks; a car is where his girlfriend builds a fire. Hah hah.

DANGER IN MANILA ROADS

Dateline, 1989

UNEXPECTED DANGERS LURKED throughout the Manila roads. My American friends and co- missionaries, Drs. Allan Garvin, Joe Jennings, Kirk Marshall, and I had a close call on a freeway. After a long day of heavy missionary work in Antipolo, we were invited to have dinner in a restaurant owned by one of the members of our medical mission. Frank Rivera's restaurant was located in Valenzuela, Bulacan, about ten miles from Manila. Since the four of us were all exhausted, we decided to leave the group and return to Sulo Hotel in Quezon City.

Kirk flagged a couple of taxis that refused to give us a ride through the heavy traffic on the North diversion freeway; however, Kirk finally got one, a run-down, dilapidated taxi that needed major repairs. It was 10 o'clock in the evening, a time when big delivery and supply trucks were scheduled to enter Manila. I was in the back seat with Kirk and Joe. Allan sat in front with the driver.

We were probably cruising 40 miles an hour in the middle lane of the highway.

Rig cargo trucks dwarfed us when suddenly the engine hood of the taxi flipped open, obstructing our view and the driver's front view. We all panicked, knowing to stop the car in the middle of the freeway would be a disaster. I was shouting at the top of my voice, telling the driver to slowly drive to the side of the road. Dr. Garvin was preparing to jump out of the car. The car finally stopped at the "shoulder" dirt side of the freeway. It was a miracle that we survived! We really believed that "somebody up there" saved us.

Dr. Kenneth Romero, a member of our medical mission, teasingly told me the lighter side of street traffic. He said that one time he had to fight his way between jeepneys and other vehicles to avoid being hit in Manila's streets. Dr. Joseph Jennings, another medical mission participant, had a funny way of appeasing his angry and frightened colleague. "In California the pedestrian has the right of way, and he is darn right. In Manila, however, he is DEAD right." Of course everybody knows that the pedestrian's right of way in Manila simply does not exist.

CHAPTER THREE

VISION, VALUES AND VENTILATED MUSINGS

Not every book has to be loaded with symbolism, irony,
or musical language, but it seems to me that every
book—at least every one worth reading—is about
something.

- STEPHEN KING

ORGANIZED MEDICINE

Dateline, July 1981

In 1981, this was one of the editorials I wrote. This appeal was directed to Filipino American physicians. During this period, about 11,000 Filipino doctors were practicing in America. I was a member of the board of governors of the Association of Philippine Physicians in America (APPA) and a member of the membership committee. The appeal was published in the *Philippine Medical Society of Southern California Newsletter* 4, no. 2 July 1981.

IT IS A FACT THAT about 11,000 Filipino physicians are practicing in the U.S. today. It is also a sad fact that there are only 1,000 members of the Association of Philippine Practicing Physicians in America (APPA). It must be of considerable concern to every APPA member when some 10,000 Filipino physicians in this country choose not to spend thirteen cents a day to join the national association and thus participate in preserving the freedoms of our profession in this country. It should be of distressing concern to those 10,000 Philippine practicing physicians in America who elect to ignore the reality that for about twenty-six cents a day - including APPA and State PMA dues - organized medicine within our group is a real bargain.

Realistically, it is a fact that we, as an ethnic group practicing under the umbrella of American medicine, are threatened daily at county, state and national levels of our profession's rights and interests. In the years to come, we are bound to become an endangered species. We could no longer tolerate the recent changes in the immigration laws designed to limit the number of Foreign Medical Graduates (FMGs), not only coming here for postgraduate training, but also remaining here afterwards. The APPA has initiated and begun defending those who opt not to join the association and pay their dues to support their efforts. All Filipino physicians in this country, including those who do not join their medical association, benefit directly from accomplishments promoted by a small-organized group protecting our principles in this country. The destiny of the Filipino physicians rests on what we do today and plan for tomorrow. The FMG problems and the constraints by governmental agencies are frightening. We must not be fence sitters or gripers about discrimination, racial prejudice and unequal treatment. We cannot afford to be mistreated, abused or even ignored. For us to try to react only when threatened and not to prepare for these inroads and crisis is shortsighted. Those of you who have already reached the success of life, enjoying the economic well being in your respective private practices in this country must join the mainstream of organized medicine and should not shy away from it.

The time has come for Filipino doctors to be vigilant and active, to re-learn the true meaning of 'BAYANIHAN' (working together) as the embodiment of Dr. Jose Rizal, a true and noble Filipino. The fighting spirit of Lapu-Lapu for human rights still looms within us.

For this reason, the APPA is embarking upon an extensive membership development program during this convention in

Anaheim, California. We need every Filipino physician practicing in the U.S. to actively support organized medicine. We must have that support if we are to continue to protect and defend our profession and its future, including those who follow us--our children.

In all candor, I do not see how anyone can ignore the existence of the Association for all Filipino physicians practicing in America. I cannot understand how not anyone can comprehend the meaning of strength and unity. Obviously, these facts are being directed to the 10,000 Filipino physicians in this country who are not APPA members.

Yet, I know of no other way to solicit new membership except by personal contact.

It is my sincere hope that every APPA member will actively participate in our membership goals.

POWER and CLOUT mean quality membership – in unity and in numbers–is a top priority."

Indeed, our membership was a problem. Was it because Filipino doctors were bustling in their private practice?

FIL-AM NURSES SHOULD HELP BUILD COMMUNITIES

Dateline, 1990

I was a guest speaker of the Philippine American Nurses Association of San Diego during its 21st anniversary.

...**I AM DELIGHTED** to be here this evening, and indeed it is with great pleasure and distinct honor to be invited as your speaker on the occasion of your 21st anniversary celebration. As a matter of fact, I am very elated to see some of you. We have worked together in the Samahan Health Clinic, and we have been together in some community activities. I feel very much at home here this evening.

As a physician practicing for many years in this community, I have watched your association grow over the years, and you have shown great strides in leadership and service to the community.

Your association has produced leaders who have advanced to senior leadership in National organizations. Carmen B. Toledo Galang DNSE, RN, is the current president of the Philippine Nurses Association of America (PNAA). She is from the Philippine Nurses Association of San Diego, and we must be proud of her achievements and leadership. You have been in the forefront to represent the Filipino nurses in the practice of the nursing profession in this country. In addition, I am confident that you are all ready and poised to face the current radical changes in the health care delivery in this country. We all know that you are in the largest group of health personnel. Without nurses, our modern health care system could not operate. But as managed care is hovering upon us, both the healthcare system and the role of nurses are changing. It is inevitable that the years ahead will bring more focus on health lifestyles and self-care implying that the nurse's role will be that of an enabler, facilitator and manager of health care.

But tonight, ladies and gentlemen, I am here not to speak about the changing trends and mode of the nursing profession. Rather, I am here to speak of our evolution and destiny as an ethnic group of professionals in this foreign land that we consider our adopted country. I will speak about our continued existence as an organized group like yours, the Philippine Nurses Association, the Association of Philippine Physicians in America (APPA) and others.

More than two generations ago, the Philippines gained its independence from the United States of America. This was a product of our natural quest for democracy and freedom. No one, I suppose, ever dreamt that thirty to forty years later or so, after that Independence Day, that you and I shall be here in America enjoying the freedom of this beautiful country and be blessed with opportunities and achieved success and affluence in our lives. We are indeed very fortunate if we compare ourselves with our colleagues in the Philippines, who are still yearning to come to America.

We all came to this country from all walks of life, of different professions, and with different perspectives and ambitions. We have struggled. Many of us have won in our struggles with flying colors, even exceeding our American counterparts. The rewards have been numerous. However, let us not be trapped into a state of complacency simply because we are doing well. There will always be challenges out there. There is no doubt that the contribution of the FMG and the FNG in the health system of this country is substantial. Let no one disregard this.

I truly believe we must concern ourselves to helping our country, and even more to our unfortunate colleagues who can never find decent careers in the Philippines.

Our current dilemma, which particularly affects nurses, is the prevailing constraint imposed by immigration laws on professional workers in this country. I am referring to the working visa, the H1A visa for Filipino nurses that is now being threatened and might even be curtailed. In addition, there is a new bill introduced in Congress to eliminate the three out of the four existing categories of family immigration. This will have an adverse effect upon family reunification, children of U.S. citizens, brothers and sisters, who had waited for so many years to immigrate to this country. These, ladies and gentlemen, are the so-called anti-immigrant sentiments. We must oppose this bill.

These nurses who come to this nation with a working visa must be protected; they must be supported and ensured their employer does not exploit them. Even though local nursing labor force is in a stage of glut as a result of downsizing in many institutions, there are still places and positions that can be filled by these Filipino nurses. The mere fact that these nurses can obtain the H1A visa is a milestone in their career, a chance to gain further experience and financial opportunity in this country, which are not possible back in our home country. I hope that your association takes a proactive initiative in looking into the welfare of our nurses, find out their needs and their concerns.

While we concern ourselves in helping our countrymen and their ills, we must also develop our Filipino American community in its political clout in this country if we are to be effective in fighting oppressive and adverse policies. There is much to be done if we intend to forge our Filipino American community into a strong, cohesive force that can speak with one voice on matters that concern us all.

As an organized group, we have a purpose for being. That purpose is no less than to help assure our survival as medical and nursing practitioners, as respectable human beings, to be given the opportunity without bias, to flourish and to achieve our maximum potential. The Philippine Nurses Association could make representations directly to the American Nursing Association and express their views and concerns. This is why it is very important to take active roles in our local, state, and national organization. Let us be recognized and our voices heard. Therefore, I urge each and every one of you to be active in your association. We in the community should dismiss all reservations concerning the capabilities of our associations. We must resolve our past and current jealousies and conflicts among the members of the community and overcome the apathetic Filipino syndrome to rise in the American mainstream by any means.

Finally, I'd like to share with you this consoling note: even if restrictions for our professions to enter as immigrants to this country are now behind us, we now have a second generation of Filipino Americans who are in college of nursing and medical schools. They will carry our heritage of which we have preserved.

If we instill in our children and in our grandchildren the treasured tradition of our culture, they will always be proud as Filipinos. If we share with our children and our grandchildren the rewards and satisfaction of being in our profession, we will be encouraging them to follow in our footsteps. In this manner, there will always be a continuing supply of Fil-Am nurses in the U.S. to preserve our traditions and ideals. This scenario, if accomplished, will be a great day, and you and I can be very happy and proud of our organizations continuing in perpetuity. Thank you."

FILIPINO DOCTORS AND NURSES PROFESSIONALS IN AMERICA- A DISAPPEARING BREED?

Dateline, May 7, 2012

THE CHANGES IN immigration policies in this country as we have seen have indeed harmed the continued influx of professionals, doctors, lawyers, engineers, nurses, and others. The previous fifth preference category, others, has virtually disappeared. Why is that? Reality check says it is the fear of competition, the economic competition imposed by the professional immigrants. Now as we grow older and finally retire questions are being raised. Who is going to follow our footsteps? Are we the disappearing breed of professionals in this country?

As we know now, there is a marked decline in the number of occupational preference immigrants. However, there has been a doubling in the number of immigrants entering under family preference.

I wish to share in passing this perspective: The passage of the Immigration Act of 1965 played a very important role in Filipino immigration. Due to the act, there was a dramatic increase in the United States Filipino population to enable close to 4 millions of Filipinos to make the United States their new home.

With the act, priority was given to families, so that immigrants could sponsor family members under certain conditions. Priority was now given to family members to U.S. citizens, and permanent residents so they could sponsor/petition families back in the Philippines. It is the family reunification provisions in the United States immigration policy that facilitated for legal immigration from the Philippines.

The family is the cornerstone of US immigration. But the policy of the current administration does not seem to recognize the importance of reuniting even the closest family members. The US really needs to revisit its family immigrant policy.

Here are the problems.

Unless the person being petitioned is a minor child, parent, spouse or fiancé, the waiting period for an immigrant visa can take five, 10 or even 20 years. The reason for this protracted wait is that there are more visa applicants than the number of visas available each year. For December 2011, the US Department of State is processing visa petitions for Filipino nationals that were filed on or before March 1, 1997, July 8, 1992 and September 8, 1988 for unmarried children, married children and siblings of US citizens, respectively. The longest waiting period is 23 years for siblings of US citizens. For married children the wait is approximately 19 years.

There are perennial cases of undocumented immigrants; usually family members who try to enter through the backdoor. There is no excuse for violating existing laws. But in reality, the desire to be reunited with family members compel many to use extra-legal means- the TNTs (*tago nang tago*) undocumented aliens.

Who are going to follow our footsteps?

The Association of American Medical Colleges estimates there is a shortage of 13,700 doctors nationwide in all specialties. That number is predicted to hit 63,000 by 2015, and more than double, reaching 130,000, by 2025. Will the influx of Foreign Medical Graduates be back again? There are some states that expect shortage in physicians in year 2020 and those Filipino doctors who became nurses with working visas, and with no immigrant visas that are available right now, may be they shall have a chance to become doctors again. Another visa available is the J-1 Visa in all states where there are medically underserved areas or health professional shortage areas. Those physicians in the temporary worker visa or H-1B, is an alternative to J-1 visa, which is a two-year residency program in the U.S.

In order to obtain the H-1B status, the physician must pass all parts of either the FLEX, the NBME, or the USMLE examinations. Upon completion of their residency programs, these physicians are able to obtain H-1Bvisas and permanent resident status through employer sponsorship. Others are able to immigrate to the U.S. through close relatives who are U.S. citizens or permanent residents. To Filipino doctors who are seeking employment in the US should bear in mind that there are special licensing requirements, and because of this they must start planning before the completion of medical school. Getting an H-1B visa is not always easy and even getting H-1B status is not free from problems. For further assistance, consult your immigration lawyers.

For Filipino nurses: With the worldwide aspiration to go to the US competing at each other, we can only imagine that the backlog (retrogression) of US Visa will continue to be a major hindrance for many Filipinos to go to the States. The only real hope in the horizon is the passing of the US Emergency Nursing Supply Release Act of 2008 or HR 5924.

The retrogression continues to be the reasons why no visas for competent nurses applying for work in the US are available, thus resulting to delay in their employment overseas.

The retirement of registered nurses (RNs), compounded by the increasing demand for health care services account for the large vacuum in such shortage.

The U.S. Census Bureau reported that the 2007 American Community Survey, identified approximately 3.1 million persons as "Filipino alone or in any combination." The census also found that about 80% of the Filipino American communities are United States citizens. Also in 2007, the U.S. State Department estimated the size of the Filipino American community at 4 million or 1.5% of the United States population. It has been estimated that 22,000 Filipino American doctors practiced in America and 40,000 Philippine nurses.

TORPOR OF IMPERATIVE CHANGE - UNITY

Dateline, January 8, 2012

"UNITY GIVES FIRMNESS and solidity to the humblest men," which is a quotation from Laberius. Filipinos living in the United States today seem to be blessed and contented people. We have achieved success and affluence. Almost everyone has a good paying job, a fine home, a car or two in the garage, and a little saving for the rainy day. Because of our diverse backgrounds, we Filipinos in America have successfully established societies of social, cultural, scientific, professional and humanitarian organizations scattered throughout every nook and cranny of this country.

These are accomplished, first because of our common roots, the Filipino blood flowing vibrantly in our veins. Second, there accomplishments stem from our ability to attain some measures of success and prestige.

Despite the many years of living in this country, so far away from the Philippines, we are and always will be Filipinos. We love our mother country. We want peace and we value the return of democracy. We are indeed united in this belief. That is the reason why we say there is only one Filipino. Yet our unity, harmony, and progress in this country remain to be an elusive dream. How often do we see rifts in our leadership developing to a point of internecine confrontation between leaders? It is happening within our midst. It has been proven time and time again that the multitude that does not condescend itself to unity only reaps conclusion, while the unity that does not bother to depend on the multitude tends to invite tyranny. Certainly, one of the ringing challenges that the modern-day society faces is to foster harmony among its members; without it, it would be impossible to achieve anything for the common good. Disunity or factionalism in a community could dissipate available energies and resources that could otherwise be applied to the tasks of uplifting the socioeconomic conditions of the people.

For the significant time I spent with civic and social organizations in San Diego and with my involvement in the Association of Philippine Physicians in America (APPA), I had entertained the impression that among the Filipinos living in America, only a few still possess the credibility, spirit and the will for unity. The dream still remained elusive.

We witness Inaugural Ball and Recognition Night in Fil-Am organizations with the theme, *"Unity-Pagkakaisa"* which means "Unity-Oneness". Philippine Faire had its theme, *"Ginintuang Layunin- Pagkakaisa,"* meaning "The Golden Principle is Unity." These are common charm that existed in communities for almost twenty years and has not stopped dreaming for unity.

It had been an uphill battle on rough and stormy seas for Filipinos in this country in their dream for unity. This subject was talked about in Filipino American communities all over the United States. It was in their agenda for more than a quarter of a century, particularly for the "Third and Fourth Wave" Filipino immigrants. This theme appeared in editorials and writings in various publications and was discussed in speeches and in conversations, all expressing their wishes and aspirations for unity. Very soon, these Filipino immigrants comprising the Filipino American Organizations may fade away as they approach the twilight of their lives.

When talking of unity, harmony and solidarity, we expressed them in hyperbolic terms especially around election time in our respective associations. Often we delivered the subject in masterly oratory and erudition to the point that it sounded like a dream that seemed real in our minds, yet at the same time are so far away and illusory like a mirage on a hot desert. No matter how we sweeten the language, the dreams really never change year after year. We dream of national unification or greater political clout of harmony among ourselves, of more concerted humanitarian work here and abroad in helping to rebuild the Philippines, and of pooled financial resources to build a Filipino Cultural Center in our respective communities...the list goes on. There is that torpor for improvement in Filipino harmony, cohesiveness and camaraderie.

While Filipino Americans have made strides numerically, their sense of community and larger identity remain elusive. An elusive dream is a goal or vision we would like to achieve or fulfill but always remain just out of our grasp no matter how much we struggle to reach it. Although there are clear signs that as a group, we Filipinos in America are slowly beginning to coalesce, many still remain rooted in ethnic identities. The obstacles to drawing them together are geographical, dialect differences, and customs, plus continuous political rivalries. It has frustrated the efforts of some Fil-Am leaders, who don't benefit from the sense of solidarity often found in African American and Latino communities. Asian Americans, especially Filipinos, are more divided than blacks and Hispanics at the polls and often struggle at being recognized nationally.

Today, we Filipino Americans are beginning to yield considerable influence. As we work toward our common goal of progress and advancement in the community, our unity and numbers should lead us to greater political and economic power. While the city government is now reaching out to minority groups for participation and representation and while we are given these opportunities, we must not "miss the boat." Our image in America must be solid, based on our unity. This is the time to speak as one.

It is important to understand that basically we are an ethnic minority. We must, therefore, use our skills, experience and expertise to promote our heritage, improve our image in the community and our place in American Society. We must establish a political clout whether we like it or not. Politics play a major role in American way of life. The appointment of Filipinos in city positions are events that should stir us and be utilized as "Pinoy" arousal to rally on, to get involved, to be active in our community organizations, in politics and in mainstream America.

As flexible and resourceful people that we are, we should never give up this struggle for unity. Despite our interpersonal problems, I do believe our people reside in our pride, love passion and compassion for one another. These are the bonds that hold us together, our strength of purpose and love of family. There is a subtlety in the ways we do, not evident to other foreigners. We are the ultimate and supreme arbiters of our fate. Filipinos are passionate people and history has shown that they have the capacity to channel their emotional and physical energy toward defined objectives. And this reality, I know shall long endure with the passing of time.

Change we must. Change, however, does not seem to fit the Filipino Diaspora. Uncertainty continues to define who and what we are. The future is ours to channel in the direction we want to go.

PEACEMAKING –EVOLUTIONARY BEHAVIOR
HUMANS AND OUR RELATIVES -
THE PRIMATES

Dateline, February 24, 2012

In my article, "TORPOR OF IMPERATIVE CHANGE - UNITY OF FILIPINO AMERICANS (PMAC News March, 2012), I wrote, "How often do we see rifts in our leadership developing to a point of internecine confrontation between leaders. It is happening within our midst..."

HUMOROUS THIS ARTICLE may portray, it is straight from the horse's mouth. This phrase also has little to do with horses when used in English literature and conversation. It is used as a way to say that information is from a reliable source.

Once I was asked by a group of concerned citizens of a Filipino American Community Organizations of San Diego to be a member of an Ad Hoc Committee to help mediate and bring together two groups of community leaders. They were in the midst of a divisive controversy that was leading to a crisis in leadership in the umbrella organization in the County. As Filipinos coming from a diversity of origin in the different islands of the country, these difficulties were products of the Filipino psyche, "our pride, our intelligence, our *"amor propio,"* our culture, our loss of face, and concern for our sign of weakness or surrender." The myriads of small and separate unions are uniquely Filipino. It is our expressed manifestation of the ethnic and linguistic boundaries that separate us; our strong adherence to traditions and customs also blind us.

There is an amusing similarity between primates and humans in peacemaking abilities/scenario.

I wrote a commentary entitled, "Primates do better job of resolving differences than human counterparts" published in the Filipino Press in San Diego, where I was a contributing columnist for a long time. The parody in the title catches your eye. My colleague friend Dr.

Ching Baquiran, a writer, posted a similar story some years ago. He inspired me to read the volumes of De Waals, primate observations. I paraphrased a few of Ching's astuteness.

Emory University primatologist Frans de Waal, an author of a fascinating and marvelous book entitled "Peacemaking among Primates", have an excellent take on the visible elements, leaving the roots the business of the likes of Darwin and Dawkins.

As part of intermediaries in the Filipino leader's dispute, we labored hard. Did we accomplish our mission? It was perceived that we did in one way or another, but there were those who said otherwise.

These efforts we spent on mediation between two humans, had prompted me to write this piece about our peace-making abilities. If it is not blasphemy, I would like to extrapolate the behavior of non-human primates regarding peacemaking to human efforts. I'd say the former know how to do it, the latter does it in a complex transaction.

For our perspective, it is an interesting phenomenon that primates are able to form a stable social relationship. This observation has been described by ethnologists and primatologists based on keen observations of non-human primates in captivity. For instance in a group of primates, "...the members are simultaneous friends and rivals, squabbling and fighting for food and water, but thereafter, becomes friends and comfort each other by means of body contact."

Some have theorized that these animals realize they cannot win a fight without losing a friend; therefore, they have developed some forms of behavior, which are either to reduce damage afterwards. "The first solution is known as tolerance, the second, reconciliation." With these traits, they maintain their communities and manage to live in a cohesive fashion for many years in spite of non-ending and veritable battlegrounds.

Lately, de Waals observed similar moral indignation when Occupy Wall Street - Wall Street Occupation movement - a dramatic moment of unknown long-term effects spread all over the nation. It has been played out over the past year. The phenomenon looked familiar and similar moral outrage over economic inequity expressed by monkeys and chimps. And he thinks we could learn a lesson or two from our fellow primates. Basically the Wall Street protest is similar as based on primate studies, "that goes for the haves as well as the have-nots. Far from being a uniquely human quality, a sense of fairness is something biologists have seen in studies of primates as well as crows and dogs. Even elephants may have an appreciation of inequity, although de Waal said he and his colleagues haven't done such a study with that species because "you don't want to piss off an elephant."

Another surveillance is that like the Occupy movement, inequality causes tension and stress. For example a monkey angrily jumps on cage walls when she saw that another monkey was consistently getting grapes while she was getting only cucumber slices - that's a protest. This scene of what these authors described get a human laugh including myself.

Somehow, there appears to be a "cooling system, a highly developed one that prevents overheating, explosions or disintegration of the social machinery." Aggression in these primates does not lead to dispersal. The healing process somehow is swift; it does not wait for the time to heal the wounds.

"The peacemaking strategies of the chimpanzees, the bonobos, Rhesus monkeys and stump-tailed monkeys, ranging from pant grunt, intense sexual contact, grooming the fur of their rival and bottom hold respectively are amusingly interesting."

Now consider the human behavior. "They hug and kiss, test and offer through intermediaries, smile or offer an aloof handshake and apologies." There is no difference between apes and humans peacemaking strategies, except that we humans approach it with great complexities and difficulties compared with primates. I beg your pardon for this amusing comparison. The juxtaposition of the peacemaking behavior of humans and primates, trivial and mundane, we have to reconcile, for it is not paradoxical.

If we do not learn to make our reconciliation processes work, then I venture to say that we should learn from our closest relatives, the primates. If they can do it, why can't we-the "fifth species" - does it? We must stir to these strategies in every Fil-Am association. We Filipino Americans have much to learn from our fellow primates: each has unique and sometimes novel means for conflict resolution. As the saying goes, a gentleman is a man who can "disagree without being disagreeable" by James Conant.

VALENTINE'S DAY REMEMBERED

Dateline, February 15, 2012

VALENTINE'S DAY, ALBEIT celebrated yesterday shall not be forgotten for February is a month of romance.

Julio Iglesias the formidable singer from Spain made worldwide popularity with a song "To All The Girls I've Loved Before". I will add "My Funny Valentine" a song that became a popular jazz standard, sung by Frank Sinatra when I was young. It originated from a show tune from the 1937 Richard Rodgers and Lorenz Hart musical Babes in Arms in which it was introduced by former child star Mitzi Green. I am one of those frustrated singer and I sing all these songs accompanying myself in my favorite incredible and a complete marvel Kawaii Grand piano. I remember that the birthday of one of my girlfriends was in February 14. Am I stupid to recollect all these things now? My brain cells synapses demonstrate the famous Alzheimer is not here with me yet.

In a recent analysis in USA Today those celebrating Valentine's Day will "spend an average of $126.03, up 8.5% from 2011 based on recent survey of National Retail Federation (NRF) which began 10 years ago. Total spending is expected to reach $17.6 billion.

Men will outspend women on the holiday by almost double, spending an average of about $169 vs. about $86 for women."

Taking opportunity of the festival people express gratitude and love for sweethearts, spouses, teachers, parents or any other person close to them. Virtually no different from what we Filipino Americans celebrate the love day.

The crux of the matter: Now, Cupid wants your money. Or are we able to do this now in the current financial crisis? The U.S. economy is facing some formidable challenges in 2012. But that doesn't mean that your love ones will not spend the money.

Can we Fil-Am spend that much? How does Filipinos celebrate this event so called love holiday? It is a day when Pinoy gentlemen is deeply ingrained out on what perfect gift they could send for their beloved special ones ... definitely not surprising to that usual Filipino celebration of Valentines Day.

A friend told me, "However, if you don't have enough money during this economy, and time to have your partner for an exclusive date, you can send cards and Valentines Text Messages or Funny Valentine's Day Quotes to them without spending much money from your own pocket!"

A phenomenal song, "Love is a many Splendored Thing", is an understatement for this special day. This holiday we observe with our heart and soul is an ultimate Splendor of celebrating, rekindling love and devotion, fresh intimate affection and relations, and new memories made to place us into the horizon of the moonlight. Love your love once. The greatest science in the world both in heaven and on earth - is love.

I wish to share some of my favorite quotations I've found on the subject of love from my search engine:

- For you see, each day I love you more today more than yesterday and less than tomorrow. -Rose monde Gerard.
- Love is a symbol of eternity. It wipes out all sense of time, destroying all memory of a beginning and all fear of an end. - Author Unknown
- Love - a wildly misunderstood although highly desirable malfunction of the heart which weakens the brain, causes eyes to sparkle, cheeks to glow, blood pressure to rise and the lips to pucker. - Author Unknown.

PINOY PRIDE CELEBRATION IN LAS VEGAS

IT'S SO NICE TO BE IN AMERICA

Dateline, May 8, 2012

THE RECENT MAY 5-6, 2012, PINOY PRIDE CELEBRATION was a huge success. It was an outdoor Philippine socio-cultural Heritage Fair at the Town Square in Las Vegas. It was organized to be the Biggest Filipino Celebration in Nevada in honor of Asian Pacific Heritage Month. Darna Productions presented the biggest Filipino celebration as a demonstration of the great gifts of Asian Pacific culture! "The mission is to showcase the best local and mainstream Filipino talents through art, music, television, film and dance. Portion of the proceeds from this event will benefit Three Square Food Bank. This is a non-profit organization that offers food & nutrition services to children & seniors in Las Vegas," according to Darna Productions.

An estimated twenty thousands of Filipino Americans, young and old and Pan-Asians and others came with their families. There were fun rides, retail, food booths, contest, bands, Kundiman songs and dancing. By far it was the ultimate celebration ever. The highlight of the event was the Santacruzan, a religious parade that is an annual tradition in the Philippines.

Creation of activities in the Fil-Am community in the Clark County is a great move that will undoubtedly produce more consciousness about Fil-Am community in Las Vegas and improve its image, visibility and leadership. As a socio-economic-cultural undertaking **PINOY PRIDE** will indeed enhance the Filipino American unity, and harmony, stature, pride, recognition, and visibleness in the community, *vis-à-vis* its culture and tradition. It is a "Pinoy" arousal to rally on, to get involved, and to be active in our community organizations, in politics and in mainstream America.

This has been a product of the increasing number of Filipino-Americans residing in this city. The are now 87,000 Filipino Americans in Clark county according to recent 2010 census, representing the majority of Pan-Asian population. It is the fourth largest in the U.S.

We are also looking forward to the **FIESTA FILIPINO** festivities on June 2 & 3, 2012 to be sponsored by NaFFAA Nevada chapter– a commemoration of the Philippine Independence Day. Community Fil-Am organization like the latter is now in the doorsill of most Filipino-Americans homes in Las Vegas.

Politically, the Filipino organizations in Las Vegas created impact in the eyes of politicians formally recognizing the difference they make in their community and nationally.

As Fil-Am community grows in number, they also become active in matters that impact the lives of the people. What a great CHANGE and improvement in our quest to be recognized by state, county and city government. Filipino empowerments are in our dreams, goals and aspirations.

In the early years Filipinos were called the "forgotten Asian Americans." The history of how they came to the U.S. was never kept alive among the Filipino-Americans of today. What appears to some to be underlying confusion underscores the fact that so little is known about the history of Filipinos in America. Ergo, so much research still remains to be done before the multi-faceted, and long history of Filipinos in America can fully unfold for Filipino students and everyone else to learn. Yet one might persistently ask, "Who are the Filipino Americans? What makes them appear different, yet one and the same?" They will know it at the **PINOY PRIDE CELEBRATION!**

Celebration like **PRIDE OF PINOY** is a Filipino arousal that starts the ball rolling by openly expressing who we are, our talents, values, our pride and our culture. In an event like this one is fundamentally significant in that it will be a revelation to the American born Filipinos.

Years ago, back to the 60s & 70s, Filipinos in America were described in an amusing way by Northern California Pilipino American Students organization stated: "We are hidden in the shadows of our Pacific Islander brothers and sisters. If possible, we would like to be able to tell our friends and neighbors that there is more to being a Filipino than just *lumpia* (egg-roll) and *pancit* (rice noodle). We want to be able to tell our friends and family that we have a unique Asian Pacific Islander heritage - a heritage that reflects our being Filipino. A heritage that goes deep into the hearts of all Pinoys, whether we speak English or *Tagalog*, whether we were born in America or in the Philippines, or whether we eat "*kare-kare*"(ox-tail dish with peanuts) and "*pinakbet*" (Ilocano vegetable dish), or hamburgers and french fries. We want to be able to tell our friends that our history is no mystery."

It had changed since then.

We have great Filipino American leaders in our community in Las Vegas (NaFFAA). They have abilities, the transparency and dedication to induce subordinates to work with confidence and zeal. They are faithful to the group members and activities that lead to gain inspiration and also inspires others in the process.

We Filipinos in America have successfully established societies of social, cultural, scientific, professional and humanitarian organizations. Hundreds of Filipino American Communities & Organizations are in every large cities of America. Certainly, one of the ringing challenges that the modern-day society faces is to foster harmony among its members; without it, it would be impossible to achieve anything for the common good.

Filipino immigrants who reach their destination in America will find out first-hand about realities of Life in America. Filipino-Americans are now learning to adapt to life in the United States and find an identity that enables them to fit in to society, while staying true to their cultural roots. The celebration of **Asian-Pacific Heritage Month** is a welcome exposition. It is important to understand that basically we are an ethnic minority. We must, therefore, use our expertise to promote our heritage, improve our Filipino Diaspora in the community and our place in American Society. Close to 9 million of them around the world. "Diaspora" is usually associated with the Jewish people. Like the Jews, we are now practically in every corner of the world managing not only to survive but even becoming successful in various professions and businesses — especially for those who went to the U.S.

It's so nice to be in America- the land of milk and honey, the land of the brave and the free.

FIESTA FILIPINO IN LAS VEGAS

Dateline, June 2, 2012

THE FIESTA FILIPINO celebration on June 2 & 3, 2012 in Las Vegas will be another special community event to enjoy. This is commemorating the Philippines Independence Day – an inexhaustible project of the National Federation of Filipino American Associations (NaFFAA) Nevada Chapter being highlighted in the City - a city of neon lights blazing around the clock, a metropolis that looks like an exotic jewel dropped into the middle of the vast Mojave Desert. This is a repeat performance with a theme of "COMMUNITY OF ONE". It is made possible by the leaders of Fil-Am community with the active and caring participation they extend to the life and activities of Filipino Americans of Las Vegas. The venue is at Boulevard Mall 3528 S. Maryland Pkwy, Las Vegas. Thousands are expected to be in attendance.

Among the several Filipino American organizations in La Vegas, NaFFAA is the organization that took the chair of planning, and manages, organizes, produces, executes, directs and presents the annual commemoration of Philippine Independence to Filipino-Americans and the mainstream community.

It will be featuring live entertainments, the display and the delight in our heritage, cultural and popularity pageant, vendors and lots of great food. Remember, New Carnival Rides for our children!

The theme has chosen these values "one bread, one body, one people- the need for oneness."

Las Vegas is diverse ethnic heritages that strengthen our state and enriches our culture. The distinctive traditions of the Filipino culture contribute significantly to our diversity and enhance our precious ethnic community. In particular the concerned efforts of leaders of NaFFAA Las Vegas on behalf of the Fil Am Community are greatly appreciated by one an all here in this county as well as nationally. NaFFAA Nevada has met with great success and has earned the sincere appreciation of all Nevadans.

As NaFFAA gather to raise funds to continue espousing its projects – a number of programs for development, assistance, political, entrepreneurial training, scholarship and youth assistance in the Fil-Am landscape in our community are ours to savor with joy and pride. The organization's vigor and commitment provide the strength and encouragement to meet the challenges of the future.

As NaFFAA NV undertakes development oriented projects designed to help our people in this community- Clark County, we earnestly hope NaFFAA will be an effective venue for Filipinos to play a pivotal role in political empowerment. Indeed, such expression of NaFFAA' concern and solidarity among us Fil- Am can only lead to the achievement of our goals for Filipinos in America.

We are proud of our multi-cultural diversity and we are especially blessed with a large number of Filipino people in this county. They bring joyful, resilient and devout dimension to our local community in Las Vegas. I have attended one meeting of NaFFAA NV, Meet & Greet at Salo-Salo restaurant and have been impressed of the increased number of young leaders with motivation and dedication among them. I believe leaders are made, not born. I can see the collaborative efforts of so many diverse groups that undoubtedly enhanced the Filipino sense of identity and the quality and level of their participation in this community. Our common roots, the Filipino blood, and our accomplishments stem from our ability to attain some measures of success and prestige. In these days and age, we must foster harmony; without it, it would be impossible to achieve anything for the common good.

Today, we Filipino Americans are beginning to yield considerable influence. As we work toward our common goal of progress and advancement in the community, our unity and numbers should lead us to greater political and economic power. Our image in America must be solid, based on our unity.

Our great need for oneness among us is an understatement. We are not simply individuals only concerned for ourselves. By nature, we are related to one another by ties of blood, of friendship, of social relationships. As God's people, however, we belong to the community and we are bound to one another in the Lord and in Unity.

We would like to continue supporting our leaders, our organizations in these projects which in some ways strengthen the democratic institutions and ideals that the Filipino people stand for but we can only do these through the generous support of the Filipino community and with the goodness of your heart. To quote the "Amazing" Chairman of NaFFAA Nevada, Amie P. Belmonte, "Together, let us renew our commitment to serve our community in greater measure... spur one another unto good works always..."

MABUHAY !

MY POLITICAL INVOLVEMENT

Dateline, 1982

THIS ARTICLE WAS written to inspire you, the readers, especially the Filipino American readers. To quote Sylvia Hemery, "A world is like a stage. All men and women are merely players. They have their exits and entrances, and one man in his time plays many parts." I hope that my missions are achieved whenever you turn a page, and that the windows of your heart, mind, and soul are opened, if only a little.

What impressed me most while writing my life story was the inspiration I received unexpectedly. It moved me up to another stage in my life. From a poor and lowly beginning into the finer aspects of my life, my strong belief of dreams really coming true has been confirmed.

When America became my second homeland, there came a change in my attitude, a willingness to make changes in my personal style, personality and moral consciousness to help those in need in the U.S. and the Philippines. The dream of helping those in need became the highlight of my career as a physician, as seen when I organized a community health clinic, the Operation Samahan Community Health Clinic. It was popularly dubbed as from "ethnic to the mainstream," a shining example that American minorities should emulate.

My extracurricular activities included my involvement in politics, which play a key role in developing strong communities. National and state legislations directly affect our lives. Legislation can have a profound effect on our policies and operations. As Fil-Am community grows in number, they also become active in matters that impact the lives of the people. In the recent past, Filipinos do not participate. Nowadays, we simply partake in the political process in many different ways. Political participation is the active involvement of the people in the political process of decision-making. I partake in a conventional way by participating in campaign activities and communal activities.

It was at this moment that I realized leadership was so very important. People strangely rise to leadership. These select people have certain characteristics - confidence, morality, discipline and respect - that help people recognize them as leaders. Believe in the kindness of people. Respect people. Give everyone the opportunity of the idea to improve his life. I do believe that a leader is a person who directs others, someone who people will follow or somebody who is in charge of others, for instance as the head of an organization.

In 1982 I co-chaired with a friend, Glenn Barroga, in a fundraising for Mayor Tom Bradley of Los Angeles, a candidate for governor of California. I was also a co-chairman of the March Fong Eu Committee when she was running for state secretary. My friend Jim Bates, a city councilman, was active in the Filipino American organizations. He became a congressman and assigned me as a liaison to the Filipino American community. State Senator Wadie Dehdeh was very helpful when I asked for his help on behalf of my colleague who had a problem with his private practice.

In my view, political participation can broadly be defined as the active participation and the involvement of the public in politics to help define societal goals and carry it out in a democracy. The active involvement of the public in the process of democracy helps to establish and keep legitimacy and trust in the political system. Citizens in any political system that is democratically based place a lot of value on the right to have the democratic freedom to help decide their own future.

Congressman Bob Filner was friendly ever since he was elected as city councilman of San Diego, and he supported my election as a commissioner (Board of Governor) of the San Diego Stadium Authority. Last but not least, I was close to Philippine Senator Raul Manglapuz who visited San Diego months before the People Power revolution (EDSA Revolution). He appointed me as a member of the National Executive Board of Movement For Free Philippines (MFP). All these close and personal associations were products of the fundraising held in my home in Del Cerro.

My activities and involvement in medical and charitable organizations, on both local and national levels, contributed to my being recognized and known to the Filipino American community.

Since 1972, I had been active in several civic, social, professional, philanthropic and humanitarian organizations. I had an ingrained passion with commitments to help others in their needs. I was extremely active in the Association of Philippine Physicians in America (APPA), a premier national organization of Filipino doctors. I was the president of the Filipino Medical Association of San Diego for two separate terms as well. Was it leadership in action? Well, leaders have a responsibility to make decisions on behalf of their constituents while recognizing the interests of the organization. I tried to inspire everyone and bring out the best in others.

EMPOWERMENT - WE MUST HAVE

Dateline, April 2012

In my article "PINOY PRIDE CELEBRATION-ASIAN PACIFIC HERITAGE MONTH" I wrote, "As Fil-Am community grows in number, they also become active in matters that impact the lives of the people. What a great CHANGE and improvement in our quest to be recognized by state, county and city government. Filipino empowerments are in our dreams, goals and aspirations."

THE SOPHISTICATED EDUCATION and cultural awareness of increasing numbers of Filipinos in America and in the advent of Information Age have helped us being recognized in the mainstream. We are doing it in Las Vegas, Nevada. The leaders of NaFFAA NV have come of age serving the community in greater manner.

The indispensable role of many Filipino American writers, intellectuals wage ongoing promotions with collective voices heard loud and clear by the American public and city government. Thus far, we have survived and managed to keep our image as competent leaders. I truly feel that we should continue to strive to maintain our parity with our American counterparts. Yes, there is still plenty of room for improvement and pave us to a brighter tomorrow.

The socio-cultural associations we organize enhances Filipinos' positive image and becomes a source of selecting a minority when mainstream and governmental political leaders need to find a representation from the Filipino American community. This is empowerment. It is a contemporary buzzword. Its modern use originated in the civil rights movement, which sought political *empowerment* for its followers.

We must be proactive in creating a positive change and empowering the Filipino American community through the political process. Participate in political action activities that create a strong and effective voice for the Filipino American Community Empowerment and the Filipino Community that it represents. We must support the efforts of Filipino Americans leaders in this community in achieving fair and more equal representation for their community in politics. It's time we walk the talk when it applies to building political empowerment within the Filipino Americans. My question: Any Filipino American has ever been elected to the Nevada State Assembly a body representing a state that is home to increasing number of American of Filipino heritage? I will repeat what I said before: to wit: "from ethnic to mainstream, we must show our skills, our experience and expertise to promote our visibility, heritage, improve our image in the community and our place in American Society." To paraphrase the mission of Rising Asian Pacific American Coalition For Diversity (RAPACD) of Las Vegas, states, whose president is the entrepreneur and brilliant Salve Edelman, "We must Represent and serve as Advocate for the Asian Pacific American community. We must Engage. Educate. Empower. Inspire!"

Modesty aside, I have been in state and city positions of what one may call political empowerment building. I was in a Filipino American Community of San Diego County with the largest Pan-Asian ethnic subgroup of an estimated 100,000 Filipinos.

How I wish to stay humble or demure, albeit as I see it I can "sing my own praises." Not braggadocio. Simply to inspire and spur all leaders and for community to reflect how empowerment can be achieve, breaking barriers, gaining respect and achieving acceptance from mainstream America.

CALIFORNIA BOARD OF MEDICAL EXAMINER
FIELD COMMISSIONER (ORAL/CLINICAL EXAMINER)

On September 26, 1978 barely eight years in my practice in San Diego, this author was honored to be appointed as Field Commissioner under the State Medical Board of California. This appointment involved conducting the oral and comprehensive clinical examination process (Examiner) to candidates applying for licensure in California to both Foreign Medical Graduates (FMGs) and American doctors from other states. It was my understanding I was the first Filipino American physician appointed to this position in the State of California under Governor Jerry Brown's administration.

This empowerment given to a Foreign Medical Graduate (FMG) was unexpected. I served for more than twelve years, until I relinquished my position.

In January 1989, a city position I was appointed was as follows:

BOARD OF GOVERNOR – CITY COMMISSIONER SAN DIEGO STADIUM AUTHORITY

In February 1989, the Filipino American newspapers reported: "The large Filipino American community of more than 130,000 the largest Asian group in the County of San Diego, rejoices in the naming of Dr. Cesar D. Candari by the City Council of San Diego to the board of governors of the Jack Murphy Stadium Authority. He will serve for four years."

I was on the floor during the session of the city council, with the active endorsements of council members Bob Filner, Abby Wolfsheimer, Linda Bernhardt, John Hartley and Wes Pratt. Wolfsheimer made the nomination, presided by the San Diego city Mayor Maureen O'Connor.

The late Ernie Flores, Jr. editor and publisher of Filipino Press, a Filipino community newspaper in San Diego, stated: "Dr. Candari has the distinction of being the first Pan-Asian to be named to the prestigious board." The board makes policies for the San Diego Jack Murphy Stadium, where events like football's Super Bowl and the San Diego Padres games were held.

In a press interview, I stated that now was the right time for Filipinos to participate and be represented in the policy-making body of the city.

A Filipino businessman commented: "It is an honor for the Filipinos here in San Diego to have one of their own people contributing major decisions that affect the profitability of San Diego's famous stadium, a major source of revenue for the city." He further added: "Dr Candari's evident visibility in the city and state's political arena has been producing positive image results for Filipinos everywhere."

How I functioned and contributed to the city's profitability was an exciting experience for a Filipino American physician. I met a number of politicians and businessmen in the city and befriended Alex Spanos, the CEO and owner of the San Diego Chargers. It was four years of loyal and dedicated service to the City.

LIAISON FOR ASIAN COMMUNITY

I served for Congressman Jim Bates in 1982 as liaison for the Asian Community in San Diego and as a member of the Asian-American Advisory Committee.

He was a member of the U.S. House of Representatives from California's 44th congressional district from 1983–1991.

I was able to connect with him regarding the situation of discrimination on Foreign Medical Graduates (FMGs). Eventually, all of our concerted efforts against discrimination of FMGs led to the passage of an anti-discrimination legislation signed into law in 1992- the Health Profession Reauthorization Act.

It was community leadership, visibility, stature, recognition and involvement in politics and mainstream America that catapulted me to the prestigious positions. We must establish a political clout whether we like it or not. Politics play a major role in American way of life. I hope that our youth and young professionals, inspires a new generation of individuals to be new and rising leaders for the community. I hope one day, we see a Filipino American in the Chambers of the Senate and Assembly.

MODEST COMPETENCE

Dateline, July 2011

WITH ALL CANDOR and humility, I claim with pride my modest lists of achievements as a healthy mix of story-based stuff and truthful facts. In my substantial number of reflection and introspective analysis of how I had been able to achieve success in my journey, my brain synapses have given me the following information flow that described my values and beliefs that seemed worthwhile to share with every reader.

One grows as an individual and achieved a "modest competence" that implies a set of skills or abilities. It can be seen as a measure of personal autonomy and agency in general as well as the capacity to be competent in being a contributing member of society. Leadership is fundamental in one's desire to do better in humanity.

If I had not listened to my inner self and had let myself be completely taken over by the words of others, I probably would not have achieved what I have all in my life, desired to achieve, to escape poverty and to make something on my hometown.

The following are values to ponder. Believe in the kindness of people. Respect people. Give everyone the opportunity of the idea to improve his life. I do believe that a leader is a person who directs others, someone who people will follow or somebody who is in charge of others, for instance as the head of an organization. Leaders have a responsibility to make decisions on behalf of the people who have appointed them to the position and the interests of the organization.

I tried to inspire everyone and bring out the best in others. I kept the members focused on moving the organization towards its ideal future, motivating them to overcome whatever obstacles lie in the way. Life can be changed if you want it and you believe it. What I believe is that if I keep myself at peace with everyone, including me, I can easily listen to my inner self, despite the confusions that others may give.

Belief is the greatest source of achieving and maintaining positive attitude. A person with strong belief is most likely to take action. At the end of the day, what does count in our life is our action. How life can be change from one moment to another! In the short period of time that I wrote my first book, I traveled the moment of my time!

All leaders need respect, respect for themselves, respect for others, and most importantly, respect from others. People adhere only to those whom they respect; therefore, a leader must earn the respect of others through consistent and continued accountability.

Whatever you have heard about you, whatever was said to you, what count most in life is that you believe in yourself. If you don't, may be no one will. Sometimes people hurt you of what they said. Console yourself that God did not promise days without pain, laughter without sorrow, sun without rain, But He did promise strength for the day, comfort the ears, and light for the way. A true leader must be willing to do what is best for everyone, not just his own personal benefit. To be a good leader requires a tremendous sense of dedication ... you don't even consider the dimension of time. You do everything you can, without limit, to do what's best for everyone. These select people have certain characteristics that help people to recognize them leaders. Amongst these are confidence, morality, discipline and respect.

Leaders are made, not born. Leadership is forged in times of crisis. When a leader believes in himself/herself, others will follow suit. Leaders cannot expect others to believe in them if they doubt themselves or the decisions they make. In addition, in order to lead, one must have a sturdy set of moral values. A steady set of values will always be a reference when one is faced with tough decision-making. People should be able to predict how their leader will react to certain situations because they know what creed they live by. A leader with moral values gives those who they lead assurance that the decisions they make will be desirable ones.

I learned from my dear mother of another trait that a good leader must have - discipline. Leaders must be able to first discipline themselves and then those who they lead. With little effort, a leader should be able to put others on the right track. It is their choice to use them effectively or not to use them at all. It is the ability of the leader to induce subordinates to work with confidence and zeal.

Finally, a good leader must be faithful to his group members and activities. Having faith in self-abilities and the world around him/her the leader gains inspiration and also inspires others in the process.

"Be gentle and you can be bold; be frugal and you can be liberal; Avoid putting yourself before others and you can become a leader among men." – Lao Tze.

I pray I have done my part.

OBAMACARE

IT'S IMPACT TO DOCTORS AND PATIENTS

Dateline, March, 2012

AS I WRITE this opinion today (March 31, 2012), the U.S. Supreme Court's conservative majority appears ready to toss out the entire federal healthcare plan -- the plan Republicans delight in calling "Obamacare. In my view, the healthcare law has leaved a lot to be desired. A senior citizen is limited to be treated in a facility/hospital/center because he does not have supplemental insurance coverage; a patient with a major, complicated ailment or difficult surgical procedure needs services of a Medical Center. An ordinary senior citizen cannot have one, unless he/she has Medicare Supplemental Insurance Coverage in the likes of Medigap. There are up to ten unique plans for Medigap coverage. You will have to make sure the plan you want is even available where you live. It still has to follow a set of standards made by the federal government. My brother at age 82 had a coronary artery by-pass as well as aortic valve replacement. UCLA medical center would have been the best to perform the surgery. His Medicare insurance will not allow it. He died after a complication of postoperative surgery in a community Hospital. What this means is that the options provided by the Medicare Supplement Insurance can be different depending which state you are in. It costs a lot more of premiums from patient's pockets. Before purchasing a supplemental policy, it is important to understand the limitations and benefits of such insurance. For example, your supplemental policy may not cover all the expenses you expected; it may impose waiting periods before payments start; or, contain limit on how much you paid and for how long.

What is needed is a comprehensive solution.

One thing to watch out for with Medicare is that while the federal government oversees it, this insurance is actually provided and sold by individual private insurance companies, which are governed by each states law.

Seventy percent of doctors in the US disapprove the Obamacare. So much complexities, but at the end of the day it is the fundamental problem that is in the   Obamacare. The High Cost of Health Care captures the true complexities facing the challenges of the American health care system. Do you believe Medicare, Medicaid - single-payer government-administered health care programs, is more predictable, uniform and reliable than the for-profit health care insurance companies? The former is proclaimed better for doctors and hospitals and certainly better for the patients. Many questions are raised. Again, what is needed is a comprehensive solution.

We are aware of the passions and paranoia that has become nearly impossible for all people, especially the lay people to understand and to talk about healthcare rationally, at least in the political landscape. As a physician, I totally agree with the U.S. Supreme Court's conservative majority to strangle OBAMACARE.

A colleague made this statement: "The notion that there are third parties (Health insurance, government: Medicare / Medicaid) paying for health consumption removes the healthcare recipients (patients) from the concept of PRICE of healthcare demand and consumptions. The SELLERS of medical products / services (e.g.: pharmas, medical device companies) have no incentive to reduce PRICE; in fact they tend to maximize PRICE since there are ready payers (Health insurance, government: Medicare / Medicaid) -- leading to an ever spiraling healthcare costs."   Government in cahoots with private insurance companies is hurting the doctors in this country

In a recent article in CNNMoney, published in New York stated: "Doctors in America are harboring an embarrassing secret: Many of them are going broke. With the recent steep 35% to 40% cuts in Medicare reimbursements for key cardiovascular services, such as stress tests and echocardiograms, have taken a substantial toll on revenue.

This quiet reality, which is spreading nationwide, is claiming a wide range of casualties, including family physicians, cardiologists and oncologists." Currently, a 27.4% Medicare pay cut for doctors started on March 1, 2012. This means primary care doctors particularly the Family practice and Internist is predestined. It is hopeless. Physicians will plummet to the bottom of doom.

Doctors cannot survive this cut due to the flawed estimated Sustainable Growth Rate (SGR) of Medicare. By 2014, 30 million people without insurance will be covered by the ObamaCare. Physician's services fee will undoubtedly be reduced. The impact to seniors in regards to their premium insurance are as follows:

"The per person Medicare insurance premium will increase from the present monthly fee of $96.40, rising to: $104.20 in 2012; $120.20 in 2013 and $247.00 in 2014." This is in ObamaCare Legislation.

Beau Donegan, senior executive with a hospital cancer center in Newport Beach, California, is well aware of physicians' financial woes."Many are too proud to admit that they are on the verge of bankruptcy," she said. "These physicians see no way out of the downward spiral of reimbursement, escalating costs of treating patients and insurance companies deciding when and how much they will pay them."

As the practice of medicine in this country becomes less and less exciting, less satisfying, and more non-rewarding, you will realize that it isn't fun anymore. Nearly one-in-three primary care physicians limit the number of Medicare patients they are able to see. It is a fact that $500 billion were cut from Medicare since 2010.

The crux of the matter is the need to resist this intolerant and regressive progressive liberal arrogance and its assumption of superiority on the rate-setting formula that has transformed into a budget-busting juggernaut that will hit doctors with a lower pay cut for their Medicare patients. We must address the whole health care delivery system, a system of coordinated care, and eliminate cost shifting that results from treating the uninsured. The disturbing problem is insurance industry will fight anything that threatens their profit. If the 30 million people can choose not to be insured and a mandate that providers treat them, which will undoubtedly push the costs onto the rest of us.

May be change will come. What about this idea of doctors would be salaried and organized into large multispecialty group practices similar to the Mayo Clinic and other private clinics; care would be delivered by a single-payer nonprofit system, financed by the taxpayers. Eliminate the private insurance industry, "a parasite on the health care system." Indeed reform is not near, nor will it ever be achieved until there is a fundamental compromise on matters needing a comprehensive solution.

Choose well 7 months from now, for President of the United States of America.

"GOLD IN THE SHADOW"

Dateline, December 21, 2012

Written in Global Balita, Las Vegas, NV. "CESAR D. CANDARI MD of Class'61, Far Eastern University Medical School, was the 2011 Alumnus of the Year. The Golden Jubilee was celebrated at the Monte Carlo Hotel Resort and Casino in Las Vegas, Nevada onJune-15-18, 2011. The award was given during the 32nd annual convention and scientific seminar of the FEUDNRSM Alumni Foundation."

"A second Presidential award from United Class'61 was also bestowed upon his laudable services, exemplary achievements, and valuable contributions to his Alma Mater and the FEUDNRS Alumni Foundation."

The following is Dr. Candari's commentary:

I COULD HARDLY believe that a man from the shadow in medical school could achieve such semblance of fame, coupled with momentous and incontrovertible honor. I was never known in my class other than a serious student of medicine. I had neither the time nor the inclination to be a student leader. As a result I did not join the fraternities, Beta Sigma or Sigma Mu Sigma, and the Student PMA. I was satisfied to be hidden in the 'shadows'. It was neither the dissolution of my persona nor the launch of the individuation process - the dark shadow which everybody carries with him, the inferior and therefore hidden aspect of the personality. It was more of a constructive aspect for I believed a person's shadow might represent hidden positive qualities. This has been referred to as the "gold in the shadow". Was I receiving little attention because someone else is bettering known or more skillful? Absolutely not. I have chosen to be invisible compared to the active officers of our United Class '61. I was not in any class organization such as the Student Council.

Though student politics was in my heart ever since I was in my secondary school years (at the highest echelon of my class), there was no room or time for it in Medical school. I can write, but never contributed to the official newsletter of the FEU Institute of Medicine 'Medical Student.' Remember an idiom - the cream of the crop? Yes, I was never in that vigorous and energetic group of leaders. I never joined the R&R of the class that was popular to everyone. I was solidly ingrained in the passion of commitments, spending few quiet moments alone. I was driven by a consuming desire to become a doctor and make all sacrifices necessary.

My landing in America and the American Dream changed my life, as my template brain started firing synapses. I expected the best from events, people and myself. I trusted my intuition by listening to my inner voice and its direction. I changed my attitudes, habitual thinking and feelings. I was willing to change my personal style, personality and appearance. I fulfilled the calling, which in turn fascinated me.

My struggle to achieve a medical education and become one of the pioneering Filipino American doctors in America is something I wish to inspire others and seek their own paths in life. My experiences were perhaps one of the first Filipino American doctors in breaking barriers, gaining respect and achieving acceptance from mainstream America. My story is for my children's children- for posterity, for my friends, regarding my life history, modest achievements, noble deeds, contributions to society, lessons in life, dreams, joys, woes, etc. I linked up to the future, touch tomorrow today--- leave a legacy.

From the shadows when I was in medical school, there came a change in my attitudes, willing to make changes in my personal style, personality and moral consciousness to help those in need here in the U.S. and in our country. The dream of helping those in need in an aura of the American Dream became the highlight of my career as a physician organizing a community health clinic- the Operation Samahan Community Health Clinic- popularly dubbed as from "ethnic to the mainstream", a shining example worth emulating by all other minorities in America.

If all of us, Golden Jubilarians are in the dawn of our lives- there is still that full-fledged sunrise which is even better for years to come. Nonetheless, now we are in the shadow of light, our 'existence is but a brief crack of light between two eternities of darkness' *vis-à-vis* that tragedy of life. When those befall upon anyone of us, then your classmates will sing not the Gold in the Shadow, instead that lovely and emotional song, "The Shadow -- of Your Smile."

MY YOUTH TIME

Dateline, September 8, 2011

AS WE ARE now living in the modern ethos, we find ourselves leaving the past, which shows how we are today. I am very much engrossed with wonderful, philosophical wisdom about how youth can influence our lives. Whereas some dazzling image and aura might come across us, no one can ever think it is a phase in our life that God has granted us. I trust the following brilliant quotations will give us the needed inspiration to boost our understanding of the younger chapter of our existence.

"Youth" by Samuel Ullman goes as follows: "Youth is not a time of life; it is a state of mind. It is not a matter of rosy cheeks, red lips and supple knees; it is a matter of the will, a quality of the imagination, a vigor of the emotions; it is the freshness of deep springs of life."

I will add my own clarity of the nature of youth: Youth is the time of life when one is young, especially the period between childhood and maturity. Mine started at the end of WWII after which I developed my mettle. The time my maturity began was an indefinable moment. I fathom to say it was in 1952 when I graduated from secondary school at Pandan Bay Institute as a valedictorian.

I was a typical Filipino youth in a non-metropolis landscape. I had a number of dreams in my younger life. I have always been lustful for life. Or is it because I had that feeling of being deprived? To go over in the lighter side of my life during my youth, I developed an interest in music and would have liked to become a good musician. It was at a time when all we had in our home was a radio, where music of the 50's gave us the joy of listening to the big band music of the early 1950's through the rockability of the late 50s. The music was fast and the beat was swing baby swing. Crooners like Sinatra, Como and Patti Page slowly gave way to artists like Little Richard and Jerry Lee Lewis. The romantic sounds of Xavier Cugat, Rumba, Perfidia and the Combacheros group were enamoring.

I was and still am a music lover, and I struggled to learn to sing. Indeed, I was in my high school operetta programs, and these struggles to sing and the love for music led to become trumpet player with Lolo Genaro Villamon, my *maestro* - mentor. He was the founder and bandleader of the KAHIRUP Orchestra, an accomplished high-class band and well known in the province of Antique, Philippines. Learning from him is tough. He was so strict, a true perfectionist that any mistake would result in his striking one's instrument or even upper extremities with his baton. I learned the basics and started to play with the band. As beginners I participated in the Filipino funeral procession with a band in the background providing the music. This was a traditional practice that Filipinos observed in relation to bereavement, honoring, respecting, interring, and remembering their departed loved ones, relatives, and friends. Things did not go along well. I finally gave it up as a trumpeter despite my musing of Louis Armstrong and Miles Davis, famous trumpeters of the 50s.

I became a bugler during my entire secondary school years. No marches for buglers, which suited me just fine. My interest in music did not stop there. My friends called me a superb harmonica player, and I played a homemade bamboo flute, basic guitar player while continuing to sing. I still do to this day. At one time, when "combo" was a common and popular group of music entertainer, I organized a small group of youth friends familiar with cha-cha, rumba and other Latin American music. I led the group as a harmonica player. We had a guitarist; a drummer, a percussion player and we all were singers. You might call us "COMBACHEROS," and we enjoyed doing it. Perhaps this was the very first time that I had proved to be a leader in music. As Arthur O'Shanessey stated, "We are the music makers, and we are the dreamers of the dream..." We entertained and provided music to any group parties for free. Those days were never complex. In our youth, nothing was known about marijuana, aderall and methamphetamines. Indeed, we had all the positive attitudes, a happy outlook in life. We were so lucky. We were serenaders. It was indeed happy moments of my life. This was life eternal. This was all that youth will give you. It was the season for music, a moment in one's life with my youth friends.

MY DAD

Dateline, June 2012

EVERY ONE OF us have a story to tell about our father. I cannot remember a person in my life that had a more significant influence on me than my father. My father (I call him Papa)) has been the driving force behind my academic achievement. Everything I have been able to accomplish with regards to school, I have him to thank for. Throughout my life, my father has been understanding, responsible, and caring. He gave me the inspiration, allowed me to grow and expand my future possibilities. My father is a kind-hearted person. All I want to tell you is about someone who means a great deal to me.

My father Praxides Oirola Candari was the oldest son of four other siblings. He was a schoolteacher. While my dad was studying to be a teacher in San Jose de Buenavista, the capital of the province of Antique, he was recognized as an athletic student. He was a sprinter and a baseball player. I remembered my father while teaching in Pandan public elementary school, served as an umpire in every baseball and softball games in the capital province of Antique in every Western Visayas Regional Athletic competition. Incidentally, the Candari clans were sporty; my father's cousin German Candari from my hometown was an established and well-known Philippine track & field athlete in the early 1930's. German (we fondly call him Tio Maning), was the first Filipino track star to lower the speed of 400 meter dash (now 400 meter run) below 50 seconds became known as the "White Horse" of speed then. He was one of the athletic giants of the era in Far Eastern Games (the Asian Olympics). He won over his competition from Japan, China, Indonesia, Burma and others in the 400-meter dash.

My grandfather was an elected mayor of our town in the early 1914. A strong, dynamic, and feared leader, Presidente Municipal Simeon Candari was also known to be a protector of the poor and was highly respected and loved. My father's younger brother—and my favorite uncle—was Francisco Candari, and he also became mayor of Pandan in 1940, a year before the beginning of the Second World War. He was an advocate for and defender of the poor. He was not impoverished. I readily recall riding in his Ford automobile with pride and dignity. He and his lovely wife Auntie Anna had no children and wanted to adopt me as their son. He was well respected and had dedicated his service to others, particularly the oppressed and underprivileged. Do I have a political pedigree? Those were the kinds of roots I belonged to of which I am full of pride.

My dad taught me many things: the value of having good character, that hard work paid off in great dividends, that although bad things will happen in life, how we react and respond is what will make us or break us. I learned humility from him as he learned humility. My dad shared his own experiences in life to teach me the importance of moral purity. Because of his and my mom's honesty and caring, I decided to face the realities of life's pressures in my delayed schooling – a decision I'm glad I made. He has taught me how to maintain balance in my life.

His heritage gave him the concern to help the needy and the poor people in the barrios. He is a loving man and kind; he listens, suggests, and defends. He became their guru, particularly in their medical problems. He would suggest what medicine or herbal things to take. Perhaps his knowledge of basic medicine came from having six children who were frequently sick in one way or another and learned from the medications the doctor would prescribe. Aside from being a schoolteacher for thirty-five years, I considered my dad a healer. Am I referring to a faith healer? No, rather, he spoke to the poor people and comforted them. I truly believe in the power of prayer in the overall well being of patients, whether it is physical, mental or spiritual. My father believed in Spiritism but he was not an *Espiritista,* which had been practiced in the Philippines for hundred years. Additionally, his interest in palmistry was merely for fun.

It was ironic that my dad, fondly called as Nong Praxis (respectful address to an elder person; Praxis, (short for Praxides) by the poor people of *barangay* Minoro was an appropriate name, because the word praxis is entwined with communication to the poorest of the poor.

My dad was very popular to the fishermen in barrio Minoro. Every early morning he would go to the barrio near the beach and brought home with a bunch of freshly caught fish given to him at no charge. The people liked him, which was why he made a cut above the rest.

After 35 years of service as a public elementary school teacher he retired in 1960 and move with us in Manila. We rented a small house in Quezon City. I was then on my rotating internship and my three other siblings were in college.

In 1963, one year after I arrived in America, my father visited us in Chicago when my son Roy was born. After a short stay in Chicago and California, my father became a permanent resident, petitioned by my older sister Eden living in California. He became a U.S. citizen. Eventually, he went home to Pandan and built a new house in a compound of his property where our small house was located. Uncle Dadong and a cousin an architect helped my dad draw up the plan and developed the property. Finally, a four-bedroom two-story house with one bathroom and shower was completed. He was too proud of his children. My dad with my name and my older brother a dentist both in America designed a medical signage for two doctors. This signage was placed in the frontage at outside wall of our home. Funny, but true.

It was my unrelenting dream to build a house as I had once promised my mother, a sickly mom but with strong positive influence on my life, who I look forward to seeing some day, if only to tell her about my achievements. But I know she knows already.

My father was a pious man. He taught me if I didn't know how to be a boon to mankind, I shouldn't be a bane either. He taught me to be helpful to the poor. I considered him a believer in the wisdom and in the words of John Quincy Adams "In charity to all mankind, bearing no malice or ill-will to any human being, and even compassionating those who hold in bondage their fellow-men, not knowing what they do."

My father taught me to live a simple and straightforward life. The greatest thing I have learned from my father was respect, to treat people kindly and with respect, and to work hard to achieve my goals. I respected my father so much. He was very intelligent. Why he did not consider being in politics was an interesting question. Did he have any political praxis like his dad and his younger bother? He . simply could not afford the substantial costs of being a candidate for the election. Perhaps it was due to his dedication as a teacher that he avoided politics.

If there is one more reason to remember my dad proudly, it is his inborn talent of being an artist. This was well known all over town. For every décor necessary for social programs and activities, he was in-charge of the unique lithographic printings, background designs in canvass, flat woods and cardboards. He is a broad-spectrum category of an artist. One painting I cannot forget was "The Last Supper," which was donated to Auntie Saling Candari Villamon. The robes of the disciples and Jesus Christ were in aluminum foil of different colors taken from candy wrappers with acrylic painting in the background of the last supper. In 1969 when we moved to a new home in San Diego, my dad was with me. While the house was being built, he picked up thrown wood-roof and designed a wood art in which he put together pieces of material from 'flat- wood-roof' cut in different sizes and lengths, glued to an oversize frame and fashioned a '3-D black/silver/gold painted skyline of New York City.' Awesome! This work of art is still hanging in our living room in the last 43 years.

My dad's talent as an artist possibly fascinated my brother, Marcelo, and he became a gifted painter. He is another artist of outstanding abilities, a creative painter, from abstract, realist, scenic, and landscapist, miniaturist. I considered his paintings as inspirational, decorative and nostalgic.

Indeed, my brother's painting talent and my musical abilities are priceless gift of God and from the very extraordinary hands of our dad. But then, there is a popular expression that talent is learned, not inborn.

I am amazed how my brother developed this feat. Marcelo D. Candari sounds like an Italian name (like for instance the legendary Italian painter Michelangelo Buariarroti), however, it is indisputably certain that Dr. M. Candari, DMD is a painter from Pandan, Antique, Philippines. Marcelo is a self-taught artist and continues to learn and expand his talent. If he holds exhibition after exhibition and on the strength of his art alone, he can prove his art to the world, that education is not everything, inborn talent can also prevail. His uniqueness and talent is simply amazing.

No words of mine will be adequate, but for what it's worth, my father had a semblance of a well-rounded person.

One comical thing that his grandchildren enjoyed very much, and humorously so, was his tobacco chewing. He told them to bury his cigar with him when he dies. Indeed, the children seriously inquired whether his cigar was buried with him. His last will and testament is still in the minds of his grandchildren up to this writing and they enjoy laughing about it.

In 1978 my dear father, at age of seventy-four, had a car accident in Los Angeles and died shortly after. It was devastating. He was in good health. My world crumbled under me. He was a wonderful and compassionate human being.

MUSIC BRINGS JOY TO ONE'S HEART

Dateline, May 6, 2012

I HAPPENED TO have two marvelous friends, board mates and classmates in medical school, one an extremely excellent pianist Dr. Manolo Catalan, the other a superb violinist, the late Dr. Boni Gamo. Of course I was so green with envy that I dreamt to be like one of them. In my impoverished town, not a single family has a piano. My dad played guitar and the slightest of violin.

The following tales are factual; all reflect the amusing development of an ordinary musician, which is nostalgic and family-oriented. In today's culture, music is a large part of our lives. Not everyone has the drive to be a musician. But, I do. When someone becomes a musician he learns many things, which non-musicians would never know. That is what I called latent talent. That is I. For many years, no one ever knew, I can play the piano in a simple way.

In 1975 when my children were taught at home on their piano lessons, I would set down after their instruction and start fingering out the chords. It was in the late1980s that inspired me to learn more by myself. The advent of high-powered musical electronics – the Keyboard- made my life in music. It was when I retired and moved to Las Vegas where my exposures to several shows and one-man-band exhibitions made my re-born inspiration for music. I could not believe myself. My fingering, in ad-libs tempo and rhythm has been perfected. Incredible! Ad-libbing is, basically, "playing around with the tune", using licks, riffs and scales (and/or whatever comes to mind) usually in a dramatic or emotional part of a song. You can learn to do it all by ear, but if you don't know where to start and it's all a complete mystery, you can train your ear by listening to the chords and practicing syncopation, i.e. rhythm. All these were developed tremendously despite of the major infirmities in my post retirement life. For ten years, I have done the playing constantly, daily, to enjoy as music brings joy to one's heart. I provided music in family parties and some social organizations, simply to entertain the audience. It's a One-Man-Band- an entertainment that I feel will unite each and everyone into one heart—one people. It gives me an opportunity to connect with friends and old familiar faces. With joy and excitement I listen and learn to the tune that touched our lives. Wherever you are, no mater what life we are in, music will always bring joy to one's heart with a smile.

My style of my music was influenced by the 60's and 70's but I'm not sure I could pin-point what aspect or even who I'm influenced by.

A friend wrote the following: Imagine attending a concert in which if you were to close your eyes, you would assume that the music you are hearing is being created by a cast of band members, each playing their respective instruments. CESAR IS THE MASTER KEYBOARDIST - A PIANIST, SINGER/ CROONER establishes and fuses elements of JASS, BOOGIE, CHA-CHA, LINE DANCE AND FOLK SONGS, KUNDIMAN, LATIN, VISAYAN STANDARD OLDIES SONGS OF THE '50s AND THE '60s. His DELIVERY OF THE lyrics is usually lighthearted, inventive and conjuring vocal sound of a splendored thing. CESAR'S ability to perform improvisational LIVE MUSICAL DISPLAY comparable to solo musicians have mastered such a multi-dimensional sound and captivating live, making him standout among his colleagues of musician doctors. What separates CESAR from the rest of the ONE-MAN-BAND genus is his ability and latent innate talent to play music. It is this skill that makes him unique – God blessed with multiple talents - notable writer, ardent musician, crooner, civic activist, book author, ideal husband to Cely, loving father, a reliable friend, philanthropist, a man of age, and a paragon retired physician. I thank my friend and classmate Tom B. who wrote these kind words. I wish to stay humble and in obscurity all the time, albeit when it is straight from a horse's mouth, I maybe allowed to "toot my own horn."

Life is full of fun and happy times. Not always. I had my share of despair. It is the music that rebounds one from misery. A quote from Billy Joel: "I think music in itself is healing. It's an explosive expression of humanity. It's something we are all touched by. No matter what culture we're from, everyone loves music."

In short, music to ears. It is the art of arranging sounds in time so as to produce a continuous, unified, and evocative composition, as through melody, harmony, rhythm, and timbre. I love it so much; my piano playing is at par with other accomplished friend pianists; I play my two keyboards (placed side by side) with my right and left hand, everyday. I don't play golf. I live in Las Vegas. I am not one of Filipino American gamblers haunted by the specter of compulsion. I don't gamble, however, I love to entertain. A quote goes: "There's music in all things, if men had ears; their earth is but an echo of the spheres."

In our family reunion every year held at Pacific Beach House in San Diego, California, two doctors and a nurse (Candari brothers, Marcelo and me, and sister Loida) entertained by singing English and native songs of the fifties, while I played along on an electronic instrument – the Roland-10 Synthesizer and Yamaha Portable Grand DGX -203. Such was the beauty of getting together and singing all our hearts out. It is always a dreamer. My grandson Caleb C. Coyle baptismal party in one of these reunions was absolutely grand. It could be compared in a saying by Gioacchino Rossini: "Eating, loving, singing and digesting are, in truth, the four acts of the comic opera known as life and they pass like bubbles of a bottle of champagne. Whoever lets them break without having enjoyed them is a complete fool."

THE FIGHT IS NOT OVER YET FOR
FILIPINO VETERANS

Dateline, 2001

FILIPINO AMERICANS IN this country should show an unqualified admiration and a hand salute to Honorable Congressman Bob Filner of the 51st district, San Diego, California, when he let himself be arrested and jailed while trying to join the Filipino World War II veterans during a recent chain-in demonstration in front of the gate of the White House in Washington, D.C. The Congregant is my good friend.

The long story and plight of these unfortunate defenders of democracy in the Philippines during World War II, warrants our attention and unqualified support as Filipino Americans residing in this country as professionals, law-abiding and tax-paying citizens of this nation. There is a blatant inequity in the treatment of Filipino World War II Veterans. It is unfair and discriminatory treatment, an injustice for those to whom this nation owes a debt of gratitude. All veterans of other foreign countries who fought alongside with American soldiers during the Second World War were virtually accorded the military benefits similar to the homegrown U.S. veterans. In fact the Filipino veterans did not.

It is discouraging to note the discriminatory treatment of Filipino Americans in this country. It is more so disgusting when this government takes this brazen disregard of the rights of our compatriots who fought alongside the American soldiers in defending the Philippines from the Japanese invasion; some survived the Bataan Death March.

The story of the 240,000 Filipino veterans of World War II came about when in 1941 President Delano D. Roosevelt called for mobilization of Philippine soldiers to fight along with the Americans in defending the Philippines, a country under U.S. territory then. These men fought under the American flag. Congress in 1942 granted U.S. citizenship to those recruited soldiers of Filipino nationality as an expression of gratitude and appreciation.

After the war, however, in 1946, U.S. congress passed the Recession Act, denying full benefits to Filipino veterans their pensions, hospital benefits and death benefits, a promise it reneged. Worst yet, they were denied becoming U.S. citizens.

After years of lobbying by a few spirited Filipino Americans, the war veterans were finally eligible to apply for U.S. citizenship in 1990. This was one of the most significant overhauls in the immigration laws that eventually allowed Filipino veterans to become U.S. citizens. We succeeded in our long battle for naturalization of Filipino veterans of World War II, but it was too late. Many of the 240,000 veterans had already died, and those still living, 70,000 in total, were too old, poor and sickly; yet still yearning for the full benefits accorded to war veterans. 28,000 are now U.S. Citizens residing in this country at an average of seventy-five years old. Sadly, they are fending for themselves while waiting their just compensation. They have left their families and love ones in the Philippines in order to obtain their U.S. citizenship and whatever little benefits they have while residing in this country.

The policy of the Department of the Veterans Affairs, in opposing the Equity bill, reeks of discrimination. Many of us had already written letters to our congressmen and senators; thousands of phone calls were placed. We need time, effort and even money to achieve our goals, and we should be willing to give that much if this is the price for recognition of our rights. Yes, these chain-in demonstrations, marches and hunger strikes are big moves. But in politics, it's not the big moves that count.

We must educate the American people to sympathize with our cause to tell this government to finally grant these veterans their benefits denied them for fifty-one years before they die in vain.

STORM HIT NEAR MY ISLAND OF
PARADISE

Dateline, December 21, 2012

THE HORRENDOUS DEVASTATION that swept these two cities of Cagayan de Oro and Iligan City, in the recent tropical storm Sendong / Washi (International name) conveys a very sad story. The death toll so far is estimated to more than a thousand; almost 400,000 people are displaced and damaged nearly P2 million in agriculture, and tens of millions in property. The devastation brought by the typhoon has compounded the miseries of the people. It was proclaimed a state of calamity. Entire communities, not only of homes and schools but incalculable repositories of culture and human memories, were gone in a mad instance of Nature, washed to the lowland of Cagayan de Oro, poor people living along riverbeds suffered. We ask if there will be deliverance from these crippling maladies. So many poor people died. Some bodies were found on the shores of **Camiguin Island,** 77 kilometers away.

In spite of calamities like this one, life must go on. We pray that the people of Northern Mindanao and Eastern Visayas are strong to face the reality in life. In times like this all that we can say is – pray. Calamities are part of this world. And it's just us humans who can't accept that sad truth. The Philippines is often hit by storm because warm bodies of ocean water surround it. But mostly, in the east part of the Philippines is always visited because it is facing in the Pacific Ocean. Cagayan de Oro and Iligan are vulnerable to storm surges and flooding. Such storms are becoming more frequent, fiercer, and more destructive. The fury of Typhoons Ondoy, Peping, Peding, Reming, Quiel, and now Sendong were adding wretchedness to our *kababayans*.

We must help our unfortunate countrymen. While government agencies are working on the affected areas, the global Filipinos are collecting relief goods as well as cash contributions to be sent to the devastated areas. That is *"bayanihan"* in action. We must simply learn the true meaning of Bayanihan (working together), the embodiment of what a true Filipino like you and I should be. The words "Bayanihan" have inspired and spirited our people in forging the Philippines into a great nation. Building mutual goodwill all the time and as Filipino Americans, we must help our poor countrymen, not just during calamities like this one in Mindanao but also work for a change of mindsets and as the Filipino Diaspora, we must continue to rebuild our nation recover from these calamities and the specter of poverty.

It is common knowledge that our countrymen are facing the realities at hand concerning different narratives of tribulations in the midst of natural wealth and beauty of our land: conflict, war, poverty, and as the events of the last week have shown, increasing environmental damage. The enormity of problems continued to reel from the terrible legacy left by the undesirable former presidents of our country - the massive institutionalized corruption, crony capitalism, bad or weak leadership and a host of other problems - it is time to wake up. And now to add this tragedy of Nature, the typhoon Sendong is a misery and disaster to our poor *kababayans*.

Let it be known that living in a democratic government in the Philippines is not enough. We need reforming our erratic and ineffective justice system. Political reform must be done. Noynoy Aquino is right in saying, "The core principle of this reform program is this -- the guilty should be made accountable because if not, it would like we have kept the door open for anyone who would want to abuse our people... We are all working for a new Philippines, one where there is equality, where whoever does wrong, whatever his status in life may be, is punished, a country where justice rules." HALLELUJAH.

Calamities like these come and go and do not affect a relationship one has with God unless one starts to blame God. Our *'bayanihan spirit'* as Filipinos will stay!

A CHALLENGE

Speech, Philippine Medical Association (PMA)
San Diego

Dateline, 1987

Following excerpted from my speech:

...ONCE AGAIN I consider it an honor, a privilege and a tremendous challenge to be at the helm of the PMA of San Diego for the next two years. More than ever before, I am now aware of the greater significance of our association in this part of the country. I promise you a dedicated leadership, but I shall also need your counsel and participative action so that we can accomplish our objectives...

In this seventh anniversary of our organization, I have these observations to make...We have been slow in our growth, yet persistent; our membership remained status-quo, but quality is high; over the years you have continued to strengthen our association; you have talents, you have leadership, you have professional responsibility, professional unity and above all, the camaraderie within our group is exemplary. There are three things, however, that appear difficult to accomplish: your monies, your involvement, and your valued time.

...These give me an opportunity to dwell on the subject and perhaps bring to you my first message. Membership in a professional association like ours is a hallmark of the profession. The organization can only be as strong as you want it to be. To survive and achieve our goals, we must continue to give our best; we need your total commitment and sustained involvement. Your service to the association provides strength to this institution and without doubt rallies us to greatness and responsibility as we pursue our professions in competition with our peers of other nationalities. The more cohesive and supportive the members of our group are, the more we shall be respected and considered...

Let us all recognize anew that a contribution to the profession--our involvement with the PMA of San Diego--is the cornerstone of professional behavior. Let us eliminate expectations from our discussion of the association; instead, we should ask ourselves how we could contribute? To paraphrase the late President Kennedy, let us not ask what the association can do for us, but instead ask what we can do for our association. I like to think that all of you are willing to do your share and participate in our undertakings. There are indeed a great number of compelling reasons why we must be involved with organized medicine. Against the current backdrop of crucial issues and nagging problems that face the minority physicians in this country, the situation is appalling. Indeed, we must be more vigilant and to continue to meet these challenges. There is no question that you and I have served and still serving an indispensable role in the health care and delivery system in this country. We are knowledgeable and compassionate members of the medical profession. Thus far, we have survived and managed to keep our image as competent. I truly feel that we should continue to strive to maintain our parity with our American colleagues. Yet, there is still plenty of room for improvement. The FMG has not been granted a section in the AMA House of Delegates. We still have to fight for equality before licensing boards, equality before specialty boards, equality in medical staff privileges, and equality in job opportunities.

...Please do not forget our unfortunate colleagues who, despite passing the many qualifying examinations, cannot get into the residency training program in this country simply because they graduated outside of the country of North America. The Association of Philippine Physicians in America and the American College of International Physicians are lobbying for the passage of a legislation introduced by our friend and supporter Honorable Congressman Jim Bates that aims to guarantee equal rights and opportunities for the FMG in this country and fight for the rescission of these discriminatory licensure laws. We certainly hope that their endeavors will merit the support of Congressman Bates and of his colleagues in Congress. All we are asking for sir, (Congressman Bates), is equality; we are not asking for superiority...

We all have the overriding moral obligation to protect our threatened profession, to direct the changes ourselves, and to defend the rights and dignity of the foreign medical graduates. Politics must be a part-time job of everyone in hospitals and in city, county, and state medical society as well as in communities and government affairs.

MAINSTREAM AMERICAN MEDICINE

Speech PMA San Diego

Dateline, 1989

Following excerpted from my address:

...TONIGHT CULMINATES MY two years of serving as president of the PMA of San Diego and with the expenditure of personal time and sacrifices, I am relinquishing the command of leadership with a profound sense of fulfillment from an honest belief that I have given the PMA, for the second time around, the best that I can.

The history of the association began a decade ago. It brought us the bold leadership of Dr. Adelito Gale, Dr. Renato Masilungan, and once again Dr. Edwin Yorobe. I have served mine and am very much proud to say that I have accomplished what I had envisioned. And that is to be able to galvanize the participation of members and promote the immaculate camaraderie of the group. We have been able to bring forth the identity of the association as we merge into the mainstream of American medicine. I feel comfortable and proud to say that we have represented the PMA of San Diego most prominently in the national organization of the Philippine Physicians in America...

...Once again, ladies and gentlemen, in this administration we have demonstrated excellence in our continuing medical education activities. As a scientific organization, we must continue to advance our knowledge in the art of medicine for the ultimate benefit of the patient. I commend you all for your participatory leadership during my administration in your active lobbying efforts for the cause of the FMG flight in this country.

My last message to you is this: In this time of abrupt changes in the practice of medicine and the outside influences and control of healthcare delivery in this country, let us continue to help one another in our endeavors in our practice, improve and strengthen our recognition and status in the profession. I thank all the officers, special mention to my CME committee and all members who, in one way or another, had given their time in the success of this association; and my family, especially my confidant and adviser, my dear wife Cely, who makes things easier for me.

The two years of stewardship of PMA of San Diego were exciting. Membership had grown and camaraderie was maintained. The monthly meetings and continuing medical education sponsored by drug companies provided excellent speakers and dinners in every local gourmet restaurants.

In my administration in the PMA, it dealt with how leadership must be achieve with success. I believed that all leaders need respect, respect for themselves, respect for others, and most importantly, respect from others. Whatever you have heard about you, whatever was said to you, what count most in life is that you believe in yourself. If you don't, may be no one will. Sometimes people hurt you of what they said. Console yourself that God did not promise days without pain, laughter without sorrow, sun without rain, But He did promise strength for the day, comfort the tears, and light for the way.

DISCRIMINATION IN FOREIGN MEDICAL GRADUATES (FMGs) OR INTERNATIONAL MEDICAL GRDUATES (IMGS)

Dateline, 2011

IN THE LATE 1982, I represented the PMA of San Diego as a delegate to the House of Delegates (HOD) in the national Association of Philippine Physicians in America (APPA). This enabled me to become not only as a member of the Electoral College to vote for the officers of the Executive Council, but also the ability to crystallize my dream for the future. I was appointed as chairman of the constitution and bylaws committee of the HOD. Dr. Noli Zosa of Los Angeles won the election for president of APPA in 1982. He was a bright leader who appointed me as his special counsel; after his term, he became the executive director of APPA for a number of years.

The Filipino American medical newsletters and magazines were inundated with editorials and commentaries about the discriminatory atmosphere in the medical profession toward foreign medical graduates (FMGs). It was not happening in full swing, however, there was the disconcerting, if not frightening, portent of fear that was having a strong impact to the FMGs. Some discrimination was evident. The FMGs, particularly those of Asian descent, were well trained and well mannered. Regardless of being in a hospital or in a private clinic practice, FMGs were highly valued in their management geared towards good quality of service and patient care. The innate intelligence and ability of many FMG practitioners had surpassed our American-born colleagues; therefore, we were perceived as threatening their economic survival.

Dr. Cosme Cagas, a sterling leader, a seasoned writer, former speaker of the HOD of APPA, and editor of APPPA/Philippine Medical, covered much of the FMG problems. His opinion pieces were hard-hitting and effusive. A few of our leaders outlined the proper course of action to take. Participation by FMGs was urged for a strong affirmative action by one and all.

In 1976 the U.S. Congress passed the Health Professions Educational Assistance Act (P.L.94-484). This barred the FMGs from entering the U.S. as immigrants or adjusting to become permanent residents unless they had passed both parts of the National Board of Medical Examiners (NBME) examinations. This had a severe negative impact to hundreds of Filipinos but was finally amended with the help of Senators Edward Kennedy, Jacob Javits and Richard Schweiker. They helped enact H.R.4975, which repealed the requirements of P.L. 94-484. There was a requirement that a physician could be considered to have passed Parts 1 and 2 of the NBME examinations, provided that on January 9,1977, he was fully and permanently licensed to practice medicine in a state and had a valid specialty certificate from a constituent board of the American Board of Medical Specialties. The latter part was patently unjust and blatantly discriminatory. Diplomate in any specialty was not a requirement to practice medicine in any state. Many American graduates were not even board-certified.

In late 1979 there were five bills in Congress of serious importance to the FMGs, and their approval largely depended on the support of the affected parties, namely all FMGs in the U.S., particularly the Filipino FMGs.

The American Medical Association (AMA) created a committee of FMGs partly because of the FMG's lobbying efforts displayed by those concerned. AMA resolution 108 was passed in 1983. Although it had some degree of protecting the FMGs, the issue of discrimination remained. The general understanding was that AMA Resolution 108 does not rescind Resolution 56; therefore, the issues of discrimination still exist.

FMGs IN THE AMA: THE FIGHT IS NOT YET OVER

Dateline, 1980

WHEN THE HOUSE of Delegates of the American Medical Association met in Las Vegas, Nevada, in late 1989, members of the medical profession again witnessed the unmistakable display of a posture that had characterized the American Medical Association's (AMA) leadership for more than a decade. It is one that may well be considered as professional jealousy and arrogance, if not discriminatory against their colleagues whose only drawback was they were graduates of foreign medical institutions (FMGs). It had been this way for the last twelve years. At least three reports on FMGs were filed before the AMA and were conveniently committed to oblivion.

In the instant case, delegates from the Michigan Medical Association, obviously with the interest of the FMGs at heart, saw it fit to bring the matter again to the forefront by filing Resolution 5, which sought the creation of a section of Foreign Medical Graduates. The rationale behind this intra-professional concession was merely to gain the imprimatur of equal membership and representation in the AMA, as well as for the FMGs to have a voice in the affairs of the AMA.

It is a generally accepted that foreign medical graduates in the United States have attained a level of professional integrity and expertise in the medical field that is not only at par but also superior to that of their American colleagues. The creation of a section on FMGs in the AMA would, therefore be commensurate with their structure in the profession

However, the House of Delegates, despite its pretensions to prestige and integrity, did not view the issue that way. Opposition to the Michigan Resolution was stiff, vehement, and fraught with allegations that the creation of the section would segregate the

FMGs from the rest of the membership. The action of the House of Delegates, with its tyranny of numbers, was only to be expected: it tabled the resolution "for further study" by the board of trustees.

Now the crux of the matter was shall we, FMGs, whether members of the AMA or not, take this brazen disregard of our right to the same opportunities and aspirations as any other practitioner of our profession lying down? Not anymore! Enough is enough! It may be relevant to recall at this time the words of the foremost Filipino hero, Jose Rizal, also a doctor like us: 'There are no tyrants where there are no slaves!' It is time to get us not being tyrannized by an arrogant majority; it is time to stand up and be counted.

Many options are available for FMGs, but complacency and meekness should not be among them. We are taxpayers, professionals and citizens as much as our other colleagues. What we require is a strong lobby if it takes that much of political maneuvering to achieve our goals. We need to write or call delegates to the AMA HOD to sympathize with our cause. We must call on influential public officials to help us prevail on the AMA leadership to give the FMGs what is rightfully due them.

We must let the local state, and even the national organization of our profession itself; know where we stand on this issue. Let them know how we feel, what we think.

Whatever the means of our involvement in furthering this cause, we need to have a strong, coordinated, and continuing commitment. We will require time, effort, and even money to achieve our goals, and we should be willing to give that much as the price for the recognitions of our rights. Yes, the Michigan initiative is a big move. They should be congratulated, as we need courageous men like them. But in all politics, it is not the big moves that count. Seldom is a fight won with one series of jabs and good footwork. This metaphor applies also to any political activity. As physicians we seem to have limited appreciation of the importance of grass roots work. This fight is not over. We must use the phone and write short letters to the AMA House of Delegates. We have capable and effective leaders in our association, but the whole of our brief phone calls and short letters is greater than the sum of all its parts.

Our profession is not only our livelihood. It is also the symbol of our commitment to the physical well being of mankind, of whatever color or creed, of whatever nationality or ethnic identity or political persuasion.

M' LADY – DECEMBER GIFT
AUXILIARY PRESIDENT

Dateline, December 10, 2012

DECEMBER! THE HOLIDAY time of the year is something very special. Our heart and soul are filled with glitter, family gatherings, the caroling, wining, and eating. Excitement, peace, hope and love are in our hearts. This is unquestionably the time of the year that manages to fill every heart and mind swarming with wishes and love. It happens every Christmas time.

You make a gift to your spouse, to charity, to friends, to your children, and grandchildren. For sure, there's no shortage of gifts to gladden the heart of your Lady. In this holiday season, my friend Edgar (Dr. Borda) made non-material gift to his loving spouse. A poem was written entitled "My Lady." It was a rhyme of a sweet and loving artistic style- poetic idioms and phrases, stunningly done! My friend expressed his all-loving words -"flawless" - a picture perfect specimen of human sagacious literary ingenuity, ... expressing those affectionate expose` of what is fitting about his graceful and amiable lady.

While my friend wrote a poem, I am going to do it in a different way.

December **6** is also my Lady's birthday. The following is my gift to her today- her brief life story. Will I opine unpopular profile? I hope not. My Lady is my sunshine.

I do believe in this saying, "You see my son," said God, "the beauty of a woman is not in the clothes she wears, the figure that she carries, or the way she combs her hair. The beauty of a woman must be seen in her eyes, because that is the doorway to her heart - the place where love resides."
Looking back at the past, Cely is a bright student who graduated as

elementary and high school valedictorian in Ago-o, La Union. She was a pre-medical student but later earned her BS in Pharmacy degree at the University of Santo Tomas in Manila, Philippines. It was at its providential time that after graduation going to America, the land of Milk and Honey was easy. She became a Medical Technologist at Elyria Memorial Hospital and Medical Center in Elyria, Ohio. On January 22, 1962, I started my internship at the same hospital with two other FEU graduates, my classmate Dr. Rodolfo Borromeo and my friend Dr. Tody Exconde.

I met Asela (Cely) Asprec in no time; a beauty caught my eye. She was a very attractive woman. Jokingly, albeit with seriousness in intentions, the three of us, new interns, decided that I must be the one to date Cely. I found an ideal woman. She has the loveliness and smartness combined. I knew I want to share all my troubles, sorrows and dreams with her. She would never let me down and I could always rely on her. Before long our two hearts became one. We got married on July 28, 1962, seven months after we met. And the rest is history.

"Being a full-time mother is one of the most highest salaried job...since the payment is pure love." Cely's chosen and important interest was a volunteer work at our children's school. It was a time when our 4 children were still young. As a proverb says, "a woman's place is in the home." But in spite of this, she made time to join me in the annual conventions and scientific seminar meetings of the Association of Philippine Physicians in America (APPA) and finally became full of zip in the APPA Auxiliary. My wife was ahead of me in the hierarchy of the Filipino American medical association. From the position of being elected as Board of Director of the Auxiliary, Cely then became a PRO and served for two terms as treasurer in 1985.

She was elected as president of the Auxiliary – The Spouses of the Filipino American physicians practicing in the United States of America in the early summer of 1987.

The 16th annual convention of the APPA and in tandem with the

FEU-DRNS Medical Alumni Foundation was held at the Hilton Harbor Castle in Toronto, Canada, on July 25-28, 1987. As if God has a purpose, this date coincided with our silver wedding anniversary on July 28 when she delivered her very inspiring inaugural speech with the theme of her administration dubbed as:

"THE YEAR OF THE FILIPINO AMERICAN PHYSICIAN'S SPOUSE."

EXCERPTS FROM HER INAGAURAL ADDRESS: "This is a special moment of my life as a physician's spouse. Tonight is also our Silver Wedding Anniversary. ... ... It is a leadership challenge that I accept...To the President of APPA Dr. Jose Evangelista, we are here to assist you in your undertakings in every way we can...During my visit to the Philippines last December, I met with the President and officers of the Philippine Medical Association Auxiliary and they expressed their need for our support of their various projects, especially nutrition programs for the needy... It is now that we must get involved in a noble cause. The upbringing of the youth is another priority that we must address today. It is difficult to raise our children in a fast-changing and competitive environment. But rather than bury our heads in the sand, we should measure up to the problems faced by our children due to the undeniable breakdown of family values and relationships. Values are taught at home, at school, by peers, and by the communication media. We need to restore the family as a primary giver of values so that our teens can get their heads on straight and make right decisions about how to live their lives. This will be a meaningful way of reaching out to our troubled teenagers. ... It is our hope to bring to the fore what everyone of us is doing in our community – be it in politics, in business, health careers, the law, real estate or in any endeavor in which we play a prominent role. But we must not also forget the scores of physicians' spouses who are homemakers and tireless volunteers and who have given unselfishly of their time and talents to make the world a better and healthier place to live...

For brevity, Cely's accomplishments will not be covered in this story, except to say that when you have a good time, a year runs fast. *Mabilis!* Cely was given a high commendation and recognition for her work that supported the goals and objectives of the APPA.

Extracted from her valedictory address, she said: ".... whichever path we follow, whether to pursue our career or remain in the home and raise a family, is an undertaking worthy of recognition. Let us look forward to the future with great hopes..."

ENTERPRENEUR: Cely is an excellent bookkeeper and was a self-taught real estate management business entrepreneur. Is she an empowered woman? By the way, especially common to a case with women, Cely wished to stay humble or demure, albeit as I see it, she can sing her own praises; it is not being arrogant or conceited, but that is not at all what it means to sing your own praises. I gave her the fruit of her hands and let her own works praise her in the gates. She is proud to say that she managed our real estate investments all by herself in different locations in the cities of California, such as National City, Escondido, Chula Vista, Spring Valley, Los Angeles, and in Indianapolis, Indiana. An Asian food store was opened in National City. Our dream home, just enough for our comfortable ménage, was built for 14 months. I was all behind her while she did all these in her own way. Of course, I learned how tough it was to be an entrepreneur. Cely had to stay long hours, and working late nights was an understatement. Stock Market Investing is not for everyone. My wife did it. Being an entrepreneur's hubby has its own challenges. She became my skilled billing manager, pathology medical coding, bookkeeping and accounting during my private pathology practice as Chief of Pathology at El Centro Regional Medical Center, El Centro California. She helped and joined me in our philanthropic activities and humanitarian medical missions to the Philippines.

For no other reason than to leave an enduring legacy and a positive influence to our children and grandchildren, I wrote this brief profile of their mom and grandma. A written story of one's life is often more valuable than a check or any other monetary asset. As a commercial would put it, "Priceless!" You must know that one day in the future, a grandchild or great-grandchild will wonder what your life was like while looking at a photograph of you, just as you do when you look at pictures of your ancestors today. My dear wife Cely has inspired my life. She helped me to stay focused in the spiritual areas of life, so that I will continually be a blessing to others and be blessed by God. Therefore, with all these being said, I appreciated, understood, and fully-supported her entrepreneurial innate talents. Cely is a remarkable woman with daunting intellect. Remember a song My Only Sunshine?

THE CODE OF KALANTIAW A HOAX?

Dateline, October 30, 2011

LEGEND, ALBEIT NOT verifiable, are not inanimate. It is an unverified story handed down from earlier times, especially one popularly believed to be historical. I wrote in my book, Success is a Journey, tidbits on Philippine history. It had fascinated a number of friends who knows their Philippine history.

Our country is basically composed of Filipinos who may be aware of their history but do not have a little bit of understanding or interest on it. Some Pinoys are out of their historical benightedness. Not cheeky, I hope you might release the endorphins to soothe and take a smile. I assume the hoax story is not unknown to many of you. The history of the Philippines maybe divided into 4 phases: the pre-Spanish period (before 1521), the Spanish period (1521-1898), the American period (1898-1946), and the year since independence (1946-present). This is a very long and wide expanse of interesting history to review written by good numbers of Philippine historians which included Teodoro Agoncillo, Horacio de la Costa, Marcelino Foronda, Nicolas Zafra, Gregorio Zaide, Nick Joaquin and the latest one by Luis Francia.

It has been established that 250,000 years ago, primitive men came to the Philippines from the Asian mainland. The first people in the Philippines (the aborigines) are the Negritos, believed to have come to the Islands 30,000 years ago from Borneo and Sumatra. They reached Luzon from Borneo over land bridges in Palawan and Mindoro. With the passing of time, land bridges submerged when the ice melted. Malays came in land bridges and later by boats. Before that, the Chinese enjoyed trade with the islands, including India, Japan, Thailand, Vietnam, and Indonesia, which settled in the ninth century A.D. 1n the 14th century the Arabs arrived, introducing Islam.

The existence of trade and travel at that time between the Philippines and its neighbors are established even before the landing of the Borneans. The Malays remained the dominant group until the Spanish arrived in the 16th century. It has always been interesting to be taught in school of the history of pre-Hispanic time.

Taken from my encyclopedic engine Google, I will limit my succinct ruminations on the Pre-Spanish colonial era- the legends that were not engraved in stone. These are stories that were not written but were spoken by each generation to its following generation. Many legends are usually nothing more than stories about the creation of the world, the first man and woman and such. Legends are stories people tell about themselves that often have improbable elements. So what happened? In our case, legendary history was demolished- the birth of Code of Laws- the rule of righteousness in the land- was pronounced a hoax. As the history of law is known to exist in ancient Greece centuries ago, our codes of Maragtas or Code of Sumakwel and Code of Kalantiaw would have been a history we Filipinos would be proud to tell. However, I wish to convey this questionable audacity of historians who have been trying to establish that all these Codes are deceptions. It is stated in the legend that the ten Datus who came and landed in Antique in the mid 1200 led by Datu Puti settled in the Island of Panay. Here, the Madya-as Confederacy was established. "The Confederation of Madya-as" was a pre-Hispanic Philippine state within the Visayan island region. It was established in the 13th century. The code of Kalantiaw was mentioned to have been established in 1433 and therefore it appears that the code of Sumakwel was established earlier than Kalantiaw's Code. To make an argument which one started first is now pointless.

Philippine historian William Henry Scott, in his doctoral dissertation at the University of Santo Tomas, made a methodical investigation into all the sources of information about the Philippines before the coming of the Spaniards. Scott proved in his dissertation that the original Maragtas book and the Confederation of Madya-as were not actual ancient documents from long ago but only legends that were collected and in some cases possibly concocted by Pedro Monteclaro, a Visayan historian. On top of that, Scott found that the Maragtas Code was but merely an invention of Guillermo Santiago-

Cuino's mind and he probably based it on Monteclaro's book and published in 1938.

It is only now that the new generations of historians have been able to set the records straight. The National Historical Institute (NHI) finally admitted that Kalantiaw was a hoax in 1998 when Chief Justice Andres Narvasa, who was about to receive the Kalantiaw Award, asked Malacanang to look into the matter. President Joseph Estrada gave him the award anyway. In 2005, the NHI, under the leadership of Ambeth Ocampo, made their opinion official when they submitted a resolution to President Arroyo to revoke the national shrine status of the Kalantiaw Shrine in Aklan, which, of course, enraged some Aklanons. The Kalantiaw hoax is still deceiving people even at the highest levels of society and government. These are just a few of the more notable examples of websites that still perpetuate the hoax either unintentionally or by willful ignorance. I come to believe that the existences of the Code are proof that our ancestors were civilized – just as many Filipinos do today, some people still cite the courage and wisdom of Kalantiaw as they continue to heap accolades upon him and the oblivious recipients of those Kalantiaw awards. Other authors throughout the 20th century, and up to the present day, recognized the story. "The Code of Kalantiaw is no longer a part of the standard history texts in the Philippines" though the myth is still believed by most Visayans. Kalantiaw's defenders insist that his legend must be true simply because he has always inspired them as a part of their heritage. In Philippine history, indeed there are periods referenced as markers of change.

Be that as it may, our legendary history is overshadowed by the 7100+ Islands in the archipelago The land surface is 115,800 square miles (300,000 square kilometers) across the warm, serene Pacific waters, a geographical landscape that we all love as Filipinos. We have displayed a Filipino Diaspora of who we are, our divine abilities to blend with all cultures, race or creed anywhere in the world. Our characters are unique, dispersed in the thousand of islands. And yet we are simply Filipinos as one, one in heart, love and devotion, one dream and one hope for the destiny of our native land. The Philippines no question, is beautiful, each island will mesmerize you. That is not a legend. It is history that will never change.

FILIPINO AMERICAN DOCTOR OF
LAS VEGAS EXONERATED

Dateline, November 18, 2011

ON SEPTERMBER 8, 2011, Francis McCabe posted on the LAS VEGAS REVIEW-JOURNAL: "Clark County prosecutors have decided to dismiss the case against a doctor charged with murder for overprescribing drugs to a patient."

Dr. Richard Sy Teh, my brilliant co-alumnus, graduated Cum Laude from the Far Eastern University, Institute of Medicine in Manila Philippines, class 1987. He is an internist practicing in Las Vegas and a diplomate of Internal Medicine.

The dismissal of his case is an overwhelming demonstration of justice served properly. I have congratulated Richard and am absolutely positive the FEU Alumni will rejoice with the wrap up of this case. His exoneration is a long overdue end to a troubling and unbelievable situation.

What happened? According to Dr. Teh's lawyer, officials at Valley Hospital and Medical Center, where the patient died, initially said the cause of death was from bi-lateral pneumonia and sepsis. A report from Overview-Journal, "a toxicology screening also showed the level of prescription drugs in patient's system were very low at the time of her death and she had been using several substances that Dr.Teh did not prescribe for her." All we know now, the prosecutor confirmed these statements as stated below.

Dr.Teh fought a medical malpractice lawsuit for almost two years; a pre-hearing settlement was made on the advice of his insurer.

On March 9, 2011, Dr Richard Teh was inexplicably arrested on a murder charge for prescribing drugs. Dr. William Van Tobel reacted on behalf of his fellow physicians in the Las Vegas Valley: "It is not just Richard Teh on trial for murder. We are all on trial."

As the investigations went on, several patients of Dr. Teh supported him wholeheartedly as a compassionate and fine physician of the highest caliber.

The case did not go to trial. After six months Clark County prosecutors dismissed the murder charge: "A lab report also showed (patient) tested positive for pseudomonas aeruginosa, a bacteria, which, with a low white blood cell count, created a lethal combination."

The prosecutor continued: "The Clark County coroner's office originally ruled the patient, 39, died in January 2007 from multiple drug intoxication but later changed the cause of death to a respiratory infection known as sepsis caused by pneumonia."

Richard's case conveys a sad story. There was simply no medical negligence; instead, we witnessed a semblance of prejudice, or horrifying or simple bad luck.

In a comment after McCabe's report under "Justice is served" written on September 9, 2011, "Undoubtedly, it is a sigh of relief, but nonetheless, the "damage", the hurt, the stress, the agony, the anxiety, and the negative public condemnation MUST have been overwhelming and destructive!"

Was there discrimination? We are FMGs, and with our Asian descent, we are well trained, with talents and treasures in service to others, well mannered, and geared towards a high quality of service to patient care. Additionally, we have been trained to fervently uphold the highest ideals of the medical profession as written in The Oath of Hippocrates. The innate intelligence and ability of those of us practicing in this country are on par with our American-born colleagues.

MY ENCOUNTER WITH A FAITH HEALER IN GUADALUPE

Dateline, 1989

DOES FAITH HEALING in the Philippines still existing? Yes, it has been ongoing for a long time but also something that doesn't seem to be dying out anytime soon. Of course as a physician, I don't believe or recommend one to be treated by any of these charlatans. The number of faith healers in the Philippines is uncertain.

When I was in Cebu City, our host entertained us with unsurpassed hospitality. He was an affluent businessman, the owner and operator of a number of inter-island passenger boats from Cebu to the other islands in that part of the Philippines. He invited us to visit his friend, whom he considered his advisor near Cebu city. As such, I had a first-hand encounter with a very popular local "faith healer" of Guadalupe. She was a middle-aged woman who also practiced palmistry. While her statements and interpretations of the markings of our palms fascinated my friends, they were so broad that they could be interpreted in numerous ways. I was more interested in her expertise as a traditional medicine lady or *"herbolaryo."*

I learned she had a number of patients, not only people who could not afford the expense of modern medicine, but also many wealthy families in the city. She specialized in activities like prayers and herbal medications.

Friends in Cebu City said there had been a rise in the practice of traditional medicine, and I could not disagree, for local newspapers indicated the proliferation of "faith healers" and "the natural approach to healing." I believe there is a rise in the practice of traditional medicine in the Philippines due to the increasing cost of conventional medical services.

Folk healing is a popular term for traditional medicine. A study by one of the local physicians in the city described folk healing, as "an indigenous approach to the health needs of a society It is generally performed by a lay person with no formal training in medical, dental, or nursing institutions, but has the knowledge and skill acquired through apprenticeship and experience under a master healer or spirit guide." In my conversation with the faith healer, I gathered that much her medicines were natural elements such as medicinal plants, oils, sunshine, and water. She also used methods like special diet, exercise, massage, and prayers. She did not practice ritualistic activities, incantations, magic's offerings and other means.

As in the United States, the practice of medicine in the Philippines is strictly regulated. Although medical schools are seemingly proliferating everywhere in the country (there are a twenty-four medical schools in the Philippines), Philippine law requires that individuals who have graduated from duly-accredited institutions must be licensed to practice medicine and pass the medical board examinations. Conventional medicine, therefore, is no different from that of the highly advanced western world. Formally trained physicians and licensed practitioners use laboratory-tested drugs and medicines, modern equipment and scientific therapies and treatments, and hospitals and clinics, just as in the United States.

During medical school, I remember writing a term paper on "the practice of quackery in the country." I opined it is difficult to remove the old culture and ancient heritage of the rural folks. These folks comprise the majority of the Philippine's society; with their economic constraints, they resort to folk medicine. Thus, despite the strict implementation of the licensure laws, the underground practice of traditional medicine cannot be eradicated. There appears to be duality in the cultural practices mainly because Filipinos have been acculturated with the Western Civilization for many years that is superimposed by their deep-seated indigenous Philippine culture.

One very interesting recommendation, which resulted in increased interest and public acceptance of the practice of folk healing in the Philippines, was that of the World Heath Organization (WHO) of the United Nations more than a decade ago. It recommends that underdeveloped countries make use of their practice of traditional medicine to supplement the inadequacies of their health service programs. Even as of today, the so-called Western science-oriented societies now give recognition to some meritorious treatments through holistic medicine.

What we see now in the Philippines is the dualistic medical system, which is somehow openly acknowledged and accepted. I know of a classmate who practices both the traditional and conventional scientific medicines in the country; he is doing extremely well. I also know that Filipino patients transfer from one side of medicine to another when they feel dissatisfied with their present treatment.

One acceptable approach of faith healers, which is also well recognized in the conventional medical system, is they prescribe sunlight and water therapies, proper diet, good sleep, massage, and herbal medicines. Psychosomatic diseases seek relief from traditional healers and are commonly resorted to by many patients.

Those with specific causes of their ailments, such as viruses and bacteria, or those needing surgery are brought for treatment by conventional medicines in hospitals and clinics. Much like licensed physicians, folk healers have their own specializations and are known to withhold treatments and reject cases not within their powers to cure.

As a physician I strongly discourage anyone to believe in supernaturalism, magic and ritualistic prayers and offerings for the cure of organic ailments. If there are indeed miraculous cures, they are anecdotal and lack scientific explanation. Today, it appears that herbal medicine and acupuncture healing are for sure on the rise in the Philippines.

CAMIGUIN ISLAND OF PARADISE

Dateline, December 2011

DESPITE THE CURRENT calamities and sadness in these areas of Mindanao due to tropical storm Sendong, last December 2011, I will share my memorable story I encountered in Cagayan de Oro in 1989. I visited Camiguin Island, not too far from Cagayan de Oro. Here was my unforgettable sojourn in the **Island of Paradise**.

I was with my friends from San Diego, Jake Jacob and Art Gairanod who are both from Misamis Oriental located in the Northern Mindanao region. From Cebu we flew to Cagayan de Oro City. We stayed at the VIP Hotel. Immediately that morning, we drove to Iligan City.

The following day, we were at the "Island of Paradise". Camiguin Island is a well-known tourist resort in the northern part of Mindanao.

After landing at the pier in Barangay Benoni, we rented a passenger jeep to the town of Mambojao. The road was passable, asphalted and single-lane. The surroundings were lush green trees and other vegetations hugging the edge of Bohol Sea where coral reefs abounded.

Apparently, Camiguin was teeming with natural wonders conducive to diverse activities, affectionate folks, and nostalgic sceneries with a romantic aura. Camiguin is a pear-shaped island that still shows evidence of volcanic eruptions from Mt. Hibok-Hibok in the not-too-distant past.

We stopped at the Department of Agriculture in the town of Mambojao and introduced ourselves. A pretty receptionist was kind enough to volunteer as our guide. We took a tricycle that was the common means of transportation in town. Our first agenda was to visit the different beach resorts. A two-kilometer trip using a motorized banca to a nearby-uninhabited white island was exciting. The islet was no more than 5,000 square feet and shaped like a dumbbell. People said it was once a rounded islet, but one night an unknown boat anchored by and sucked almost all the white sands. The blue, knee-deep water surrounded this beautiful, serene place. The blue waters from turquoise blue to sapphire blue are inviting. It is almost similar to Boracay Island's inner beauty. We swam in the warm water until some of the native fishermen landed nearby, bringing with them their fresh catches.

We checked in at the Caves Resort. After dinner that evening, our guide suggested that we go to the Ardent Hot Spring, six kilometers up in the wooded mountains using a four-wheel-drive jeep that she borrowed from the department. A female tourist from Germany and a local male guide came along.

Due to the recent rains, the rugged terrain uphill was almost impassable; still, we managed to reach the spring in thirty minutes. The spring was in its natural setting of hot water that flowed into a lagoon, a six-foot deep Olympic-size swimming pool. The heated waters originate from the vents of Hibok-Hibok Volcano. The pool was well lit but the surrounding jungle was pitch dark. The distinct chirps of crickets and other insects filled the air.

The water percolated through one's skin in a most invigorating manner at ninety-two degrees, dilating the superficial veins of the sub cutis. The soothing effect was difficult to describe. This water was noted for its therapeutic effects on various bodily ailments and on one's soul. This was an once-in-a-lifetime swim in the middle of the night, in the middle of nowhere, and in the ambience and aura of a romantic jungle environment.

The following day, prior to returning to Cagayan de Oro City, we stopped at the Benoni Lagoon. Here, we catch fish, crabs, and prawns and gather shells and have them cooked to our liking. A floating shaded raft, paddled by local boys, could be rented for twenty pesos an hour. And that was exactly what we did, as we enjoyed lunch the whole time.

There is no comparison to the joy and invigorating vacation that I had experienced in this island. This is a call for a challenge... to all Filipinos to visit our islands and know first hand what makes every island tick.   In the past few years my wife and I visited Paris, France, and Rome and the Vatican City in Italy; however, I prefer this island resort in the Philippines - a tropical paradise flooded with beautiful colorful tropical flowers. It was almost like heaven.

EDSA REVOLUTION RALLY SPEECH
FEBRUARY 22, 1986

Excerpted from my speech.

...WE HAVE FINALLY come to the final hour; the election in the Philippines, our beloved country, has ended but not over yet. Democracy has faced the toughest challenge of resurrection in the archipelago of the brave and the home of the free. It is the Filipino people's turn to make a judgment wherever they are, whether here in the United States, Canada or other parts of the world . . . What remains to be done now is to save our people from the continued Marcos rule. The reason you and I are here this afternoon is to appeal to the conscience of the people of the United States, to the leaders of the government, in particular Mr. Reagan, to stop supporting a government that has destroyed and gutted the very main fiber of democratic principles in the Philippines...

Cory Aquino, the 52-year-old widow of the fallen leader Benigno Aquino, showed a mandate of the people had it been a free-and-fair election. There were rampant intimidations of pro-Aquino supporters, with some even murdered. A good friend of mine, Evelio Javier from the province of Antique, was murdered in broad daylight at the Provincial building while he was watching and safeguarding the ballot count for Mrs. Aquino. I lost a great friend that day, the youngest governor ever elected in the Philippines at age twenty-nine. He was murdered because he was anti-Marcos . . .

Ferdinand Marcos has devoted the greater part of his twenty years of presidency in plundering the economy of the Philippines and corrupting its civic institutions. In the ultimate act of greed and larceny, he has brazenly hijacked the expressed hope of the Filipino people for a return to democratic rule. The hue and cries in the Philippines are for a change to a democracy. The country's economy is deplorable; peace and order are deteriorating all over the country; the insurgents under the NPA are growing stronger. Human rights are destroyed, and there is no justice served to those perpetuators of crime who happen to be the supporters and cronies of the Marcos administration...

The Filipinos proved beyond doubt to the entire world that they want democracy back. But what has happened? Mr. Marcos stole the election! The will of the people has been trampled.

What we want from you Mr. Reagan is to stop military and moral support of a man who has betrayed that legacy of liberty. Only then will the Philippines become a true heir to our legacy of liberty. Only then will the shadow of blood vanish from the face of the sun. We will continue to seek for that wonderful dream—a return to democracy. Marcos has deprived the Filipino people of that democratic right in the last twenty years and finally the people have awakened..."

VIRTUES OF DR. JOSE RIZAL

Dateline, December 2010

THIS YEAR IS THE sesquicentennial (150th) birth anniversary of Dr. Jose Rizal. An appropriate and timely subject to write today is the very significant occasion of commemorating Dr. Jose Rizal who gave his life for our beloved country, the Philippines in December 30th - a century and fifteen years ago. I could write of many interesting subjects about our national hero, Dr. Rizal. He was a poet, a linguist (22 languages), and philosopher, patriot and martyr, a physician and an ophthalmologist, an artist and a sculptor, an agriculturist and a surveyor, and a teacher, a novelist, a world traveler and an international figure. Dr. Jose Rizal was the embodiment of a true, noble Filipino. We commemorate this event not only to showcase the legacy of Dr. Rizal but also to reaffirm our pride as Filipinos.

Today, I write an essay as a pedagogical tool to reminisce Dr. Jose Rizal as our champion of PATRIOTISM, FREEDOM and UNITY.

To begin, let me share with you an event in our history of how we, Filipinos, came about to know democracy and freedom through our forefathers and through Dr. Rizal. As a descendant of a noble Malayan race, we must be proud of being able to savor Democracy as established in the legends- 'Code of Kalantiaw' and the 'Code of Sumakwel'. Many centuries ago Democracy was born in 510 B.C. in ancient Greece.

We must be proud of the legacy left behind by our national heroes, particularly the bravery and national sentiment of Dr. Rizal. We must be proud of our heritage. We must adapt to the various cultural climates that we have been exposed to and have culled the best from each of these divergent cultures; the combined courage and aggressiveness of Marikudo; the wisdom, integrity and gentleness of Sumakwel; the religious fervor of the Spaniards; and the sense of fair play and self-sufficiency of the Americans.

We commemorate this event every December 30th not only to showcase the bravery and wisdom of Rizal who died for our country but also to reaffirm our love for freedom and democracy.

I mention these historical legacies because I believe that awareness of our common ancestry and culture could lead us easily to develop values that could integrate into a community. These values will bind us together as Filipinos where the words *"Bayanihan"* and *"Katipunan"* (togetherness) have inspired and spirited our people in forging the Philippines into a great nation. It was Jose Rizal, as a political figure, initiated a civic organization - *La Liga Filipina,* that subsequently gave birth to the KATIPUNAN led by Bonifacio and Aguinaldo. He was a proponent of institutional reforms by peaceful means rather than by violent revolution. The general consensus among Rizal scholars, however, attributed his martyred death as the catalyst that precipitated the Revolution in the Philippines.

Dr. Rizal faced the firing squad at Bagumbayan on December 30, 1896, and finally, two years later, our forefathers won freedom from the Spanish oppression on June 12, 1898. We obtained our Independence from the United States of America in 1946. The EDSA revolution returned the democracy we had lost. All these events were part of our Divine relationship. A Roman sage said, in Latin, **"VOX POPULI VOX DEI"** ("The voice of the people is the voice of God"). I would like to think that the legacy of Rizal has influenced the Filipinos to an appointment with destiny.

Among men of wisdom and legendary heroes, Jose Rizal stood tall with Demosthenes of Greece who shouted against the Macedonian conquest, with Victor Hugo of France who defended the Magna Carta, Abraham Lincoln of the United States of America abolished slavery. Jose Rizal bravely exposed and fought the repressive Spanish rule and paid with his life three hundred years after the Spanish domination of our country.

The fight for freedom, human rights and UNITY in this world is never ending. All these speak of the inherent desire of men, of peoples of the world - be it in the prehistoric days or in the atomic/nuclear and cyberage - the desire to be free. Our forefathers down to Dr. Rizal wielded their pens and swords in their quest for freedom from the Spanish conquerors. The hero-contemporaries of our past, with Rizal as the towering figure, exemplified the essence of Democracy divinely gifted with the boon of UNITY that solidifies its whole fabric. At age eighteen, Jose Rizal in a prize-winning nationalistic poem addressed to the Filipino youth entitled, *A la Juventud Filipina*, he called upon them as *the fair hope of the Fatherland*, challenging them to higher aspirations, and to unshackle their chains in order to build nationhood. We must never forget of the two novels he wrote, that 170 passages in the *Noli Me Tangere* (Touch Me Not) and 50 passages in the *El Filibusterismo* (the Subversive) to fight for our rights and the political resolution of the problems that the Spaniards abused the Filipinos. These are social commentaries on our country, the Philippines, which formed the nucleus of literature that inspired dissent among peaceful reformists and spurred the militancy of armed revolutionaries against the Spanish colonial authorities. These writings gave him "immortality in the eyes of his people and compatriots, but made him a target of ecclesiastical vengeance."

Several years ago, we gained our independence from the United States of America. This was a product of our natural quest for freedom that we inherited from our forefathers, the courage and wisdom of Lapu-Lapu, and the bravery and nationalism of Dr. Rizal. I suppose no one ever dreamed that you and I should be here in this land of Milk and Honey talking about this great history. We have so far enjoyed the blessings of not only the freedoms and democracy of our adopted country, America, but we are also blessed with the opportunities, achieved success and affluence in our lives.

While Rizal was away from his country his zeal and clarion call was to inspire his *kababayans* to be aware, to be engaged, and to be involved in the events happening in the Fatherland. Let me remind you, that today, achieving and restoring democracy is not enough. We must also have economic freedom; we must have economic power and justice for our countrymen. This was what Dr. Jose Rizal stood for.

At age nineteen as a third-year medical student in Manila, the young Jose formed a university fraternity called *El Compañerismo* to promote civic and patriotic education, mutual aid, and cooperation. While in Madrid, Spain, he again did this time, put fuel on the spirit of PATRIOTISM and sense of pride and purpose in his Filipino co-students. He dreamt the dreams of FREEDOM in the Philippines as enunciated by the tenets of the French Revolution, that of *Liberté*, *Égalité*, *Fraternité;* ("Liberty, equality, fraternity (brotherhood)", - the national motto of France.

We must learn from Dr. Rizal who championed the tenets of UNITY. In fact when Rizal was elected *responsible* (chief) of the association of Filipinos in Madrid during his college days over his colleague, Marcelo H. del Pilar, who wanted the position very much, he abdicated the position in favor of del Pilar and stated, "I do wish you to give your full support and cooperation to my dear colleague Marcelo. Let us be united in our efforts to liberate our country". This is the kind of dignified politics within an association that we must emulate. Yes, and I could not agree more, that whatever little politics we have to contend with, we should be guided by ethics and principle, by personal aggrandizement not as a motive but for the welfare of the association and the members

We are now living in America but why is it important that we talk about the Philippines this day in memorial of the death of Dr. Rizal? It is because what is good for the Philippines is good for every Filipino wherever he/she is. While we concern ourselves with helping our countrymen and their ills, we must also develop our Filipino American community here in its economic, political, and social aspirations in this country. There is much to be done if we are to forge our Filipino American Community into a strong, cohesive force that can speak with one voice on matters that concern us all.

Rizal wrote article *El Amor Patrio* (Love of Country), sent to the Philippines from Spain, again enunciated his PATRIOTISM. But first, we must rise above the divisive elements of our Filipino heritage. If Dr. Jose Rizal is reincarnated, this is what he is going to say: the Filipinos in America must also be prepared to fully support and assume leadership roles in achieving the inevitable destiny of the Philippines. This is a responsibility that every Filipino must take.

We are aware of the problems of leadership that beset our Filipino communities in general. It is lamentable that we are still plagued with simmering disunity, discord and internal crises in leadership. How can we presume to bring a united front against enemies from without when as a group we look for conflicts and become adversarial? The negative publicity that comes out of this imbroglio jeopardizes the image of the Filipino community.

However, I realize that where there is growth and progress, we also expect things to be more complicated. In every case in our social and civic organizations there are inherent and natural growing pains and should be taken as such, otherwise we will lose the proper perspective of things and be disillusioned. As James Conant said, "Democracy is a small core of common agreement surrounded by a rich variety of individual differences."

Tipping the balance of scale to the right are the positive reflections of the organization like the Phil-American Community of San Diego, Inc., who invited me for two consecutive years as the speaker of Dr. Rizal memorial celebration. This organization's performance, stature, and decorum has become the face of the Filipino community in San Diego, merit our admiration and pride to all of us. What we need in our leadership are those who have the courage and wisdom to carry the flag of unity. The Visayans have a saying we can profit from: *Ang kusog ara sa pagbinuligay.* In Tagalog, *Nasa pagkakaisa ang lakas.* (In Unity there is strength - there is strength in working together.)

Lastly, let us not forget the last word. On the eve of his execution, while confined in Fort Santiago, **Rizal** wrote "**Último adiós**" ("Last Farewell"), a masterpiece of 19th-century Spanish verse. His last word- to die is to rest-*mamatay ay ganap na katahimikan.*

PACQUIAO'S DEFEAT A CHEAT

Dateline, June 10, 2012

IS THIS THE tip of the iceberg in this boxing sport with bias judging? After watching the fans react to last night's decision, it was pretty clear that even the most diehard boxing fans are getting fed up with the current state of their sport. The city of Las Vegas unquestionably will be impacted financially. I am not a boxing aficionado. My son-law-in law, an American invited my wife and me last night to watch the Manny Pacquiao-Bradley match. Since it was well publicized in the local media and I guess all over the world because of the popularity of the Filipino boxer Pac-man, I was very excited to see a *kababayan* (countryman) to win the fight. I saw the unofficial round by round score on TV screen with only one round (10nth round) won by the American boxer.

I was of course shock and all of us in the family TV room of my son-in-law to hear the judge's decision. The following morning media coverage stated that around the world boxing fans and pundits were shock of the wrong decision and also expressed shock over the result of the Manny Pacquiao-Timothy Bradley fight that took place in Las Vegas, Nevada. It has turned the boxing world upside down and inside out.

I am a Filipino-American physician. As a specialist in pathology, we analyze our judgment USING OUR EYES based upon what we see in the microscope very meticulously done to make a right diagnosis whether it is malignant or benign. Once in a while a subject of controversy comes in when it is a difficult case. When that happens, consultations among more than three pathologists are done. It is not subjective analysis. It is objective quality control practice. Boxing judges must have an 'honest quality control practice.'

Now, unlike, the Pacquiao decision that he lost the fight, to me is a shock because, it appears clear (despite not a boxing enthusiast) that the judges made a mistake, if not a blatant blindness of the two judges with a microscope in the ringside. I suggest the State Boxing Commission must look into this matter.

Is boxing a most subjective and controversial in terms of making a judgment? It has been known that there are bias judges and /or corrupt to some percentages. I do not accuse the judges in the P-B fight last night, but something has to be reviewed when loud boos came from the audience, TV commentators and reporters, "punchstat" statistics declared that Pacquiao won the fight.

There has to be a modernized procedure on how to score, effective punching as being the core. There must be an extra judge to review. All judges must have a comprehensive training, standardized training, uniformity of criteria. I agree the judges are experienced men, albeit it does not make them free from bias mind. I admit we are humans and subject to fallibility, and yes, bias. Objective judging is a must.

By the way, boxing is a breeding ground for controversy. But, not this one last night. It should not be within that milieu. Asked those who watched in television all over the world? In my personal view, Pac-man won by score and hard punches.

Everybody knows the fight has gone the wrong way.... I read in my search engine about bias boxing decisions and some down right blatant wrong (as in corrupt) decisions... Is there any governing body doing investigations into these so-called high rolling judges?

With all of the hype surrounding last night's sport event, the boxing fans and all Filipinos here in the US and in the Philippines and all over the globe are downright disgusted. I was not sure whether the 40 Philippine congressmen who flew from Manila to watch the fight. Were they accompanied by their spouses and/or their kabit? I am certain it was time to rub elbows with the glitterati and much more than that in the Sin City. I would have warned them of that canard of mobsters who might tip them to place their bets for the underdog with a bigger payoff.

Frankly, the only truly damning result for the sport would be for the fight to end in a controversial decision that gets the crowd thinking that the fight was fixed or is there a conspiracy to result a rematch, business buildup, money for promoters and to those behind the fights? The Mafia?

Funny, but true, I will compare the 3 judges as the matching part of the three Philippine Senator Judges Santiago, Arroyo and Marcos who voted not guilty to CJ Corona in the impeachment in the Senate Assembly while there is that overwhelming evidence of guilt of the man being impeached. These 2 boxing judges disregard what Pac-man did, where "punchstat"scoring or CompuBox and Associated Press (AP) have counted it a win for Pac-man. Do you think the two judges have " hangin" (hot air) in their head like Senator Miriam Defensor Santiago?

Could we believe Promoter Arum when he stated last night "The decision was a ridiculous decision? You guys all know who won this fight. So let's be honest about the situation. Hopefully we'll revisit it in November…. I hope boxing recovers, because this isn't arguing about a close decision. This is something that's an absurdity, that's ridiculous, and everybody that's involved in boxing should feel ashamed." He continued: "I went over to Bradley before the decision and he (Bradley) said, 'I tried hard but I couldn't beat the guy."

To quote a friend, "The fact that the judges made an obvious and shameless travesty of Manny's obvious control of the fight and having landed the more telling shots reeks of obvious tampering and corruption." Pacquiao is seriously planning to retire. Therefore one may conclude that to win this fight, he will certainly retire. Losing it, a rematch was already in the Promoters agreement in a contract with Bradley.

Whether the rematch was preplanne is the big question. Manny has been Arum's boom to earn a lot of money. Greed? For Pac-man to accept a rematch in November and loss a fight will be a big embarrassment for him and the Filipinos since we thought that he really won the fight. I can see Pac-man appeared weaker, unable to have a knock-out punch not like previous fights. He is getting older. I'd say, forget the millions of dollars. You have it already. People around the world declared you a winner last Saturday's fight. My personal advice is for you (Pacquiao) to completely retire now. You are a Filipino icon in World Boxing.

<u>CHAPTER FOUR</u> ★

ENVIRONMENTAL ACTIVIST

"If a tree falls in the woods, and there's no one there to hear it, how will the Environmentalists react?"

— ANONYMOUS

ANTI-MINING IN ANTIQUE PROVINCE, PHILIPPINES

IN THE LATE 2011, the mining exploration was initiated in the municipality of Libertad, province of Antique, adjacent to my hometown Pandan. Government officials approved licenses with a high possibility of expansion to the nearby mountains in barangays of Pandan. The Mayor of our town will approve responsible mining.

You may call me an environmental activist, someone who is resisting outside interference, since I have been solidly entrenched with my civic activism in my hometown even though I am here in the U.S. In my opinion, the importance of doing activist work allows me to give back and to consider myself not as a single individual who may have achieved whatever I have aspired for, but to be a part of a movement that sees problems that are not being addressed and help make our voice heard.

I wrote the following series of articles in my column in Philippine Times Southern Nevada weekly newspaper, Asian Journal San Diego and FEU Newsletters.

NO TO MINING IN MY HOMETOWN

Dateline, February 17, 2012

FOR THOSE OF US Filipinos who recognize the economic situation in our homeland, we welcome mining as an important economic activity - mining industry in the Philippines. Our land is one of the world's most highly mineralized countries, with untapped mineral wealth estimated at more than $840 billion. We also recognize that mining can provide an important source of jobs and income, but sometimes the biggest losers of all are isolated rural communities in the vicinity of mining projects, where too-rapid social and environmental change can tear at the fabric of traditional daily life. Irresponsible mining (e.g. in watersheds, above food production areas, in densely populated areas, high rainfall, seismically active areas, ethnic minority areas, and areas of social conflict etc.) is already severely damaging the Philippines.

Such incidents have fueled an often-contentious debate about how to identify areas that should be declared off-limits to mining because of their environmental and social sensitivity. This is basically the situation in my hometown in the province Antique, Philippines. Many of our provinces in the Philippines are facing this problem. This is a very serious issue. This has been an issue that is more prominent in provinces where big companies can hide from the public what they have been doing to the land they are mining.

Citing evidence of destruction from mining activities, the Save Palawan Movement insists there should be no mining in areas of biodiversity and island ecosystems like Palawan. Dr. Gerardo "Doc Gerry" Ortega, a civic leader, environmentalist and broadcaster was killed January 2011? Was this an extrajudicial killing? This sent a strong message to the governments of the Philippines and Palawan of the need to stop mining activities in Palawan and help protect its natural resources. Dr. Ortega's daughter said, "We live in a culture of death. We need to change that and go back to a culture of life.

The most important thing is not gold, copper, cell phone or a laptop. It's food, air, and water--things we are losing already. The costs always outweigh the benefits. Let's bring back a culture of life.

Like Dr. Ortega, I have my dream to have a Philippines where natural resources are protected. You may call me an environmental activist, someone who is resisting outside interference, since I have been solidly entrenched with my civic activism in my hometown even though I am here in the U.S. In my opinion, the importance of doing activist work allows me to give back and to consider myself not as a single individual who may have achieved whatever I have aspired for, but to be a part of a movement that sees problems that are not being addressed and help make our voice heard.

I am a believer of grassroots empowerment and strengthened civil societies. Environmentalist David Brower was once asked, "Why are you conservationists always against things?" He replied, "If you are against something, you are always for something. If you are against a dam, you are for a river."

I will tell you my 'environmental encounters' that have resulted to my strong contention and protestations to speak up and raise arms against tyrants and dictators. I happened to be one in the forefront of an e-group of *kababayans* -town mates- living abroad and we are passionate about our cause and its lasting value because we can't just accept the way things are if they are to the detriment of our loved ones and the destruction of things we hold dear. We are solidly behind "No to Mining" in our area in the Northwest Panay Peninsula.

I delivered my views with clarity and intimacy to my community in the province of Antique, particularly my beloved hometown Pandan. You may call my environmental feature editorials and opinions to be demonstrative, reflective, and with a litany of rants and raves against the mining venture in our area.

Together with my friends and town mates here and abroad we have raised our voices to give vent to our stubborn and ongoing passion to preserve our beautiful forested mountain that sustains endemic wildlife, our land, rivers and sea from environmental intimidations. Foremost is the mine's familiar catastrophic impact on the environment and the serious health vulnerability it will create on the residents of the municipalities of Pandan and Libertad in my province of Antique. It will bring about unacceptable environmental impact and destruction such as permanent alteration of terrain, stripping of vegetation, soil erosion from floods and landslides, and water pollution from the mine's tailings and wastes. These are just a few of the numerous unacceptable environmental perils wrought by mining. There is a Kalikasan People's Network for the Environment (Kalikasan-PNE) and the Defend Patrimony Alliance that emphasized mining is a great detriment to the welfare of the people and to the environment.

The transnational mining corporations (TNCs) are broadly opposed by the communities in the Philippines. Operations by these mining TNCs have overwhelming support from the government.

FRAGILITY OF ECOSYSTEM

Dateline, February 24, 2012

THE NORTHWESTERN VISAYAS Peninsula Park (NWPP)---declared, as a Natural Park per Presidential Proclamation No. 186 issued on April 15, 2002---by law must not be disturbed by the current mining exploration in the area. According to the Department of Natural Resources, the Park is home to diverse and endemic wildlife, including the Tarictic Hornbill, the Negros Bleeding Heart Pigeon, and the Serpent Eagle. This protected peninsula covers the towns of Libertad and Pandan in Antique and the towns of Nabas, Malay, and Buruanga in Aklan.

In spite of this law, mining continues, and there are still applications for mining permits being filed even in core protection zones.

Why in the world was permission issued by the government officials of Antique to Mayor Jesry Palmares of Passi City in Iloilo, the President of Archlegan Mines Corp. (AMC)? The exploration permit (EP) covers the barangays of San Roque and Pajo in Libertad, and barangays Luhod-Bayang, Duyong, Tingib and Mag-aba in the neighboring town of Pandan. It was endorsed by the regional MGB to its central office on June 30 for approval of the bureau. Not only that, another Mining company---JC Hartman Mines Inc. (JCHMI) with Mayor Palmares and others as incorporators---are also interested in San Roque and four other barangays of Libertad (the site of Tudor Mineral Exploration Corp.) for expansion of their mining projects. A Hong Kong national, Chan Ka Che Ong, is the chairman of the corporation. It is the extraction and processing of metallic and nonmetallic minerals including gold, copper, chromite, manganese, iron, marble, silica and limestone that attract these individuals with one and only purpose...to quench their own glorious quest for the big moolah.

I am extremely concerned about the mine's familiar catastrophic impacts on the environment and the serious health vulnerability it creates on the residents. Contaminations from the leakage of chemicals are tremendous health risks. The degradation of land and water resources may last for decades. The fragility of the ecosystem makes the environment hazardous that we pray for the tide of public and political opinion to turn and be against the continuation of the mining venture in the area.

I am aware of the mining industries in the Philippines that had been cited for human rights abuses in local communities, especially to indigenous people.   Extra-judicial killings of protestors and corruption in the local, provincial and national government are well known. These "judicial killings" of those who oppose rampant deforestation and mining concessions had been tolerated by corrupt politicos.

It is notoriously known that mining companies have a very poor record with regard to environmental protection and clean up. There are some 800 abandoned mines in the Philippines that are not cleaned up and damage is never fully reversed.   Water contamination is inevitable. With some mine areas close to the sea, damage to valuable marine resources is a constant threat.

Around five million hectares in the Philippines are potential mining areas open to local and foreign investors. If only the DNR and other departments in the Philippine government that are overlooking the mining industry in our country can be trusted. But nay! Thus the elites with their dominance towards exploitative behavior cannot be controlled. Now, the mining approval in Libertad and Pandan can only be aborted if our government officials can be converted to sway and believe in the negative impact of mining to our environment. Yes, there is this so-called responsible mining. It has never been implemented strictly.

It's a never-ending controversy between the mining industry claiming economic benefits and the citizens who oppose the mine, pointing out its lasting major environmental and health hazards to the people.

The interest of mining firms to venture into Antique remains as a conflagration in the region. I am absolutely happy of the popular supports from the Antiquenos and the residents of nearby provinces who have overwhelmingly expressed the bad effects of large-scale mining. I hope we shall be victorious in our "No Mining in the Northwest Panay Peninsula" campaign.

Our *kababayans* in Pandan under the leadership of Mimi Ortiga, Ms. Condez and others recently organized a protest rally in the capital of the province, San Jose de Buenavista. An appeal to the Honorable Governor Exequiel Javier to reconsider his support of mining in Libertad/Pandan was delivered. According to PNA and U.S. News Agency / Asian, Antique Governor Exequiel B. Javier said that he will revoke the mining permit that he has granted to a group in the northern town of Libertad as requested by the people in the area.

I am one of the sons of Pandan. This is my home region, and as we Antiquenos of indigenous origin would claim, we are all Pandananons, born to the place and grew up in it. We are children of the great outdoors where our mountains are endless and forested, where Pandan boasts of its eco-tourist attractions, like the Malumpati Health Spring and Tourist Resort and the Bugang River, which won the national award of "Gawad Pangulo sa Kapaligiran" as the cleanest inland body of water in the Philippines. Every tourist will be amazed and impressed by the river's blue, clear, and tranquil water that illuminates its purity.

For heaven's sake, let no one poison our land and our waters!

A SCOURGE AND A TRAVESTY

Dateline, February 17, 2012

Once upon a time, Milagros Tambo-ong of Barangay San Roque, Libertad, Antique, would look at the blooming forest canopy of Mount Pinupo in appreciation for the sustenance it provided to her village. Today, Milagros is saddened with the mining activities that many political forces are trying carry to out, despite the inevitable catastrophic economic and environmental harm.

This is indeed a tragedy. How can we mitigate environmental hazards brought about by mining in our country? Are there any assurances for minimizing such hazards during mining? Can the government monitor the proper implementation of responsible mining? Do mining firms even bother caring about protecting the environment and people? My answer, sad to say, is a resounding NO!

The rich people of the Philippines, Cojuangco and Ang (San Miguel Stallwarts) made money on mining, and they made a lot of it. The mining foray bodes especially well for the country, says Mark Mobius, who oversees about $50 billion as executive chairman of Franklin Templeton Investments' Emerging Markets Group: "We believe in commodities, whether nickel, iron ore or coal.

That's where the Philippines' potential is." However, Mr. Mobius seems not to care about how these mining applications in places like Panay and Guimaras Islands will affect environmentally critical areas inhabited by indigenous people. It seems the quest for profit is greater than the care for his fellow man.

How can we Filipinos fight these individuals high in the government monarchy? It really depends on leadership and governance of our country. Everyone is corrupt, as our so-called leaders are little more than thieves, liars, crooks, plunderers, scam, opportunists, smugglers and tax cheats. While proponents of mining operations, including

Libertad Mayor Norberto Raymundo, utter some nonsense about giving short term employment to the residents and supporting responsible mining, we all know these are just sound bites meant to cover their motivations and justify their behavior.

During the Arroyo administration we were witness to the political backing and financial support of the mining industry, despite the communities in the Philippines broadly opposing these transnational mining corporations (TNCs). Since 1995, the private banks and other financial institutions have grown every year and become large-scale operations, proliferating all over the country. These mining TNCs intend to cover the whole archipelago with their mining projects and plunder the country's mineral resources in order to rake in billions in profit.

And who is there to protect us? Surely not the government, which has supported these intensified operations. Mayor Tan supports responsible mining. Fortunately, those affected by the mining have remained valiant and steadfast in their struggle against them, and such opposition continues to widen.

Mining in Northwest Panay, albeit protected under various acts of government mandates, is a scourge and a travesty of the rights of the residents.

EARTH DAY AND THE TRAGEDY OF A
FAMOUS RIVER

Dateline, April 1, 2012

EARTH DAY IS a commitment to a clean and healthy environment. It is a worldwide celebration held annually every April 22, dedicated to the appreciation and promotion of awareness for the conservation of the environment. Senator Gaylord Nelson originally founded it in 1970 in the United States. Today, Earth Day is celebrated in many countries.
Last March 15, 2011 was the 18th Annual Pasig River Fluvial Parade. The parade was co-organized by the Department of the Environment and Natural Resources (DENR) through its River Basin Control Office (RBCO), and the *Sagip Ilog Pilipinas Movement* (SIPM), formerly known as the *Sagip Pasig Movement.* That was in observance of the International Day of Action for Rivers, as well as part of a series of activities commemorating World Water Day on the same month. March 22, (DENR) posted in PNoy News Philippines stated "what better location to drum up awareness and advocacy regarding the state of the country's rivers than on the Philippines' most famous yet most abused and neglected river – Pasig River."

Three hundred representatives from both public and private sectors gamely participated, boarded 35 boats to take part in festivities.

To say Pasig River is an abused and neglected river is an understatement. During this Earth Day, April 2012 will be a sad situation at the Pasig River.

Twenty-two years ago, the Pasig River Rehabilitation Commission was established supposed to clean and rehabilitate the river. Nothing happened. It was a huge task to accomplish.

Eight decades ago, it was a river for people – well known as a place from which sustenance for food - fish and all to everyone. Those chow are now dangerously pathological carriers of infectious organisms and venomous chemical transporter that will kill the people. It is the true facts of life. To this day, Pasig River is hopeless. A friend writer said, "the toxicity of the river originates from the various industrial plants that sprouted around Laguna de Bay, and is made worse by unhygienic and mindless human habitation." To continue the sad situation, DENR Secretary Ramon J. P. Paje had earlier proclaimed, "The Pasig River plays a very important role in the lives of Filipinos in Metro Manila and its environs, commercially and environmentally speaking. Ideally, we should be able to drink from, and bathe in, this river, yet we have turned it into one big septic tank."

Pasig River is described as stretching for 25 kilometers (15.5 mi); it is lined by Metro Manila on each side. Its major tributaries are the Marikina River and San Juan River. A total of 16 bridges cross the river. In my search engine, the foremost landmark on the banks of the river is the walled district of Intramuros, located near the mouth of the river on its southern bank. The Spanish colonial government in the 16th century built it. Further upstream is the Hospicio de San Jose, an orphanage located on Pasig's sole island, the Isla de Convalescencia. On the northern bank stands Malacanang Palace, the official residence of the President of the Philippines.

Pollution of the river is the basic fundamental problem. In the 1930s, observers noticed the increasing pollution of the river, as fish migration from Laguna de Bay diminished. People ceased using the river's water for laundering in the 1960s. Massive population growth, infrastructure construction, and the dispersal of economic activities to Manila's suburbs left the river neglected. The banks of the river attracted informal settlers-total of estimated 800,000 and the remaining factories dumped their wastes into the river, making it effectively a huge sewer system. Such resulted to the "ruination of human lives, health, dignity and a culture."

Despite increased environmental awareness, simply stated, the Pasig River became a repository for unwanted items, trash and litter;

including couches and mattresses; bicycles; shopping carts; cars and car parts; bags of stolen property; fuel containers; and paint cans. There are tons of them- a semblance of the Payatas on top of land. They are unsightly and are a sign of human neglect or disregard for aesthetic values and natural ecosystems. I have to look at facts that are, like the sun, too painful for my direct gaze; instinctively, I look away.

The Pasig River Rehabilitation Program (PRRP) was established in 1989. Notable was when on April 16, 1990, President Corazon C. Aquino issued Proclamation No. 553, officially mandating April 22 of every year as Earth Day in the Philippines. Was it meant to bring awareness of what was happening in Pasig River? I am a believer of former President Cory Aquino as a recognized clean President, albeit Pasig River at the back of Malacanang Palace was already dirtier than ever when the Land Reform of the President was dump over the filthy river.

The former President, Joseph Estrada signed Executive Order No. 54 establishing the PRRC to replace the old PRRP with additional expanded powers such as managing of wastes and resettling of squatters. Nada happened.

In my 'mini exchanges threads' with my colleague and friend, he summarized it brilliantly and coming from a horse's mouth: "Pres. B. Aquino III was severely criticized for appointing Gina Lopez (ABS-CBN) to head the PRRC. Miss Lopez, it is claimed, and her family (the powerful Lopez dynasty) are inherently tied to the big businesses along the banks of Pasig River that contribute to the continuing degradation of the river with the dumping of toxic wastes. Was this a mistaken political appointment because of conflict of interests? Through decades of monumental abuse and neglect, the public and business community kept a blind eye to the numerous laws and regulations in place enacted to protect the river and its ecosystem. Ergo, the biological death of the all-too-important Pasig River was inevitable."

I am overwhelmingly sad. But, I am a small fry to make a difference. What can we Filipinos do? Could there be room for change to a cleaner Pasig River? We have more questions than answers.

CHANGE! **C-** Continuing degradation abort **H-** Help **A-** Assurance **N-** No to informal settlers; **G-** Good Governance **E-** Environmental Empowerment

I am a believer of grassroots empowerment and strengthened civil societies. Environmentalist David Brower was once asked, "Why are you conservationists always against things?" He replied, "If you are against something, you are always for something. If you are against a dam, you are for a river." I am for a river. I am for a clean Pasig River.

My opinions are demonstrative, reflective, and with a litany of rants and raves against the degradation of Pasig River. I zealously hope my environmental feature chronicle will serve as a lesson to us all.

The month of April will provide an unprecedented showcase for the clean energy options available to individuals, businesses and the government, Manila must listen. Save Pasig River. From the Bible, "Are the consolations of God small with thee? Is there any secret thing with thee? / Why doth thine heart carry thee away? and what do thy eyes wink at, / That thou turnest thy spirit against God, and lettest such words go out of thy mouth? / What is man, that he should be clean? and he which is born of a woman, that he should be righteous? / Behold, he putteth no trust in his saints; yea, the heavens are not clean in his sight."

I'd be remiss if I do not mention the cleanest inland waterway in the Philippines which is the "BUGANG RIVER", in my hometown Pandan, province of Antique, Philippines. "In 2005, Bugang River was the winner of the "Dangal Ng Ilog" Award during the 1st National Summit on the State of Philippine Rivers." Already considered the country's cleanest inland body of water, Bugang River once again coveted an award from the prestigious Green Environment Apple Awards in the United Kingdom.

THE DUMPSITE OF MANILA'S GARBAGE
Environmental Havoc to our Land and Sea

Dateline, January 2000

THIS IS MY MEMOIR of a huge milestone in Antique's history when in November 2000 Metro Manila Development Authority's (MMDA) of Jejomar Binay planned to dump Metro Manila's garbage on Semirara Island in Antique province. Semirara Island is approximately 300 kilometers away from Manila by air. Located at the northern end of the province of Antique, it is only two kilometers away from Pandan Bay in Pandan, my hometown and fewer than forty kilometers from the world-famous Boracay Island Resort in the province of Aklan. As chairman of Pandan Antique Foundation (PAF), I took a strong initiative of protest in open letters to the powers that be in Philippine political leaders.

It started this way:

It was in mid 2000 that a hot topic about what to do with Metro Manila's trash problem was under consideration by the Metro Manila Management Authority (MMDA). Remember the Payatas and the Smokey Mountain's sad stories about their garbage? During that year, the San Mateo landfill in Rizal province will be closed by the end of the year and Manila's garbage must be dumped somewhere. No municipality near Manila would agree to be the garbage dump, no matter how much bribe was offered to them. Therefore, the Manila garbage must be dumped elsewhere. It was reported that the Philippine government has earmarked P1 billion to fund the operations of a proposed disposal facility to be operational on January 1, 2001.

Now the crux of the matter! The MMDA plans to use the island of Semirara of Caluya town, in the province of Antique, as the new dumping ground for the trash. What in the world did MMDA chairman Jejomar Binay think of when he considered the province of Antique to be Manila's dumping site? Does he really think that the Antiquenos are that gullible and he expects them to say nothing about this preposterous decision? I said it was foul!

It is interesting to note that DMCI-RII Builders Consortium and Waste Action Recycling, Inc. (WAR), the two big companies vying for the contract for dumping of waste, are tipping a fee of P950 per metric ton. We are talking about 2,000 metric tons of garbage to be dumped daily. One can imagine the financial gains these companies will net from the garbage contract that they may be blinded by the money and become indifferent to the many environmental hazards the people in the Antique region will be exposed to.

Caluya and its neighboring islands like Boracay, have pristine beaches, coral formations, and marine life that provide a fertile fishing ground for the islanders' food and their fishing industry. Seashells abound, and some of them are rare species.

Caluya has also been declared by the Philippine Ministry of Natural Resources as a bird and turtle sanctuary. Its beaches have white sand and its waters are ideal for scuba diving and spear fishing. What will happen if one of the barges loaded with garbage gets caught in the rough sea and sinks, or if the crew decides to dump the garbage into the sea? The millions of pounds of garbage per year from the Metropolis are potential pollutants of toxins and carcinogens that could leach into the groundwater. The incineration can release dioxins into the atmosphere.

The people of Caluya have been complaining about the operations of the Semirara Coal Corporation (SCC) in Semirara. It has dumped extracted soil from its mine into the sea, destroying the coral reefs and killing the fishes. However, despite the mounting oppositions from the islanders, the government's Department of Environment and Natural Resources granted SCC an environmental compliance certificate. Lo and behold! SCC is a subsidiary of DMCI Holdings, the consortium that is interested in the Semirara dumpsite contract. And now dump in Semirara the garbage from Manila? Antiquenos, are we going to take this lying down? This is a brazen disregard for our basic right to live in a clean environment.

Remember that big money is being considered in this dumpsite project. We hope that our local leaders and politicians will not be swayed or lured by the big bucks being dangled before them in exchange for their approval of the plan.

We, the Pandan Antique Foundation, Inc. (PAF) and Pagtatap USA, based in California, and the Pagtatap Foundation, Inc. in Manila, Philippines, and all the Antiquenos abroad were outraged and vehemently opposed to Metro Manila Development Authority's (MMDA) plan to use Semirara Island as the dumping site for Metro Manila's waste.

As professionals who were born and raised in Pandan and now living abroad, we have made tour mission to help improve the lives and well being of those in Pandan. We are vigilant in preserving Pandan's environment and natural resources.

Now with the potential of hazardous and toxic run-off, not only is the coral reef threatened, but also so are the fishing and resort industry of the waters surrounding Semirara, Caluya, Sibay, Boracay, and indeed the whole bay of Pandan.

We asked MMDA the following questions: Why can't Metro Manila dump its own garbage in its own backyard? Why do you want to pass on your toxic waste and refuse to the residents of a neglected and underdeveloped province of Antique? Is it because you can't stand the sight and smell of your own garbage? If so, what right do you have to sully the waters of Pandan Bay and destroy the town's fishing industry and main source of food supply? How can you justify destroying Pandan's quality of life and polluting its ecosystem? Do you think that Antiquenos are gullible that you expect them to say nothing and just accept your preposterous decision?

With the barges still in Semirara, a threat loomed that President Estrada was going to issue a special proclamation to use Semirara as a dumpsite to accommodate the worsening garbage crisis in Manila. The dreaded presidential mandate almost became a certainty; we thought we had lost the fight and were doomed. However, we mustered up our strength to yet rise up again and salvage the remnants of our resolve to fight till our last breath. And we prayed. Then, Philippines' little President Angara came to our side. And finally, Presidential Legislative Liaison to the Senate, Sally Zaldivar-Perez, a native of Pandan, told the Manila press that the president released the order for the barges to return to Manila.

Reflecting upon our crusade to save Semirara, we knew right from the start that embarking upon a mission of this magnitude was an uphill battle. As we relied on each other for spirit and stamina, we came to develop a special level of affection for each other and a greater appreciation for what life is all about. We clung to each other for our constant source of sustenance and perseverance as we tackled the tumultuous urgency and demands of our plight.

I cannot forget the emotionally powerful protest of Pandananons all over the world. So many letters, editorials, commentaries were written coming from people abroad and the tireless work of Pandananons in Manila Philippines, led by Dr. Bobby Alojipan. It was a hard-fought battle against formidable odds, but with Pandan Antique Foundation (PAF) in California, Pagtatap USA, Pagtatap Philippines, and United Antiquenos rallying behind, along with the financial support from Pandananons (natives of Pandan) and their friends all over the world, Semirara Island was left untouched and unsullied. The strength, staying power, and success of PAF's endeavors are greatly dependent on individuals and organizations that are generous of their time, talent, and resources to help accomplish PAF's goals. The Semirara saga had its moments of glory, despair and anger. It was a test of our faith in God and each other.

Coming out as victors, we realize we have built a treasury of power, talents, goodwill, and respect towards each other over the weeks that we "fought as one" to outmaneuver and topple our formidable enemy. This is one of the proudest moments of our lives, knowing that we have turned the tides to free Semirara and return this peaceful, beautiful island to its people.

From this moment of rare significance, we have become aware that within us exists this potent, albeit latent, impetus to rise and respond to calls to defend the land of our birth whenever we sense it as being threatened. We know now, more than ever, that with this awakening, Antique will never be left alone and defenseless against aggression and invasion of tyranny and plunder.

For this, history will remember the sweet victory of our Semirara crusade.

THE NAPOCOR DIESEL PLANT

On September 20, 2002, the National Power Corporation (Napocor) wrote a letter addressed to Mayor Plaridel "John" Sanchez of Pandan, Antique, requesting his endorsement from the Sangguniang Bayan (SB) of Pandan to erect in the municipality, specifically at Danao, Patria, a 110 Megawatt diesel power plant. Reportedly, the plan was to transfer to Pandan a 9-year-old diesel power plant, which was constructed by the Enron Power Development Corporation, from the province of Batangas.

The PAF and Pagtatap USA/Philippines and Pandananons all over the world reacted badly to the proposal. The impact was like the Semirara Dumpsite nightmare resurrected before its bitter taste had settled into oblivion in the minds of the protesters. Once again, letters of protest reached the mayor and the council members.

The Napocor project was discontinued.

CHAPTER FIVE ★

CAREER HIGHLIGHT

Start where you are. Use what you have. Do what you can."

- ARTHUR ASHE

FROM ETHNIC TO MAINSTREAM
"OPERATION SAMAHAN" STORY

UP TO A CERTAIN POINT one's environment and heredity shape a man's life. But the time comes when he must figure out the kind of person he wishes to be. As I allowed my dream to take me to my journey, I also permitted the true spirit inside me, the spirit that stemmed from my roots, to reach out and serve the underprivileged.

In 1972, three years after we arrived in San Diego, there were only four Filipino foreign medical graduates practicing in the city: Dr Romeo Quini and his wife Dr. Mila Quini, Dr. Adelito Gale, and of course me.

160,000 Filipino Americans were living in San Diego County, mostly in the South Bay area of the city. They were predominantly U.S. Navy retirees and their families, and from different regions of the Philippines.

At that time there were about 75 Filipino American organizations in San Diego County. To bring together the different organizations to foster unity, harmony and mutual cooperation, the Council of Filipino American Organizations of San Diego County (COPAO) was founded in 1971. Eventually I became a member of the board.

Meanwhile, the three of us Filipino American doctors, Dr. Quini, Dr. Gale and me, noticed the sad situation of many old timers, or *"manongs"* (Filipino men in their senior years) who had worked in farms, restaurants or other menial jobs. They were living in the depressed areas of the city and shied away from the social scene. These manongs had never sought medical treatment or check ups due to a combination of indifference and also financial difficulties, limited knowledge of English and problematic cultural barriers.

Because of our keen awareness of their situation, in 1973 the three of us started a makeshift clinic in the backroom of a Filipino-owned barbershop on Market Street in downtown San Diego. Using our own time and resources, we made our consultation services available to patients on Friday nights. Here, at least one of us, along with other volunteers, manned our tiny and understaffed clinic. From the beginning, our purpose was to provide free medical care to those without medical insurance and who could not afford assisted medical fees.

I am convinced that people like to do what they are meant to do. They can be extremely patient when doing what they like. When people are fulfilling a calling, it fascinates them. The three of us were completely fascinated by our calling. Wanting to give something to the community that had given us so much in life, we, the three medical musketeers, pursued this mission. Other physicians - Dr. Iluminada Arenas, Dr. Mila Quini, Dr. Emma Matel, Dr. Ceferina Ruiz - rendered their help. Filipino American RNs also responded and joined as volunteers.

The Filipino American community quickly learned there was a free medical clinic operated by three caring Filipino physicians, nurses and staff. A growing number of patients soon besieged our evening clinic, far more than we could handle alone. At this point we sought for help from more members of the community and government agencies that could provide us much-needed funds for expansion.

COPAO Chairman Filemon Adrid and Vice Chairman Paul Bayani were among the first to answer our pleas for help. Grace

Blaszkowski, a Filipina and Chief of the City of San Diego's Office of Asian-American Affairs, along with other concerned citizens, held a rally and lobbied for city and county funding. It proved to be not an easy task.

People with passion, however, do what they do out of love for the work they are performing and for the expected results. Thus, in 1973, Operation Samahan was born and incorporated the same year into a 501(c)(3) non-profit freestanding private community clinic. The humble clinic, which was the hub of health screening and informal health education gatherings, was relocated to a larger space in National City, south of San Diego. The mayor of National City, Kile Morgan, offered us the use of the Boys and Girls Club building free for two years. Operation Samahan's first executive director provided the administrative support and machinery for the management of the clinic.

We organized the first Filipino Medical Foundation Inc., to administer the clinic; I became the founding president. I also became the first chairman of the board of the Clinic called Operation Samahan. *Samahan* is a Filipino or Tagalog word that can be translated to "togetherness," "helping one another," and "working together."

The programs and services made available to the community included medical, educational, cultural and multi-social activities. In 1975, the clinic moved to a 3,000 square foot medical professional building at 2340 Eight Street in National City. To continue meeting the growing need for the clinic's good and affordable services, a branch of Operation Samahan expanded to Mira Mesa north of San Diego two years later. Like National City, it was a venue for thousands of Filipino immigrants and other minorities of Pan-Asian descent. At its inception, most patients were predominantly Filipino Americans, and it became a beacon for patients of all backgrounds and races, especially new immigrants. Due to space limitations and its expansion into a multi-service health and family-service center for low-income families and individuals from diverse ethnic backgrounds, both the National City and Mira Mesa's 800 square-foot clinic required considerable upkeep. The patients were Latinos, Asians and Pacific Islanders, Laotians, African-Americans, Caucasians and refugees from the Middle East and other countries. They were so diversified that the signs and pamphlets of the Operation Samahan were in English, Spanish, Tagalog and Lao. Significant numbers of these people were unable to communicate in English, thereby requiring Operation Samahan to employ those bilingual.

There were ups and downs in the clinic's activities, especially when the earlier members of the board of directors were not actively participating in the administration and supervision of the day-to-day operation. I had mostly spent my time at Operation Samahan as chairman of the board. After a decade of volunteer services, I decided to slow down to embark on other projects, and took a sabbatical leave. Together with the other two founders, we entrusted the management of the clinic to civic oriented Filipino Americans in the community.

In August of 1984, barely two years after the three of us left for sabbatical, an inspection and audit of the financial status of the clinic revealed fiscal problems and administrative deficiencies. As a result, the county discontinued the Revenue Sharing Program for Samahan.

There was a vigorous and forthright request by the public for myself, Dr. Quini and Dr. Gale to return. In response to the emergency situation, the three of us came back and the entire board of directors resigned en mass except for our friend, Mauro "Jake" Jacob. I hastily became the chairman of the board. With the help of some previous board members and other local activists - Mr. and Mrs. Ben Cendreda, Ben Monzon, attorney Henry Empeno, educator Sal Flor, Fem Ramirez RN and Perla Torres RN - we were able to achieve a compromise. The problems were resolved.

In September 26, 1984, the County of Supervisors, under the leadership of the Honorable Brian Bilbray, restored the Revenue Sharing Contract with Samahan. In a short span of time, the clinic continued to function under its new executive director, Romeo G. Cruz, who successfully served Samahan.

An important instance that has lived in my memory was when I wrote a memorandum to all the members of the board regarding their individual commitment and renewed interest to Samahan in between October 1986 through July 1987

July 23, 1987

"Dear board members:

I am writing this letter to reiterate my concern for your individual commitment and renewed interest to Samahan. A review of our records of the board of directors and committee meetings reveals the following attendance reports, which are enclosed for your own information. I feel these records reveal a standard, which is far below the expectations of the funding agencies.

I find it necessary to ask each of you to evaluate your priorities and determine if you can still fit in your scheduled commitment to Samahan. We all realize how precious your time is, and the voluntary service that you have given to Samahan has been exemplary. If possible, we expect you to be able to attend at least a minimum of two meetings a month, at an average of two hours per session. If you can continue to dedicate yourself towards the future of our organization, we can bring this community project to greater heights

Meanwhile, we will pursue our established goals. We will continue to be sensitive to the needs of our community and will create policies compatible with those needs and the philosophy and goals of the corporation.

Feel free to call me if you have any questions."

Lord Chesterfield, an English statesman and author, said: "Know the true value of time; snatch, seize, and enjoy every moment of it. No idleness, no laziness, no procrastination; never put off till tomorrow what you can do today."

We continued to operate with funding assistance from United Way, the Human Services Program of the County and City of San Diego, and National City's private agencies and individuals. In addition, Medical, Medicare and third–party insurance groups helped finance daily operations and keep optimum services at minimum costs. Subsequently the clinic was able to pay staff salaries while maintaining a pool of volunteers.

About forty percent of Operation Samahan's patients were uninsured. A patient whose annual income was twice the federal's poverty level or below qualifies for Operation Samahan's sliding scale, though he must also pay a small percentage of the cost of treatment. The uninsured that did not qualify for the sliding scale program paid $65.00 per visit, with the clinic paying for the rest.

BUILDING PROJECT EXPANSION

It was hard to believe that the old 5-bedroom house bought in 1978 became a 3,000 square-foot medical building. It was purchased in 1975 for $40,000 with a down payment of $10,000, and it originally served as a medical office and outreach clinic. The three of us, the original founders, funded the $30,000 balance by obtaining a mortgage loan at Peninsula Bank. We each had to guarantee $10,000 by putting up our own medical practices as collateral. The plan was to expand it to ten additional rooms for clinic operations with an office.

As chairman of the board, I felt that the dream of San Diego's Filipino American Community would soon become a reality once the $220,000 project expansion was completed. Under the aegis of Mayor George Waters, the National City Block Grant contributed $120,000 while Operation Samahan was able to raise $100,000 through loans and fund raising.

Executive Director Cruz resigned from Samahan after he and I had fervently worked with Joe Martinez, our architect. The blueprint of the clinic's building plan was completed, and the groundbreaking ceremony was held in the summer of 1989. With the approval of the board of directors, I hired Joel San Juan as the interim director for one year with the option to renew his contract. His job was to implement the policies set forth by the board. His initial duties would include conducting a comprehensive audit of clinic operations including its finances, administration, marketing, personnel and organization structure. After scrutinizing the program, we expected him to provide a specific plan for stabilizing revenue, expenses, cash flow and debts.

On May 6, 1990, hundreds of people attended the grand opening of the newly expanded and renovated Samahan Health Clinic. With my assistance as chairman of the board, Mayor Waters officiated the ribbon-cutting ceremony. A flurry of donations started when Dr. Manuel Sison, a formidable physician of Los Angeles, the chairman of the Education Research Foundation (ERF), was introduced, approached the podium, and raised an envelope in his hand. He said, "I'd like to start the ball rolling by donating $250 to Samahan Health Clinic. I hope others will follow suit."

And so they did! Mayor Waters came forward, donated $100, and hurled a challenge to the members of the City Council to do likewise. Two city councilmen accepted the Mayor's challenge. Councilman Fred Pruitt came forward with a check of $200, followed by Councilman Ralph Inzunza with $250.

In my welcome address, I emphasized how proud I was to share this moment, our new expansion, with everyone there. It was a milestone that could only happen with these good people working together in the spirit of "samahan." The mayor and councilmen were highly praised and received a laudable welcome for their support of our project.

Joel San Juan eventually became the executive director, and the rest of the stories about the two clinics were overwhelmingly successful.

More grants were accumulated, additional services were multiplied, and a new building across the clinic in Highland Avenue in National City was purchased for service expansion.

CITY MEDIA COVERAGE

Union–Tribune Staff Writer Gil Griffin reported on December 8, 1998. I was interviewed by Griffin. He quoted me when I stated, "this is the highlight of my career!"

"Twenty-five years ago, Operation Samahan was simply a dream of three Filipino American doctors. They wanted to find a way to provide affordable medical care to the poor and uninsured.... while the clinic as an outreach to the Filipino community, it has become a beacon for all uninsured patients of all backgrounds, especially newly arrived immigrants..."

Looking back, it gives me great pride to have helped organize a community health clinic that served the poor and the disadvantaged.

In August 1999, Philip Pinpin, a businessman and writer, wrote the Operation Samahan story "From ethnic to the mainstream." In my view, it was a fascinating article that remains lodged in my mind. Extracts of this article, thus:

"Therein lies the secret for awe-inspiring success of the medical clinic of Operation Samahan. From a purely ethnic Filipino manned and oriented operation, the project has metamorphosed into a mainstream player and its doors are now open to all the diverse peoples that make up the American landscape. What started as a Friday-night-only clinic in 1972 by the three pioneers, Drs. Candari, Quini and Gale, after a quarter of a century, has grown into a full-blown operation with professional staff of regular doctors, nurses and support persons.

"The emergence of Operation Samahan from a dream to a shoe-string, makeshift clinic to a multi-racial, mainstream health provider under Filipino American initiative and leadership demonstrates what our people can do to succeed if they put their minds and hearts into it. All it takes is vision, courage and determination.

"The Samahan proves to all and sundry, beyond any shadow of doubt, that Filipinos can actually unite and preserve a worthy and noble cause. It is a living antidote to the common belief that Filipinos have no sense of unity and merely a *"ningas cogon"* (initially enthusiastic but don't follow through) in their work ethic.

"...What Filipinos in San Diego have accomplished with Operation Samahan is probably a very small step if viewed in the light of the unlimited potential for service waiting to be unleashed in all of our Filipino American communities across the United States. But it is one giant leap to inspire all Filipinos everywhere, and it is a shining example for emulation by all other minorities in America..."

Several letters from readers all over the U.S. were sent to Filipino Reporter in which Operation Samahan received acclaim. Criselda Fuentes wrote: "Your special report about the Operation Samahan organized by three Filipino doctors in San Diego was very impressive and touching.

"In my 30 years here in the East Coast, I have never known of any Filipino medical group in this area with this kind of voluntarism and humanitarian devotion in helping poor immigrants...

"Although there are few commendable groups that go on medical missions to the Philippines, the achievements of these three Filipino doctors and others who joined the Operation Samahan cannot be surpassed."

Like a germ placed in a favorable condition, a good deed is contagious, highly infectious! Every person's life touches some other life that needs love today.

As of this writing, an on-line business information shows Operation Samahan serves over 20,000 patients and provides 45,000 visits a year. Current estimates show that Samahan has an annual revenue ranging from $10 to $20 million and employs a staff of approximately fifty to ninety-nine.

In 1991, I decided to endorse the administrative operation of the organization to the active members of the board. Those who I could remember include: Elvie Magsarili, Perla Torres, Medi Monaco, Ludy de Perio, and Fem Ramirez. The first few nurses who volunteered were namely the following: Amy Galang, Rose Seba, Betty Barrera, Connie Mirasol, Chris Cuesta, Medi Monaco, Cely Pablo, and Tessie Abella.

I am mighty pleased to paraphrase the wonderful words from Philip Pinpin's "From ethnic to the mainstream."

The success of Samahan Community Health Clinic originated from the three Filipino American doctors with dreams, beliefs and leadership. A true leader must be willing to do what is best for everyone, not just his own personal benefit. To be a good leader requires a tremendous sense of dedication ... you don't even consider the dimension of time. You do everything you can, without limit, to do what's best for everyone. These select people have certain characteristics that help people to recognize them leaders. Amongst these are confidence, morality, discipline and respect.

I left Samahan to switch my interests concerning the overall status of Filipino physicians practicing in the United States.

We faced many challenges. Like other Foreign Medical Graduates (FMGs) our American Colleagues threatened the Filipinos with some degree of discrimination, subtle as they may be. I became an active officer of the Association of Philippine Physicians in America (APPA).

By the way it was in 1972 that my previous mentor, Dr. Lucito Gamboa, founded the Association of Philippine Physicians in America (APPA). I became a member of the association, which was organized for charitable, educational and scientific purposes. One of the major objectives was to render free medical care to indigent people. It did not take long for Filipino American physicians in America to learn about these three doctors in San Diego. In 1975, the first APPA Community Service Award was bestowed to Dr. Cesar D. Candari, Dr. Romeo Quini, and Dr. Adelito Gale during the 3rd APPA annual convention in San Francisco.

CHAPTER SIX

HUMANITARIAN

Never respect men merely for their riches, but rather for their philanthropy; we do not value the sun for its height, but for its use.

- GAMALIEL BAILEY

PUSO
PHILIPPINES

Dr. Cesar D. Candari, guest speaker, delivered the following speech on October 15, 2011 - 25th anniversary of PUSO Philippines

I AM INDEED GREATLY honored to be your guest Speaker this evening. Tonight's occasion, the 25th anniversary of PUSO Philippines, is another memorable event of this humanitarian organization. To say it's a memorable event is an understatement. It is a shining silver anniversary. Indeed this occasion is to inspire us; it is to sanctify or consecrate us to the service of God and our fellow countrymen.

I am here tonight to share with you glimpses of an interesting short story. Along with it, however, will grab to the limelight of the sad specter of poverty in our country.

I am here to talk about PUSO Philippines of how it came about and why it was founded. It reminded me of an oddity, the peculiarity of series of events in the history of mankind - the fight for freedom, human rights and democracy in this world starting in the prehistoric days down to the atomic/nuclear, and cyber-robotic-digital age. Prehistoric man in the stone age invented fire in order to be alive from the freezing cold nights; while fire was used by Magellan in burning the homes of our forefathers in Mactan, Lapu-Lapu took up arms and killed Magellan and his men along the shores of Mactan Island. When Japan reduced the Far eastern people into subjection with their cannons and bullets, the United States of America, invented the atomic bomb and reduced Japan into ashes. Today, people in the US want to occupy Wall Street, they're concerned that the middle class in America is shrinking –with the rich getting richer and the poor getting poorer and growing in numbers. Now the "Occupy movement" goes global.

All these ladies and gentlemen, these sequential fates of events- are due to the yearning not only for liberty but also to live in better life and democracy. The People Power revolution in February 1986 was part of those fortunate events in the Philippine history that resulted to the establishment of PUSO Philippines. It came at its virtuous time. In the darkened days of gloom- as the story goes- we lost our freedom during the Marcos dictatorship. It lasted for almost 20 years. The dictator destroyed the economy of our country. But because of our inherent love for freedom and liberty, we rediscovered Democracy once again through Ninoy Aquino's assassination-- after which a few years later the indomitable People Power revolution surfaced.

Ten thousand miles away from the EDSA, we did our rally here in San Diego, delivered our speeches on that very day of February 22, 1986 (I was one of the Speakers) telling the whole world that the dictator abused our country.

And finally Marcos was ousted. The dictator fled the country on February 25, 1986.

On that date, Filipinos in the whole world were triumphant. We celebrated here in San Diego. A thanksgiving mass was held at St, Mary's Church in National City. Thereafter with all sincerity, with all our passion, and with all our compassion in our hearts, immediately after that thanksgiving mass, PUSO Philippines of San Diego was designed, blueprinted and built by a group of indefatigable, the untiring founders - a revolution of sort for the start of our humanitarian help to the poor people of our native land. It was a historic occasion for CHARITY. A popular word of wisdom says: "Every good act is charity. A man's true wealth hereafter is the good that he does in this world to his fellows."

Beside charity, PUSO Philippines believed in the spirit of ideals and goals to achieve her destiny. PUSO Philippines wrote her own destiny. PUSO did not reach that destiny by chance; Destiny is a matter of choice; it is a thing to be achieved. Yes, indeed PUSO Philippines achieved that destiny. Now, all these events appeared to me to be a part of our Divine affiliation. In our history, we Filipinos came about to know democracy and freedom from our forefathers and through Dr. Rizal. We must be proud of the legacy left behind by our national heroes, particularly the bravery and national sentiment of Dr. Rizal.

In recollection the "people power" movement was driven by the desire to live in peace and nay- to find relief from the specter of poverty. The popular uprising of more than a million of Filipino people brought Corazon Aquino to power in an almost-bloodless revolution. People Power was our shining glory! The whole world applauded our saintly courage, our dignified defiance, and our bloodless solution to expel a dictator. We were the toast of all freedom-loving countries, the envy of all oppressed people. These made news headlines as "the revolution that surprised the world." By inspiration, a moving reality, the name PUSO was born coming from the new President's name, Corazon. PUSO is literally simple, in an idiom, "in (one's) heart of hearts – is in the seat of one's truest feelings." A very symbolic Corazon- a heart that beats and deliver that fluid red blood cells into the circulatory system of our poor kababayans.

Personally, I have to confess to you, as a participant in the founding of PUSO, this was the start of my heart's desire to establish my humanitarian medical missions to our country. I am very proud of it and PUSO, I REPEAT, PUSO inspired me.

Now, another story of why PUSO Philippines was born. It was because we wanted to help our fellow countrymen from the ravages of poverty. For many years, the population of our country is represented virtually by 70%-80% of our countrymen trapped in the vicious cycle of poverty and exploitation. We are burdened with vast economic, social and political conflicts, and so we are not completely free. Filipinos continue to wallow in sordid living conditions and unimaginable conditions of poverty, complicated by insurgencies, unresolved civil strife and most blatantly graft and corruption in our government officials.   There is a sense of hopelessness in the business community, with so much greed, dishonesty, opportunism and frustration in the government.   Just imagine the filth and squalor of poverty in the slums of Manila; the shards of destitution litter our cities. Hunger, disease, pollution, and congestion in the city are appalling. The faces on the city streets tell many tales.

Today, the economy is lower than Pakistan - and 25% of the 100 million people live on less than $1.25 a day.

Well, PUSO Philippines remained to its goal of helping the poor people, fulfilling its affirmed mission, to pursue charitable projects in the Philippines. Since then, this charitable organization has been sending donations and funding charities in our home country.

Let me tell you, it's a travesty of life in the waste dump in Payatas the Manila's main waste dump with garbage piled as high as seven stories building. Close to 30,000 impoverished squatters, the poor families live in this area with their malnourished children. Scholarship programs for these children were supported by PUSO Philippines. PUSO Philippines helped the orphanage Hospicio de San Jose in Manila, for the destitute and abandoned children. And there are more in the name of CHARITY. Scholarship program to the youths are supported at the Don Bosco Vocational Technical School. In Malolos, Bulacan PUSO helped Fr. Ricardo "K.C." Moraga took care of the abandoned sick, and elderly citizens.

While Filipinos now enjoy democracy, life is still difficult. There is an expression of despair in their eyes: We ask if there will be deliverance from these crippling maladies.

Every Filipino in his dream must support the current President of the Philippines, Noynoy Aquino when he stated, *and Kung walang corrupt walang mahirap*! I put this question to our new president. *Ano ang mangyari sa ating Pobreng kababayan?*

Lastly, I'd say, end the poverty! Democracy restored is not all that they need; the people must be free from hunger and want.

Meanwhile we must continue with our messianic zeal, passion and devotion to be determined to support PUSO whose vision is to help our poor people in our beloved native land. As a popular quote from PUSO-- PUSO is the heart that beats for the Filipinos ten thousand miles away.

TODAY, we inform Filipinos from all over the world to pray, as a people, for the economic recovery and moral reformation of our nation. THANK YOU.

PRESIDENTIAL ADDRESS, PVLC LIONS CLUB

Dateline, 2000

It was in the millennium year, 2000, that I was elected president of Paradise Valley Lions Club Dist. 4-L6. Following were extracted from my speech.

TONIGHT HAVING BEEN entrusted to carry the banner of leadership of Paradise Valley Lions in this new Millennium, I humbly accept this challenging responsibility.

Tonight is also another special occasion where we articulate our joys, our dreams, and our shared values. It is a time to reaffirm our vision, our sense of duty, and our commitment to serve. It is time to reflect upon our organization's accomplishments with pride; and because of our dedication, you have made a lot of people happier and you have improved the lives of many people around you. Ladies and gentleman, the PVLC deserves to be congratulated!

I wish to speak tonight about the virtue of CHARITY combined with LEADERSHIP. I feel that this is most appropriate for any service organization like ours. Real charity is not something you give away, it is something that you acquire and make a part of yourself. And when the virtue of charity becomes implanted in your heart, you are never the same again.

Perhaps the greatest charity comes when each and everyone of us are working together in great harmony, in the spirit of teamwork — for teamwork is the ability to work together toward a common vision. Charity is expecting the better of each and every one of us in this organization. With charity in all of us, there will be no mountains we cannot climb.

Now, having said that, this is the LEADERSHIP that I will espouse in this administration, one with power and wisdom of charity in order to motivate each and every one of you so that we can have a clear vision as we sail into this new century of service. In order to continue serving those in need, it is important that we stay strong and dedicated. By fostering membership growth and developing effective and quality leadership skills and retention, we can be sure that we will be able to continue to serve our people in need. I remember the message of Lions Club International Immediate Past President James E. Ervin when he said, " Leadership is crucial to our vision for maximum efficiency. Strong, effective and quality leadership are the foundations we all seek as Lions". Allow me to add; it must also be a leadership that will inspire interest, involvement and renewal. You see, in the PVLC, we have a fine tradition and strong foundation upon which to build; we have the enthusiasm, we have the dedication and we have the interest to meet these goals. I say to you my fellow Lions in the PVLC, seize this occasion, seize the opportunity; we have the force.

As your president for the incoming fiscal year, I would need your support more than ever before, on the projects we have in progress. For a small organization like ours, the success of our undertakings relies heavily on the continued support of the members. We must be aware that we need each other; we must be aware of our mutual commitment of 'we serve imperative' of Lionism. The virtues of mutual sharing and tolerance will assure us an open communication and reconciliation and will remove distrust and confrontations among us. As immigrants to this country, we must improve our image in our respective communities, promote our heritage, and establish our identity and our place in American Society. What we think, what we do, and what we portray in this club concerns everyone. During this recent medical mission, you have shown great interest for the disadvantaged, the poor people of our country. That was a noble act.

...My foremost objective is to increase our membership with carefully selected and qualified men and women. You will notice that there are thirty awardees and plaques given away this evening. Many more were awarded in the Philippines including last year's inaugural celebration. This is indeed a difficult act to follow. That shows there were just as many club members doing their job well. So, to follow this act, I appeal for your involvement and support in my administration; let me remind you that if no one tries to help, no matter how simple the job is, it becomes a lonely task. What I need for this administration is a Bayanihan- a samahan, (the spirit of working together) as true Filipinos that we are. We must remember that communities, towns, and nations are the result of combined efforts and skills of people with hope and vision. We must share the sum total of our many gifts and talents, our expertise and our spirit of unity, to build a solid and stronger PLVC…

On a personal note, I wish to take this opportunity to express my profound thanks to my dear wife for her support and understanding in all these volunteer time spent weekly for meetings and the medical missions.

Lastly, my fellow Lions, I wanted to say, I am deeply honored to serve as your leader in this organization.

I wish to leave you a famous quotation on what I believe a leader must be: " The leader are not those who strive to be first but those who are first to strive and who give their all for the success of the team. The leaders are first to see the need, envision the plan, and empower the team for action. By the strength of the leader's commitment the power of the team is unleashed."

Fellow Lions, I promise you this kind of leadership and I mean to carry it. Thank you.

MISSIONARY WORK

Dateline, 2011

FOR A NUMBER OF years before my retirement, I joined groups of medical missionaries to the Philippines. From 1987 (after the People Power Revolution) to 2002, I participated once a year to help the poor people in our country who needed medical care. I became a charter member and board member of Paradise Valley Lions Club (PVLC) of San Diego when it was founded in 1993. I deeply believe in the Lions Club Organization and its strong missionary work.

The late Dr. Eduardo Manaig, a friend, colleague, and prominent medical practitioner in National City, California, was the founder and first president of PVLC, Dist. 4-L6. I was the vice president in 1999 and became the 8th president in 2000. I was re-elected to serve until 2002. The PVLC's achievements in those eight years included medical services to poverty areas in Africa, India, Vietnam and the Philippines.

From the very start, the Lions Code of Ethics and Lions International Objectives were well known to every charter member. The medical mission was the vanguard humanitarian endeavor of the club. It showed no limits in their dedication, kindness, sympathy, charity, and genuine love for the poor people in the Spirit of Lionism. Our mission was to collaborate with individuals and organizations to improve our community and to help those we were serving.

Generally speaking, there are many members in the entire universe that make a difference in the lives of thousands of people every day. I said, without the help of these members, the suffering we see today would be tenfold. The Medical Missions of the Paradise Valley Lions Club were truly one of the most important and life-changing deeds performed by Lions anywhere across the world. Congratulations to the PVLC for turning suffering into happiness for so many people. To borrow the words from Lions International: "Whenever a Lions club gets together, problems get smaller. And communities get better. That's because we help where help is needed – in our own communities and around the world – with unmatched integrity and energy." The Paradise Valley Lions Club of San Diego won the coveted LIONS CLUB OF THE YEAR award for Lion year 1999-2000 in District 4-L6, which covers San Diego County and Imperial County in Southern California.

In 1995 when the PVLC was barely a year old, the members decided to travel to the Philippines on a medical mission. In several areas, they attended to hundreds of people who were sick and without funds for treatment. The mission went so well that the members decided to do it again the following year.

This time, they agreed to expand their mission of mercy to include more people in need in other poor countries. At the urging of one of the members, who was born in India and grew up in Nairobi, they decided to have a medical mission to Kenya and India.

In 1996, the Lions Club spent a year raising funds, collecting medical equipments and supplies for the mission to different countries. It also took almost a year to work out the logistics of making the mission feasible. I was chairman of the logistic committee. For a trip that would include three countries, PVLC remained undaunted although it realized that it would need more effort to put it all together.

To raise funds for a successful mission, PVLC sponsored bowling tournaments and raffles, sent out solicitations for donations from friends, relatives and supporters. Finally, $50,000 was raised, which was deemed enough to cover the expenses for the trip that started in 1997. Hundreds of thousands of dollars in used medical equipments and eyeglasses were also collected.

In Kenya, the group conducted medical camps in several orphanages. Nearly 300 children were treated and given gifts of toys and clothing. Many of the youngsters were disabled and had not had any medical attention for more than three years.

In India, the volunteers saw over 600 people including children from nearby orphanages at one medical camp. Another camp rendered medical treatment to more than 1,000 people and gave eyeglasses, medicine, and donations of clothing and toys.

When PVLC reached the Philippines, they conducted camps in Pampanga, Zambales, Valenzuela and Calamba. Lions joined the medical and dental unit of the Philippine Army in San Antonio, Zambales to see nearly 350 medical and 150 dental patients. They performed fourteen surgeries at a nearby hospital. In addition to surgical patients, Lions tended to 705 medical and 225 dental patients.

Here again, I have written a number of articles covering the different places of our medical missions and the messages and opinions I have expressed therein were my stories of my journey in my life.

I participated in the logistical planning, but I was not able to make it to the foreign countries, except to meet them in Manila and to the join them in the Philippine medical missions.

Looking back at my accomplishments thus far, I felt intense pleasure from knowing that I have touched many lives. It goes as far back to 1973 when I initiated the establishment of the Operation Samahan Health Clinic in San Diego.

Another momentous medical mission of the Paradise Valley Lions Club in 1999 was in Vietnam and the Philippines. A recognition night was accorded to the participants held at the Le Pavilion, Town and Country Hotel. I was a vice president and one of the recipients of the missionary award.

"Indeed, it has been a privilege and honor to be a part of the leadership of PVLC since its inception in 1993. Together with our motivated members, we nurtured this organization to what it is today - a mature, valuable and successful organization to be reckoned with in this community," my statement I made.

In those formative years, it was not easy. Like any other young organizations, hurdles were encountered. Our club starred a meteoric rise with achievements in humanitarian endeavors due to our dedication to serve the less fortunate, the magnanimous and unselfish desire of the members to extend a helping hand, not to mention time and money, but in the spirit of Lionism. This has been a feat no one can ever imagine to follow, and we were all profoundly proud of it.

PVLC was a breeding ground of creative projects and has persistently maintained the annual launching of its medical missions. The immense magnitude of the mission's positive impact on the health of the people of the countries visited will surely be long remembered.

One of its most desired goals, however, was to adopt a clinic or a hospital in our homeland, the Philippines. I have a dream, and it seemed that I was able to get the members more excited about dreams for the future than the history of our past accomplishments. It was my contention that it is incumbent upon the new leadership to remain strong and unwaveringly dedicated to carry on the banner devoted to the motto, "We Serve." The honor that everyone deserved reminds me of a saying by Mark Twain: "It is better to deserve honors and not have them than to have them and not deserve them."

MEDICAL MISSION TO BULACAN, NUEVA ECIJA & BATAAN

Dateline, March 2000

IT WAS CONCLUDED as an unprecedented labor of love when the PARADISE VALLEY LIONS CLUB (PLVC), District 4-L6 returned from a recent medical, dental and optical mission to the Philippines. Approximately 5,500 patients were seen in consultations and treatment in the depressed areas of the provinces of Bulacan, Nueva Ecija and Bataan. The missionaries served about twenty-five Barangays from February 27 to March 7, 2000. Specifically, the medical campsites were in barangay Cabu (in Cabanatuan City), Talavera, N.E. and Orion, Bataan. Tony Pizarro was our host in Bataan.

The principal sponsor of the mission was the PARADISE VALLEY HOSPITAL (PVH), ADVENTIST HEALTH of National City.

I, as president of PVLC, and Dr. Eduardo Manaig, chairman of the medical mission, organized the project. This was a regular yearly undertaking of the Paradise Valley Lions Club whose mission statement is to help alleviate the physical ailments and health problems of the needy, the poor and indigent populations of the Philippines.

The PARADISE VALLEY HOSPITAL (PVLH) Adventist Health donated $10,000 cash to this mission. Because of their belief in the noble objectives of the Lions medical mission, Mr. Terrance A. Hansen, the president and CEO of PVH, was altruistic in his desire to help the club and its leaders. Other sources of funds were from monies generated by the fundraising activities of the Club...wine-tasting at my home, luau at Dr. Manaig, Christmas party and valentine jam sessions...that netted more than $28,000 dollars.

During this medical mission, the Club transported about $500,000 worth of medicines and medical supplies to the Philippines.

Different drug companies donated for the mission. In addition, the club purchased about $9,000 worth of medicines.

The medical mission had a busy and hectic schedule. The missionaries traveled from one place to another covering hundreds of kilometers to get to a medical site. They talked to hundreds of the sick children and adults who presented a myriad of needs that could not be enumerated here. They performed blood tests for blood sugar, hemoglobin and CBC with differential. ECG was a very popular request. Most of the illnesses the medical group saw were typical of poverty caused by malnutrition and inadequate sanitation. Many anemic patients and upper respiratory infections and EENT problems were seen in the pediatric populations.

The missionaries ignored the summer-like hot weather in the Philippines. Some worked to the point of intense exhaustion due to dehydration. Despite the physically exhaustive endeavor, the experience was gratifying for everyone. Those non-medical volunteers were highly commendable.

The project could not have been a success without the undying support of Juliet Quan of Sister Lions Club – Valenzuela United Lions. Dr. Manaig led the planning, fundraising, and gathering of medical supplies and medicines, and packaging. Indeed, members of the PVLC expended tremendous time and effort.

Realistically, any endeavor of this mammoth proportion, no matter how meticulously planned, may entail some minutia of oversight, but in the final analysis, these were dwarfed by the historic event of the medical mission. The PVLC medical missionaries are all volunteer groups who spent their own money for air transportation and other incidentals in this mission.

We received some recognition of the PVLC after the 2000 medical mission. It is not only to give recognition to the missionaries but also to celebrate our accomplishments with high pride. I am proud that the PARADISE VALLEY LIONS has always been outstanding in many ways. It has excelled in almost every endeavor in helping others in our community and even around the world. This recent medical mission to our home country was outstanding and a huge success. You gave all you can, showing no limits to your dedication, kindness, sympathy, charity, compassion and genuine love for others. Indeed, these are moments for self-glorification, moments to be remembered and appreciated. To the many fellow missionaries...you are the best! Your work was a tremendous success.

Best of all in this medical mission was when each and every one of us worked together in great harmony in the spirit of teamwork and our ability to work together toward a common vision. And at the end of the day, we could say, "it is more blessed to give than to receive. It is not what we accomplished that is really worthwhile, but rather it is what we have willingly provided for others, even at the expense of our personal comfort." The recent medical mission was terribly exhausting. Yet, this did not deter our spirit, and the tireless work went on. As your president who led this medical mission, (and I am extremely proud to be your leader) I salute all of you. You are to be congratulated for your efforts in carrying the tradition of PLVC of selfless dedicated service to our less fortunate brothers and sisters, for preserving unity in this club, and for giving your best to serve in the spirit of true Lionism.

Finally, I wish to congratulate Dr. Manaig, our mission chairman, and the rest of the officers and members of PARADISE VALLEY LIONS whose unselfish dedication and unquestionable loyalty, quality and integrity are beyond reproach. They have made the PLVC a pioneering and distinct group of committed Lions in helping the needy around the world and in our community.

HEALTH FAIR: In addition to the medical mission, the Paradise Valley Lions Health Fair on October 29, 2000 was considered a huge success. The theme was "Building a healthier community". It was held at the Boys and Girls Club building in National City. The tireless efforts of the members especially Dr. Manaig, the project chairman, contributed to the project's success. There were pharmaceutical booths and other health-related exhibits; free medical exams such as eye screening, diabetic eye exams and podiatry exams; bone density, hypertension, blood sugar and cholesterol tests. Close to 1,000 attendees, members of the mainstream community including Hispanics were present. Mayor George Waters and Lion International zone chairman John Kirk and his lady were the honored guests.

This project was successful as an excellent meeting ground for the healthcare industry and the public it serves.

I am proud that our membership in the PVLC had been reinvigorated with quality members; spirits are high and the enthusiasm great. The health information services to the community with monthly seminar programs of educating the people about understanding their health, prevention of diseases and treatment became a popular demand by the public.

COVETED LIONS CLUB OF THE YEAR AWARD
LION YEAR 1999-2000 IN SAN DIEGO COUNTY

Introduction: I was re-elected president for another term. It was at this time when, inspired by the humane vision of Lions Club International called "Saving Sight", we embarked on a missionary journey to reach a new dream. We were venturing to establish a partnership in the underprivileged areas of the world for the purpose of reducing blindness. Along the way, we would acquire a state-of-the art portable ocular laser and support equipment, train local personnel, educate the population, and perform laser surgery. Dr. Manuel Puig, a prominent ophthalmologist practicing in San Diego, was the main proponent of the project. He is a close friend, my personal physician, and also a member of the Paradise Valley Lions Club.

Following delivered at a Hawaiian luau party in the residence of Dr. and Mrs. Ed Manaig, inaugural speech.

"...**I AM GRATEFUL** because we have not only survived, but through everybody's collective effort we have become the Lions Club of the Year of District 4-L6 in San Diego and Imperial County.

Our struggle and determination to undertake the medical missions yearly to third world countries have been recognized, and we are happy that we have created a niche for ourselves in Lionism for our humanitarian endeavor.

I am delighted to see many of our friends and supporters who have come out of their way to be with us this evening. It is significant that this beautiful summertime in this backyard pool of our great host, that we celebrate once more our accomplishments, another special occasion where we articulate our dreams and visions. And so this evening, I will speak about our dreams. I am so proud of the achievements of Paradise Valley Lions Club in the past year and even prouder of the dreams and visions that we entertain for tomorrow.

When you reelected me as your leader to carry PLVC's banner once again, I accept the responsibility with a greater resolve to carry on the steady course of our club in implementing our 'We Serve' motto.

About a year before, there was this dream that came about in this club. A dream to acquire a laser – an instrument to support the popular theme of Lions International, an association recognized around the world as the Knights of the blind in the Crusade against Darkness, the Helen Keller Challenge.

The price of the laser instrument was beyond our reach; nevertheless, we went on hoping, working and dreaming. In less than a year we are almost there. We only need a few thousand dollars more to reach our goal. This eye instrument, described by the Committee Chairman Dr. Manuel Puig, will be able to treat many diseases related to eyesight that is preventable and reversible. By having this instrument available, we will serve our community and others in the poor countries where we will conduct our medical missions yearly.

I am pleased to say that our membership has been invigorated with quality recruits, the spirit of enthusiasm is high and the total involvement of members in each project has been spontaneous. Fellow Lions, I am very comfortable of you and I want to thank every one for your support. We take pride in our accomplishments and look forward to the challenges before us with confidence.

Last but not the least, I have another dream. I dream about achieving unity in the world of Lionism, particularly among Filipino Americans. We are proud to tell you that Paradise Valley Lions Club works as a team and in harmony and solidarity with our vision for the future.

My fellow Lions, Lions International President Frank Moore III said ".... leadership must be nourished and sustained in every Lions Club." We, particularly the Filipino Americans, can do this only if we observe the values of tolerance. Concern, mutual commitment, and above all, unity in our hearts are required. We must not encourage or tolerate a leadership that is cultivating vacuous posturing or motives centered on personal glory and aggrandizement. We must be guided by ETHICS, HONESTY, INTEGRITY, and enlightened PRINCIPLES.

We have another year to plan for our annual medical mission to the Philippines and to other countries. We wish to thank our benefactor, the Paradise Valley Hospital Adventist Health, for its continuing generous support.

Let us remember that in unity we could achieve social and political empowerment, an attractive platform that could encourage a stronger and dynamic image for Filipinos in America. There is a saying: "Hundreds of people may be banded together to carry out a project, but these individuals are sure to fail if there is no solidarity in their purpose and objectives." Lionism is providing us such an opportunity. With the outstanding leadership of Lion District Governor Morman and his officers, we can continue and sustain the onward thrust of Paradise Valley Lions Club in our avowed service to the community all around the world..."

MEDICAL MISSION TO ANTIQUE AND
TO MY HOMETOWN PANDAN

My article coverage of the Medical Mission

Dateline, March 2002

INDEED, A VERY successful and magnanimous achievement of humanitarian endeavor was concluded last February 26, 2002 when the Texas Association of Philippine Physicians returned from a recent medical and surgical mission to the province of Antique, Philippines, led by Dr. Leonidas Andres, a Far Eastern University alumnus.

The principal sponsor of the mission was the Antique Circle of USA (ACUSA), assisted by the Pandan Antique Foundation, Inc. (PAF) and Pagtatap USA in the Pandan mission. Dr. Cesar D. Candari is chairman of PAF from San Diego, California, and originally from Pandan, assisted in the coordination of the Pandan mission. All three organizations are based in California.

The delegation was composed of 26 physicians with various specialties and 10 RN's and local volunteers. Approximately 2576 patients were seen for consultation and treatment in the towns of San Jose, the provincial capital of Antique, and the northern towns of Culasi and Pandan (987 in San Jose, 681 in Culasi and 786 in Pandan).

These missionaries served several neighboring towns and barangays of each of these places from January 21 to January 25, 2002. Major and minor surgical procedures were performed in each of these places of mission, totaling 156 cases (67 major surgeries in San Jose, 39 major and 42 minor surgical procedures in Culasi, and 8 minor surgeries in Pandan). The common major cases operated were thyroidectomies, hernia repairs, hysterectomies, and gall bladder resections.

Drs. Leonidas Andres and Adelfa Yap Andres of Anahuac, Texas, planned and chaired the medical mission whose sole purpose was to help alleviate the physical ailments and health problems of the needy, the poor and indigent population of the province of Antique. The Andreses are originally from Barbaza and Culasi of Antique

Dr. Arsenio Martin, President of the Association said, "It is simply our selfless and genuine desire to be of some significant assistance to our countrymen, particularly the poor people of Antique who otherwise may not be able to obtain medical care in their lifetime." The medical mission had a busy and hectic schedule. The missionaries ministered to hundreds of the sick children and adults who presented a myriad of needs that cannot be enumerated here. The group felt that most of the illnesses they saw were typical of poverty caused by malnutrition and inadequate sanitation. Many anemic, upper respiratory infections, and EENT problems were seen in the pediatric populations. Almost every patient complained of coughing and some form of upper and lower respiratory ailments including pulmonary tuberculosis. Despite the physically exhausting endeavor, it was a satisfying experience for everyone in the medical team to see patients with gratifying and smiling faces and hear them say, *"Salamat po doctor sa inyong tulong sa amin. Hulog po kayo ng langit"* (Thank you very much for your help. You are all manna from heaven). Loida Candari, RN said, "Their faces of gratitude were indeed touching." The members of the mission were: Dr. Arsenio Martin, Dr. Fe Martin, Dr. Nellie Martin, Dr. Mario Castillo, Dr. Sonia Castillo, Dr. Cesar D. Candari, Dr. Edgar Borda, Dr. Chris Polvoroza, Dr. Licerio Castro, Dr. Daisy Castro, Dr. Dorothy Matamorosa, Dr. Fred Arcala, Dr. Avila Arcala, Dr. Archie La Madrid, Dr. Vivianne La Madrid, Dr. Jeng Conferido, Dr. Donabel Anico, Dr. Pacifico Dalisay, Dr. Vic Fermo, Dr. Rey Manzo, Dr. Ferolino Karl, Dr. Ricardo Francisco, Dr. William Candelario, Dr. Florentino Ibabao, Dr. Panes, Dr. Lim, Dr. Alcalen, Dr. Tanchuan , Jovy Fermo RN, Dina Garcinella, RN, Honeychille Andres RN, Loida Candari RN, Narzeneth P. Moscoso RN, Mary Ann Ancheta RN, Lou Manzo RN, Zenaida Tubianosa RN, Shellane Pinzon RN, Nely Imperio RN, Ruth Agustino RN, Gina Martin, Sixto Moscoso, Dr. Quirico Escano, Michael Montoya, Jinky Limos and Marilyn Tan (mission overall coordinator). The project could not have been a success without the undying support of ACUSA, the many volunteers in Antique, and the remarkable hospitality of a host of provincial and town officials led by Governor Sally Zaldivar Perez and Congressman Ex Javier, the Rotarians of Antique, and the local hospital personnel. To all of them, the Texas Association of Philippine Physicians expresses its sincere thanks and gratitude. Dr. Martin said; " I would like to thank the Antiqueños for their warm welcome and hospitality. Foremost is our appreciation of our patients for their trust in all the physicians, nurses and the whole team. The food in Antique is second to none. We will be very happy to do this again in the future".

Since the places where the mission was held were among the most impoverished towns, I find it gratifying and spiritually uplifting to have served the poor constituencies of my birthplace. I wish to thank the Paradise Valley Lions Club for helping purchase the much-needed medicines that I brought to the Philippines. It was a very successful mission.

The missionaries transported to the Philippines a total of twenty-eight *balikbayan* boxes of medicine and medical surgical supplies worth hundreds of thousands of dollars, all of which were donated by different drug companies in the U.S. In addition, the team purchased thousands of dollars of medicines in the Philippines during the mission.

The Paradise Valley Lions Club of San Diego donated the medicines that I brought to Pandan as well. Our reception in Pandan was headed by Mayor Sanchez, care of Vice Mayor Arthur Dionela and coordinated by Sonnyboy Alojipan.

MEDICAL MISSION TO KALIBO, AKLAN

Dateline, February 1998

THE FRIENDS LTD. (Graduates from different Medical Schools) made history on January 22 to 25, 1998, after traveling to Kalibo, Aklan in the Philippines and participating in an enormously successful medical and surgical mission. Record number 2,100 outpatients, children and adults alike were seen and treated in three days. The surgical team performed a total of 120 surgical cases as team members worked three and a half days treating hernias, lumps, cysts, soft tissue tumors, goiters, cleft lips, ptyridium, caesarean sections, hysterectomies, colon cancer resections and cataract operations.

This charitable mission was an effort of members of FRIENDS, an organization of an exclusive small group of friends of Filipino American physicians in the United States. Volunteer nurses and other physicians joined the group, totaling fifty participants in the mission with each one bringing a *balikbayan*-box (home travel box) of all sorts of medicines. The anesthesiologists and ophthalmologists also brought their special equipment for surgery.

The congressman of the province of Aklan, the Honorable Allen Salas Quimpo and the Governor, Florendo Miraflores, hosted the mission. Other sponsors were the Philippine Economic and Cultural Endowment (PEACE); Mission Hospital; Kalibo Rotary Club; Philippine Medical Association of Southern Virginia; North Central Virginia Association of Philippine Physicians and Virginia Association of Philippine Physicians. The missionaries worked alongside with health care workers of the Aklan Provincial Hospital and the Mission Hospital of Kalibo, all of whom provided medical care and follow-up treatments on the surgeries.

This event marked the first medical mission of FRIENDS. It was organized under the chairmanship of Dr. Jane Peralta-Legaspi of Chesapeake, Virginia, and co-chaired by Dr. Daisy Pelayo-Ramos of Bloomfield, Michigan, and Dr. Oscar M. Laserna of Fredericksburg,

Virginia. The three physicians were originally from the province of Aklan.

The overall coordinator for the Philippines was Prosecutor Edgar R. Peralta assisted by Atty. Edmund R. Peralta of New Washington, Aklan.

The surgical team performed their surgeries at the two hospitals of Kalibo, Aklan...the Provincial Hospital and the Mission Hospital. The doctors were composed of varied specialists. The members were: Dr. Cesar D. Candari, Drs. Rosario Guanzon-Laserna, Oscar M. Laserna, and Juan Montero. Rolando Casis, Virgilio Supetran, Jack Bautista, Gerrald Sy, Reynaldo Lee-Llacer, Zorayda Lee-Llacer, Glen Carwell, Monica Thom, John Van Belger, Amante Legaspi, Floviano Uy, Lenny Baquiran, and Wellie Magat.

This project could not have been a total success without the professional coordination and logistical preparation of Drs. Jane Legaspi, Daisy Ramos, and Oscar Laserna.

"Our special mention and thanks go to the Peralta brothers of New Washington, Aklan, Fiscal Edgar Peralta, the Ex Mayor Atty. Edmund Peralta, and Chito Peralta", said Dr. Rolando Santos, chairman of FRIENDS (The Peraltas were the brothers of our mission chairman Dr. Jane Legaspi).

Dr. Oscar Laserna commented, "We all felt this mission as a personally fulfilling effort and proud to be part of a team that is making a meaningful difference in people's lives in our country." Dr. Daisy Ramos added, "It is unavoidable not to be touched deeply by the very sick and poor people of our homeland."

These patients had not seen a doctor for many years. Children were barefooted and malnourished. Cely Candari, a volunteer pharmacist said, "I remember I gave a bottle of Tylenol to a baby and the mother who said with a grateful smile, *"Maraming salamat po sa inyong tulong sa mga mahirap"*(Thank you for your help to the poor).

THE PINNACLE AT LIONS CLUB
My commentary delivered to Lions Club

Dateline, January 2001

... AFTER RECOVERING FROM the rigors of the medical mission trip, I have come to realize that in barely three months, my second term as president will come to an end. Looking back at the past two years, I feel humbled by the achievements during my two successive terms. I am most appreciative of the harmony and unifying spirit prevailing among the members of our club. To me, this spirit is pivotal in the shaping up of our plans, the carrying out of the varied projects that we have carefully discussed and nurtured, and the successful completion of all of them. Naturally, we owe everything to the selfless devotion of our officers and members, and their relentless pursuit for perfection.

The late Lion Dr. Eduardo Manaig interrupted me and stated the following:

"I would like to extend thanks to President Lion Dr. Cesar Candari, for having successfully carried out club programs whose magnitude and importance will be felt by Paradise Valley Lions Club for a long time. Chiefly, Lion Cesar's term will be credited for the medical mission last year, the cool and calm exercise of his leadership. Suffice to say that Dr. Candari has already created for himself a niche in the halls of outstanding achievements in Paradise Lions Club. Lion President Cesar's term of office shall be cut three month short due to his appointment as Chief Pathologist of El Centro Regional Medical Center – a lucrative and challenging proposition difficult to refuse. For that matter, I, along with my fellow-medical practitioners, envy him for the extraordinary fortune and luck. Bon voyage in your new undertaking, Lion Cesar!"

I continued on: In more ways than one, Paradise Valley Lions Club and myself in particular, have been truly blessed and for which I am very thankful, first to God our Almighty, to you, my fellow-Lions, and to all our patrons and benefactors who have perseveringly supported our efforts through all these years. When the time comes to pass on the torch of leadership to the incoming leadership, I will yield the gavel of authority with a sense of pride of accomplishment. I promise to remain active in the club.

I expressed my sincere thanks to everyone who had helped me steer the boat in sometimes-rough waters. Nevertheless, it had been smooth sailing because they were there, committed to make a difference.

Vic Ortega, the editor of the Lions COURIER monthly newsletter had this to say: "After an emotion-filled farewell which Lion Dr. Cesar Candari delivered to fellow members in the Paradise Valley Lions Club during the March 26th Tuesday meeting, former President Lion Carl Batuyong equally delivered and bade an emotion-filled response by saying that when the Club's integrity was being questioned by former members whose agendas were to cause mischief, Lion Cesar was the president; when the Club's harmonious relationship among the member was being tested and its unity was being harangued by groundless imputations from the same jealous hate-promoters, Lion Cesar was the president; and when courage to forge ahead was needed with cool determination to succeed, Lion Cesar provided the quality leadership."

FOUNDER AND CHAIRMAN OF THE BOARD
PANDAN ANTIQUE FOUNDATION, INC.
(PAF)

Dateline, July 2000

THE PANDAN ANTIQUE FOUNDATION, Inc., a non-profit, public benefit corporation was registered in California, USA, on July 18, 2000, a 501 (c) (3) Tax-Exempt Foundation. Taxpayer I.D. # 33-0916694 . Its mission is to undertake various support programs, projects, and activities geared toward helping our beloved hometown Pandan, Antique, Philippines. It is designed to help the poor people from the ravages of poverty and make available proper health care. Modesty aside, single-handedly, I founded the Foundation.

This was how it begun. In April 2000 a good number of Pandananons went home to attend our town fiesta. Many of them were the so-called *'KYAPNETS'* (bats in our vernacular; Pandan town mates in the Internet) from all over the world, who had been interacting with each other through the Pagtatap e-groups Internet with plans for our hometown. The members of Pagtatap USA and Pagtatap Philippines were among those in attendance at the meeting. One of the primary missions of the group was to improve the general welfare of our *kasimanwa* (town mates). Among the many projects placed on the table were the health problems of the people, especially the poor in our hometown. This was at the top in our list. I volunteered to chair the committee on "adopt a hospital concept", i.e., help the municipal hospital of Pandan, so that it would become a better place to admit patients and also be a venue for our planned medical missions in the future.

Back in the April 2000 meeting, we brainstormed on how to improve the hospital's facilities. Mrs. Melinda Pechangco Liberman was present at that meeting. To make a long story short, Mrs. Liberman said she would help in this project. Furthermore, the prospect of building a surgery center in Pandan became a strong possibility.

Everybody agreed therefore that we should establish a public benefit corporation and name it as Pandan Antique Foundation, an attractive, recognizable corporate name that would appeal to American donors and benefactors. Dr. Lourdes Alojipan Burgos was the number one proponent of this project. PAF would be the fundraising arm of our group that carried two separate organizations, Pagtatap Philippines and Pagtatap USA. We envisioned that the Foundation would have stronger capacities and resources. The Foundation would design fundraising strategies by tapping humanitarian organizations and foundations in the United States. Thus, our substantial financial support would be from publicly supported organizations and from the general public. PAF was to work hand in hand with Pagtatap USA, but both entities would maintain their own autonomy, legal identity, and responsibilities. PAF would also assist Pagtatap Philippines in implementing these projects in Pandan.

ALEX LIBERMAN SURGICAL PAVILION

Our dream of having a Surgery Center in the Pandan community hospital became a reality when Mrs. Melinda Pechangco Liberman, a native of Pandan and the widow of the late Alex Liberman of New York, is benevolence personified kept her word at that April meeting. She fully funded the construction of the multi-million peso surgical unit annexed to the hospital in Pandan. This state-of-the-art edifice was aptly named the "Alex Liberman Surgical Pavilion."

Dr. Robert Peter Alojipan, my cousin and also president of Pagtatap Foundation Philippines, has been bringing his medical mission to Pandan since the 1980's. He was actively involved in the planning and design of the surgical building.

As PAF chairman of the board, and Daughlet Bautista Ordinario, PAF treasurer, both in San Diego, and Jiji Bautista Exequiel of Manila, we were in close communication with Mrs. Liberman in

New York during the building's negotiation and finalizing of the building contract.

The completion date of the Surgical Pavilion was set for April 2002 in time for Dr. Alojipan's medical mission team from the Makati Medical Center and the nurse volunteers from the U.S.

PAF takes great pride in successfully launching and preserving its mission to improve the lives and well being of the people of Pandan. We hereby convey our deepest appreciation and gratitude to Mrs. Melinda P. Liberman for her selfless and most noble commitment to donate the proposed ALEXANDER LIBERMAN MEMORIAL SURGICAL CENTER to the people of Pandan. The late Alexander Liberman was a world-renowned artist, a magazine editor and designer of popular magazines in the U.S. He was a famous sculptor whose works of art are displayed in public places all over the world.

The newly constructed Alex Liberman Surgical Pavilion finally opened its doors to start operations. It was a fitting homage to Dr. Alojipan who was actively involved in this ALSP project from start to finish, and to Melinda Pechangco Liberman for funding the pavilion. The arrival of the medical team will be a testimonial to the efficacy of the new edifice, a dream that has finally come true. At the end of one year as chairman of the board of the Pandan Antique Foundation, Inc. (PAF), I sent through the Internet a message to every Pandananon participating in the Pagtatap e-group communications. This was also my opportunity to inform the members of Pagtatap who may not have been fully aware of the workings of PAF. I said the following:

We are from a small town. We all know each other very well. We become a model for Antique by organizing the three organizations from a group of visionaries and dreamers. Simply stated, we have but one purpose - to help our *kasimanwa* back home. Did you ever get a sense that we are being easily looked down upon even in our own province? We get the last share of the pie from the capitol. Our hospital is neglected, and we are routinely taken for granted. If you feel this to be true, we really have nobody to blame but ourselves.

Now is the time to stand up and be counted. The Semirara issue has added insult to injury. Our disunity and apathy now will surely bring all of us down. Look what we have accomplished with the Semirara dumpsite issue. I know that we are seriously committed about our unity, our future, and our freedom. Notice the dedication of Doc Bobby Alojipan, Cadoy Candari, Ed Rodillon, JiJi, MiMi and others out there. The show of *Banwahanun* (love of hometown) by this group of people from Pandan should steer and utilize us towards a Pandananun "arousal" to rally behind them and be united. United we stand, divided we fall.

A case in point is Mrs. Liberman who has not forgotten her birthplace and has therefore made it possible for her less fortunate town mates to enjoy the blessings of her bounty. Her spirit of giving is indeed inspiring and gratifying.

MEDICAL EMERGENCY AID FOR THE POOR PEOPLE
BULIG SA POBRE (HELP THE POOR)

It was in February 2008 that *"Bulig sa Pobre"* (help the poor) was established. This idea came about when I received sad stories of poor people with emergency serious illnesses in my hometown were left to die because of the inability of the families to afford paying for the medicine. These were cases wherein the patient were critically ill and will surely die if the medicine is not administered.

This is a true story. I was told that in one instance, a young boy from the barrio was diagnosed with tetanus (lockjaw). It needed Tetanus immune globulin (TIG) injections. Money was not available and the patient died.

Similar other emergency medical conditions like status asthmaticus, septicemia, dehydration and many more ailments that will inevitably result to their demise without the medication prescribed by a physician must be helped. We cried for emotional mercy for those needy people. It was my dream to help and the PAF responded. As of this time, we have helped a number of poor patients. We are profoundly appreciative of the volunteer work of the custodian, Ms. Suzing Mission. Funds are available as needed.

MEDICAL EMERGENCY REVOLVING FUND AVAILABLE TO THE CUSTODIAN

Policy and Procedure:

A PAF custodian in Pandan follows the procedure of this project.

•   The financial help for the poor is limited only to emergency cases wherein the patient is critically ill and will surely die without medicine.
•   The local physician (emergency room or hospital physician) must be responsible for determining the critical condition of the patient and the immediate need of medication.
•   A prescription must be presented to the custodian of the project. The project is only responsible for the medication and nothing else.

ADOPT THE COMMUNITY HOSPITAL IN PANDAN

Dateline, May 2011

I AM THE FOUNDER and chairman of the Pandan Antique Foundation, Inc., a non-profit, public benefit corporation registered in California, USA, on July 18, 2000. By February 2001, a 501(c) (3) California Corporation was granted, I.D.(EIN) # 33-0916694.

Pandan is one of the impecunious towns, in the province of Antique located in the island of Panay of the Philippine Archipelago (Visayan region). In the 2000 census, it had a population of 27,647 people in 5,534 households with 34 *barangay*.

HISTORICAL PERSPECTIVE: Six out of ten Filipinos die without seeing a doctor. According to the Philippine Department of Health, this situation was true seventeen years ago, and it is still true to this date. One hundred thirty-two die of tuberculosis (TB) every day, and the number will increase because a more deadly strain of the disease is spreading fast in the western Pacific region. Quoting the WHO officials, the TB fatalities have nearly doubled since 1993. The Philippines has the highest number of TB fatalities in the western region, which covers East Asia, Micronesia, Australia and New Zealand, and is among the 22 countries that account for 80 percent of the world's total TB cases. In 1998 48,000 Filipinos died of TB.

About 70 percent of Filipinos live in poverty. They cannot afford to buy basic medicines and are unable to see a doctor.

MEDICAL MISSION: Throughout the years many Filipino medical organizations and other charitable humanitarian groups from the U.S. have conducted numerous medical missions to help the poor in the Philippines. It is an initiative with broad based community support both in the U.S. and in the Philippines in the spirit of voluntarism. The group has donated medicine, medical equipments, and supplies to many hospitals and clinics.

The various provincial and regional small community hospitals throughout the country provide the bulk of government-sponsored patient care to the poor. The Department of Health (DOH) of the Philippines has done a good job running these hospitals, considering the many budgetary and manpower constraints. However, the rapidly growing population and increasing patient load have stressed the resources of these hospitals to the limits. Many of these small community hospitals are neglected. Therefore, extending help to these run-down community hospitals by non-government organizations from the U.S. can alleviate some of these problems.

The surgical and medical missions conducted to many places in the Philippines are extremely needed. For one thing, the surgical interventions that are performed, for example, cataract extraction, palate repair, and hernias are God-sent and lasting cures for patients who may not otherwise see a doctor in their lifetime. However, the impact of the medical mission to the thousands of medical cases seen (out-patient) in many instances are of a "short term care," a band-aid type medicine due to the very nature of the brief visit by the missionaries. The medicines given to patients are usually limited and when the missionaries are gone, where would the patient go? Many of them would never see a doctor until another medical mission arrives. What happens to a patient who needs a constant six-month therapy (four-drug combination) for tuberculosis? This is the recommended mode of therapy for this disease. It is at this juncture that my goal in my civic organization aims to stir medical and social awareness of their plight and radiate some light in the life of the poor. Therefore the concept of "Adopt a Hospital" was an idea that came about after participating in numerous medical missions to the Philippines including my hometown where I saw the lamentable condition of the community Justice Calixto O. Zaldivar Memorial Hospital (JCOZMH) in my town Pandan.

"Adopt a hospital concept," i.e., help the municipal hospital of Pandan was and still my priority.

Everything I had worked for, all that I believed in, all the days of suffering and dreaming of the day when I'd finally be able to help my poor town mates in the town of Pandan, Antique, Philippines, is about to come true.

For the last eleven years, I'd been dreaming of the day when I'd be able to improve the deplorable condition of the community hospital. In a moment of triumph, everything I've done has led up to this very personal mission about ready to be accomplished.

If you work hard enough at your goals and ambition, if you are willing to make drastic changes in your life, and if you are willing to get out of your comfort zone to start something wonderful, you too can make your dreams a reality. You can. My story is proof that you can overcome your surroundings and make your dreams happen.

COMMUNITY HOSPITAL
JCOZMH

Dateline, February 2011

WHEN I TOOK THE pictures of the hospital's unpleasant environment and incomplete facilities from room to room it stirred a thousand, nay, a hundred thousand words. If you look at the photos, the environs must be like hell's ferment. If you are unmoved of what I have just said, your heart must be made of solid-rock, of granite. The poignant sight of this small community hospital in my small town Pandan stirred my soul and indelibly etched in my mind. It spurred me to help. It's a travesty of the health care system if compared to our adopted country where we now live. Our hearts bleed for those needy people. They cannot afford to go to another distant hospital with better facilities. The hospital must become a better place to admit patients, especially the impoverished people of the community.

I have seen firsthand the unspeakable condition of a 25-bed community hospital in year 2000.

In January 2011, I visited the Justice Calixto O. Zaldivar Community Hospital (JCOZMH) again and the situation has not improved much, with rusted spring beds without mattresses, two vastly unequipped surgical rooms, and other signs of bad conditions. We have been concerned about the substandard medical care of the needy people of our town whose family cannot afford to send them to better-equipped hospitals in other towns and in Manila.

The adopted hospital can be helped in several ways:

- The hospital can be provided with material resources that are badly needed.

- The needed items can either be bought or procured from local hospitals in the U.S. Bigger foundations like Brothers'

Brother Foundation, World Medical Relief Inc., and Direct Aid International can be approached for donations. Other foundations, drug companies and medical supply companies will be solicited to participate in this program.

- The hospital charity ward will be provided with free medicines donated by the sponsor organization and continue to follow up patients who will be seen by local doctors for diagnosis and prescriptions.

- A local nurse may be hired as an employee of the sponsoring organization to follow up patients on treatment especially those with tuberculosis. Finally, to initiate a vaccination program for children in collaboration with the government.

In April 2011, I was extremely fortunate to be connected with Rev. Thomas A. Stoeckel Executive Director of Medical Ministries International (MMI) based in San Jose, Clovis, California to be our donor, benevolence personified, to help us. MMI a Christian non-profit corporation is a relief organization that provides medical and dental assistance through missionary organizations located in Third World countries. Such assistance is provided in the form of used or refurbished medical, dental and associated equipment, donated supplies and medicines, and teams of volunteers who provide medical care. MMI takes surplus medical supplies and equipment that would end up in landfills and sends them to hospitals and clinics in third world countries. Supplies are shipped in 40-foot sea containers and are usually valued at nearly $500,000. Donations of supplies and equipment are acquired from area hospitals and doctor's offices that are either upgrading their equipment, or required to discard brand new supplies due to U.S. regulations. These hospital equipments and supplies to Pandan Community hospital under my leadership are now ready for shipment.

UPDATE OF HOSPITAL EQUIPMENTS DONATION

Dateline, June 2012

MANY ARE SUPPORTIVE of my mission and vision. I have worked arduously with writings in the media, FEU alumni and friends, to good Samaritans in this country to raise social consciousness of our projects and appeal for help. Praises and thanks to the Almighty for blessing us with this breed of good Samaritans! With this inspiration and support Pandan has all the reason to succeed and break out of obscurity so as to stand out to the world as a model of humanitarianism and social commitment. This is not a fancy outreach endeavor. It is not a grandiose effort, although it will affect the impoverished people of my town. We do not compete or seek glory. Our supporters just want to help the health conditions and comfort the weary in whatever little way in our town Pandan.

My project is taking equal billing in my life with messianic zeal, passion and total devotion. It has taken almost ten months since I established connections with our donor Medical Ministries International (MMI).

We are concerned the humanitarian donations to the hospital in Pandan will meet uphill difficulties for obtaining a tax and duty free status. Substantial delays may occur to deal with the different Philippine governmental departments. I wrote a letter to Dr. Ona, the Secretary of the Department of Health, and Senator Loren Legarda who were gracious enough to help. Unfortunately, nothing positive developed.

Finally, we have asked for help from the Governor of Antique, who suggested that the consignee should be the Province of Antique C/O Governor Exequiel Javier.

From the Philippine Consul General Office Los Angeles California, I have the following statement of policy regarding donations to the Philippines: "Food, medicine and other relief goods, books and educational materials, essential machineries/equipment, consumer goods and other articles may be granted duty-free entry by the Department of Finance and the Bureau of Customs, upon the recommendation of the Department of Social Work and Development or other concerned agency. Prospective donors can seek assistance from the Commission on Filipinos Overseas." Simple and clear as it may sound, there is indeed a tremendous red tape to overcome.

International shipment charges are expensive, thus requiring on-going appeal for donations. I wish to thank my magnanimous colleagues and other humanitarian organizations like the Filipino United Network Fund for Hope and the FEU-DNRSMAF Nevada Chapter. To my town mates in America and other countries, thank you from the bottom of my heart for your support of PAF's Adopt the Community Hospital.

We are also blessed with the knowledge that benevolent and charitable souls exist and are willing to reach out and lend a hand to our town Pandan.

The Pandan Antique Foundation under my leadership is in great anticipation of a positive assistance from the governor of Antique province. Again, this is to facilitate the duty-free entry status of the hospital equipments and supplies to be brought to *JCOZMH* community hospital.

I am a believer in the wisdom and words of Billy Graham: "God has given us two hands — one to receive with and the other to give with. We are not cisterns made for hoarding; we are channels made for giving."

It is not what we have done for ourselves that is really worthwhile, but rather what we have willingly accomplished for others, even at the expense of our personal comfort. This project is the vanguard humanitarian endeavor of our Foundation, the PAF. We become a model for the province of Antique by organizing the three organizations.

CHAPTER SEVEN

MILESTONE

Life is not a matter of milestones, but of moments.

- ROSE KENNEDY

POST GRADUATE TRAINING

THE CLARITY OF image of what is an "American Dream" is what we must know.

I never envisioned to become a U.S. citizen and partake in the American dream.

I left the Philippines in December 1961 for postgraduate training. Truslow James Adams first used the term "American Dream" in his book, "The Epic of America" that was written in 1931. He states:

> "The American Dream is that dream of a land in which
> life should be better and richer and fuller for
> everyone, with opportunity for each according to
> ability or achievement ... each man and each woman
> shall be able to attain to the fullest stature of
> which they are innately capable, and be recognized
> by others for what they are, regardless of the
> fortuitous circumstances of birth or position." In the
> United States Declaration of Independence, the
> founding fathers "held certain truths to be self-
> evident, that all Men are created equal, that they are
> endowed by a certain Creator with certain

unalienable Rights that among these are Life, Liberty
and Pursuit of Happiness."

Might this sentiment be considered the foundation of the American
Dream? Without America, many of us who were adopted as
American citizens would not have had the chance to be what we are
now--including me. Some say the American Dream has become the
pursuit of material prosperity, bigger cars, fancier homes, and fruits
of prosperity for their families, despite having little time to enjoy
such prosperity. Others say the American Dream is beyond the grasp
of the working poor, who must work two jobs to ensure their
families' survival. Others look toward a new American Dream with
less focus on financial gain and more emphasis on education and
living a simple, fulfilling life. Thomas Wolfe once said: "To every
man, regardless of his birth, his shining, golden opportunity . . . the
right to live, to work, to be himself, and to become whatever his
manhood and his vision can combine to make him."

After passing my Philippine medical board in 1961, I desired to
become a general practitioner. However, I did not have any general
training except for my rotating internship. One option was to
become a physician of my province. In the Philippines, you must
have connections. Oh yes, my father had close relatives in the higher
positions in government, but something else was already in store for
me. The ripest peach was at the highest branch of the tree, and I was
on my way to pluck it. It was during the time when the United States
of America badly needed more doctors. Through the Exchange
Visitors Program, many hospitals in the U.S. were willing to provide
post-graduate training to foreign medical graduates in the big land of
opportunity. I took the Educational Council for Foreign Medical
Graduates (ECFMG) examination. In December 1961, with two
other FEU graduates, the three of us were ready to leave for Elyria
Memorial Hospital in Elyria, Ohio. The Secretary of the Office of
the Dean of our medical school facilitated the process. The program
was a fly-now-pay-later deal. The hospital deducted $30 for airfare
from my monthly stipend of $150.

INTERNSHIP AND WEDDING

Dateline, July 2011

SOMETHING WONDERFULLY UNBELIEVABLE happened during our pre-travel orientation. I sat down beside a lady who was also leaving for the U.S. Her name is Sylvia, and she asked me where I was going. She was very excited to tell me she knew someone, a medical technologist, at Elyria Memorial Hospital. I did not pay much attention except to know that her friend graduated as a pharmacist. She gave me a piece of paper the following day with the medical technologist's name: Asela M. Asprec.

On January 22, 1962, I started my internship with two other FEU graduates, my classmate Dr. Rodolfo Borromeo and my friend Dr. Tody Exconde.

I met Asela (Cely) Asprec a few days after our arrival in a welcome party at the home of Dr. Picoy and Lina Amaro. Needless to say, among the Filipina laboratory technologists in the hospital, she was the most attractive lady.

For a laugh mixed with seriousness in intentions, the three of us new interns decided I must be the one to date her.

"You see my son," God once said, "the beauty of a woman is not in the clothes she wears, the figure that she carries, or the way she combs her hair. The beauty of a woman must be seen in her eyes, because that is the doorway to her heart - the place where love resides." I found an ideal woman. She had and still possesses the beauty and intelligence combined. I knew I want to share all my troubles, sorrows and dreams with her. She would never let me down and I could always rely on her.

This was much I have learned later. Cely was a bright student who graduated as elementary and high school valedictorian in her hometown in Ago-o, La Union. She started as a pre-medical student but instead switched course and graduated her degree as BS in Pharmacy at the University of Santo Tomas in Manila, Philippines.

Before long our two hearts became one. We got married on July 28, 1962, seven months after we met.

With a short engagement, there was less time to stress over planning a wedding. By not spending a lot of time worrying about everything, I made a forthright decision--and it was one of the best of my life. Getting hitched or tying the knot is such a major step in anyone's life. And it was the best one I ever made.

My sister Loida, arrived from the Philippines to attend the wedding, bringing with her the personally designed traditional Filipiniana bridal gown. This was a unique detailed artwork immortalized in fine embroidery and my Barong Tagalog (Filipino formal attire). She came to the U.S. under the Exchange Visitor Program as a nurse at Cook County Hospital in Chicago, Illinois.

In a way the wedding reflects who you really are and what you really value. A simple wedding reception for about fifty guests (not the traditional expensive reception) was held in an elegant venue twenty-five miles from Elyria in Cleveland, Ohio. The atmosphere and service created a lasting memory.

Known as the honeymooners' destination for nearly 200 years, Cely and I made our way to Niagara Falls in our brand new car (Corvair). Stunning and awesome Niagara! The water was the attraction, crashing and plunging without ceasing. It was indeed mesmerizing!

The year 1962 went fast. Ours is more than a good marriage. I would say there is no lovelier, affectionate and charming relationship than what we have. Love is the strongest and deepest element in all life, the harbinger of hope, joy, and ecstasy. In a saying by Harold Macmillan, "No man succeeds without a good woman behind him. Wife or mother, if it is both, he is twice blessed indeed." She is, indeed, my sunshine, my only sunshine.

Wedding, July 28, 1962, Elyria, OH
Dr. Rudy Borromeo behind-Best Man

My father visited us in 1963 when my son Roy was born in Chicago.
After a short stay in Chicago and California, my father became a

permanent resident. He later become a U.S. citizen. Eventually, he went home to Pandan and built a new house in a compound of his property where our small house was located. Uncle Dadong and a cousin, an architect helped my dad draw up the plan and develop the property.

Finally, a four-bedroom two-story house with bathroom and shower was completed. He was too proud of his children. My dad with my name and my older brother a dentist both in America designed a medical signage for two doctors. This signage was placed in the frontage at outside wall of our home. Funny, but true.

It was my unrelenting dream to build a house as I had once promised my mother, the sickly but strong inspiring woman of my life, who I look forward to seeing some day, if only to tell her about my achievements. But I know she knows already.

MEDICAL SPECIALTY

Dateline, January 2011

BEFORE COMPLETING MY rotating internship, I needed to decide what path I should take in my career. Choosing a specialty was one of the important decisions I had to make. Medicine is composed of many specialties. In fact, the American Board of Medical Specialties recognizes a total of twenty-four official specialty boards. Finding a specialty that suited me was a process of assessing my strengths and weaknesses. I had to identify my lifestyle, intellectual challenge, and research potential to find a specialty that best suited me.

I extensively analyzed pathology as my chosen specialty. People may see pathology as autopsies where crimes are solved with glamour, much like what we usually see on television. This is an incorrect, overly exaggerated notion. Pathologists are known to be the "doctor's doctor." They are physicians who diagnose and treat patients through laboratory medicine.

When a cardiologist orders a blood test, the pathologist reviews the results for abnormalities; when a surgeon removes a breast lesion for biopsy, the pathologist determines if it is cancerous; and when a gynecologist does a pap smear, the pathologist determines the result of the slide. So where is the television glamour?

Currently, many physicians are focusing on specialties that have more flexible lifestyles instead of focusing only on income level and prestige. Pathology is included in this "friendly lifestyle", which offers the physician more control over his hours and income that are commensurate with his workload and level of responsibility.

After completing my internship, my wife and I moved to Chicago. I took up residency training in Anatomic Pathology at Edgewater Hospital. My mentor was Dr. Lucito Gamboa, a Filipino American who was the director of the Department of Pathology. I was impressed with his expertise, intelligence and leadership. He was an outstanding pathologist, well liked and respected by the medical staff. I learned a lot of anatomic pathology from Dr. Gamboa. We became good friends and remain so today. He was the founder and first president of the Association of Philippine Physicians in America (APPA) in 1972.

In 1964, I transferred to Illinois Masonic Hospital and Medical Center and completed my residency in 1967. The next step was to move to a state with a better climate. I obtained a state license to practice in Indiana and also passed California's written medical board examination.

My career was thriving; my perseverance had been rewarded. I felt grateful to this country that offered me such opportunity.

Cely stopped working in 1967 after the birth of our second child Marjorie in Chicago. She dedicated her time to the caring of our children. I was hired by Dr. Gustavo Gyori, Department Chief of pathology at Illinois Masonic Hospital where I trained for four years. I was assistant pathologist, head of Blood Bank and Transfusion service. But one day, there was a problem. I received a letter from the Department of Immigration ordering me to leave the country in sixty days and return home to the Philippines as required by the ECFMG. My lawyer was able to waive the immigration order. He advised me to have more children. Funny but true. And I was just the man for the job! Candace, our third child, was born on March 1, 1969 after which we planned to move to California.

In those early years, foreign medical graduates must undergo rotating internship training as a prerequisite to practice in California. This seemed unnecessary and blatant discriminatory. For the first time, I promised myself I would face these challenges and partake in the Association of Philippine Physicians in America to fight discrimination.

SAN DIEGO PATHOLOGISTS MEDICAL GROUP, INC.

Dateline, 2011

IN MAY 1969 my family decided to move to the beautiful and the "cleanest city" in the U.S., San Diego. Roy 6, Marjorie 2, and Candace was only 2 months old when we traveled by car three to four thousand miles from Chicago.

I considered our relocation as mundane, though it cleared the path to my remarkable career advancement along with the evolution of my "inner journey." We grow when we consistently connect with higher ideals.

I was accepted as an intern at the 520-bed Mercy Hospital and Medical Center (now known as Scripps Mercy), a highly reputable teaching institution. Founded by the Sisters of Mercy in 1890, it is San Diego's oldest hospital. As a major teaching hospital, Mercy provided a primary site for the clinical education of more than fifty interns and residents and was a secondary training site for residents from the University of California, San Diego (UCSD) and the Naval Medical Center. In June 1997, Scripps Mercy Hospital was acknowledged by the physicians' magazine "California Medicine" as one of the top twenty hospitals in Southern California.

I considered myself a humble man. In addition to my past position and being board-eligible in pathology, I was accepted to function not as a rotating intern but instead positioned as acting chief resident and as a fellow with four other residents in the Department of Pathology. I was the only Filipino American physician out of the 100 house staff in the training program.

The San Diego Pathologist Medical Group, Inc., runs the Department of Pathology. There were four pathologists led by Chairman and Director Dr. Dominick De Santo. He was an extremely honorable, respectful and honest person, a brilliant pathologist and educator. Formerly, he was the Director of Medical

Education of Mercy Hospital. His compassionate and friendly demeanor gave me hope to work in his department someday. Still, I had to ask myself if opportunity lies in one's job or in the individual who looks at the possibilities instead of impossibilities?

One year went by fast. I received a Certificate of Internship in May 31, 1970. I was ready to take the oral clinical examination of the State Medical Board before practicing my specialty in California. For whatever reason, the chairman of Pathology advised me not to look for a job elsewhere and offered me a position as a locum tenens associate pathologist, pending my certification for the Oral State Board Licensure. Dr. De Santo wrote a letter to the membership committee of Mercy Hospital and Medical Center:

"Dr. Candari is a well-trained pathologist; a fine
young gentleman and we would like to recommend
him for appointment in the pathology department...
a credit to any department of pathology..."

I passed the oral clinical examination and received the California State Board Licensure on July 7, 1970.

DIPLOMATE - ANATOMIC / CLINICAL PATHOLOGY

BOARD CERTIFIED SUBSPECIALTY BLOOD BANKING

A number of milestones were happening in my life. On November 7, 1970, I successfully passed the specialty board examinations and became a diplomate of the American Board of Pathology, Anatomic and Clinical Pathology. Thereafter, I finally became an associate pathologist and eventually a partner of the San Diego Pathologist Medical Group, Inc. My contract with the SPMG Inc. was completed, with my pension benefits to be fully vested in three years.

In 1971, I was elected as Fellow of the College of American Pathologists and the American Society of Clinical Pathologists. I was privileged and honored to receive the title of Fellow Emeritus in 1995.

In January 1973, I decided to take the very first subspecialty examination in Immunohematology — Blood Banking, which was established by the American Board of Pathology. I was pleased to be the first Filipino pathologist to take the examination and passed it without difficulty. There were more than 130 candidates from all over the U.S., and I was the only participant from San Diego. The Pathology News at Mercy Hospital and Medical Center published the following:

> "Dr. Cesar Candari, one of the Mercy Hospital
> pathology staff, has recently become certified in a
> new subspecialty of the American Board of Pathology.
> This new subspecialty is immunohematology – Blood
> Banking, and the first examination was given in January
> 1973. The pathology staff is very pleased to have Dr.
> Candari's special knowledge and expertise available to
> the Mercy Hospital blood Transfusion service."

Impressed by this showing, the medical staff highly valued my practice of pathology in the hospital. I became the Medical Director of Blood Bank and chairman of the Transfusion Committee and Transfusion Service, which provided vital expertise to interface with the medical staff. These were indeed important events in my chosen career.

I seriously entertained my objective to use my extensive training, knowledge and experience in the practice of service-oriented anatomic and clinical pathology that emphasized top quality patient care in a cost-effective manner. My education provided a similar quality service to the medical staff by establishing education programs and conferences that contributed to the facility's overall compliance with accreditation and licensing requirements.

My modest administrative and supervisory skills included the ability to implement quality improvement programs and procedures in the Department of Pathology, creating an efficient turn-around time of delivery and high quality work. This is what I believe in - leadership. Leaders have a responsibility to make decisions on behalf of the people who have appointed them to the position and the interests of the corporation.

Dr. D. de Santo retired three years after I joined the San Diego pathologists Medical Group Inc. My senior partners - Dr. Jerome Heard, Dr. Daniel de la Vega, and Dr. Ralph Shishido - were all very helpful, and I considered them my benefactors.

I was responsible for determining and establishing policies and procedures governing all phases of blood banking and transfusion services. As a specialist of a large teaching community hospital with the mission to provide the safest possible blood transfusion, this was my forte. Transfusion services for cardiac surgeries and other specialties were under my attention and supervision. I received patient consultations and treatment in therapeutic pheresis. I had mastered the knowledge and application of the American Association of Blood Bank Standards and was prepared at all times for the Joint Commission on Accreditation Inspections.

Blood Transfusion Policies and Standard Practices at Mercy Hospital and Medical Center were established in a form of a booklet, which I had written. My practice of pathology with four associates was a busy one. In the early 1970's, the pathology residency program was active. Four residents were in training for combined anatomic pathology (AP) and clinical pathology (CP). Daily surgical pathology conferences were held for residents focused on acquiring the technical skills that would form the basis for their careers in pathology. They had to become knowledgeable to be able to apply these skills intelligently as physicians (not technicians) towards the goal of becoming diagnosticians. Multiple rotations on the autopsy service for residents were followed to understand dissection techniques, anatomy, and how human disease is manifested in anatomic changes. Rotation in cytopathology was a part of the AP program. Throughout the training program, the daily morning conferences provided residents with both formal instructions and longitudinal exposure to all of the areas of anatomic pathology. Residents in Clinical Pathology undergo rotation into departments, blood bank/transfusion service, microbiology/virology, hematology, and clinical chemistry/immunology. I have dedicated my time and efforts to this training program.

It was in the mid 1970's when the hospital discontinued the pathology residency-training program for economic reasons. I had truly enjoyed participating in this program.

Every one of us in the department had his own subspecialty, and we divided our responsibilities and duties to every department. We rotated on the coverage of surgical pathology, i.e., frozen sections, surgical pathology reporting, fine needle aspirations and diagnosis, cytopathology and autopsies. I emphasized the quality control process of the surgical pathology diagnosis by adhering to the pragmatic points in my article "Patient Audit Process Applied to the Pathology Department." Dr. Jerome Heard, director of the Department, and Dr. Michael Kasun, an associate pathologist, co-authored the article.

In the early years, I was assigned to chair the Clinical Pathologic Conference (CPC) for the house and medical staff. Dr. Jack Geller, Director of the Internal Medicine Teaching Program, Diplomate in Endocrinology, organized the weekly conferences. He was a brilliant director of Internal Medicine and we became fast friends. In one of his research studies, he invited me to be a co-author of a publication entitled, "Comparison of Dihydrotestosterone Levels in Prostatic Metastasis and Primary Prostate Cancer," which was accepted for publication in Prostate Vo. 15:171-175, 1989. I wrote an article entitled "Breast Carcinoma Following Simple Mastectomy for Benign Breast Disease."

I became chairman of the monthly surgical tumor and oncology conference in rotation with my associate, Dr. Tyler Youngkin, who completed his training in our Department of Pathology. The hospital newsletter "Pacemaker," published monthly by the medical staff of Mercy Hospital and Medical Center, wrote of updates and established guidelines for good transfusion practices.

Our environment in the Continuing Medical Education could be compared to a semi-academic facility. I gave lectures to second year medical and dental students at the University of California San Diego, to laboratory technology students and nurses at Mercy Hospital. After my training with Dr. Azorides Morales on immunohistology at the University of Miami Hospital, Department of Pathology, School of Medicine, I became interested in a new, advanced procedure of specific tumor markers for diagnosis by immuno-staining procedures.

The specialty I had chosen led to an extremely gratifying career. Our group maintained a billing office of twelve employees and a billing office manager. Most interesting was every pathologist who performed a procedure and diagnosis was responsible for submitting the billing codes to the billing office. It effectively streamlined workflow, reduced the chance of errors, cut costs, enhanced patient outcomes and helped run the whole practice more efficiently.

ALTERNATE DELEGATE FROM CALIFORNIA
TO THE COLLEGE OF AMERICAN PATHOLOGISTS

At the height of my practice, I received a letter from Dr. Emmett B. Reilly, Speaker of the House of Delegates, College of American Pathologists:

> "The 1989 House of Delegates Summer elections have
> come to a close, and I am pleased to notify you that
> you have been elected to serve as an Alternate Delegate
> from California."

Being a Foreign Medical graduate (FMG) elected to such a position in my chosen specialty was rather unexpected, although I was not surprised. It was an honor and a privilege. Dr. Dan de la Vega, the

Director of Pathology Department, recommended me to this position for a term of eight years.

In the same year, I received a letter from Bella L. Meese, Deputy Appointment Secretary from the Office of the Governor, George Deukmejian, who was interested in appointing me to the board of trustees of the Minority Health Professions Education Foundation. Since I was very busy, I had to decline the offer.

My practice as an associate pathologist at Mercy Hospital grew more exciting. The group opened a separate pathology practice in Encinitas, California, about thirty miles away from Mercy. Each member of the corporation was a co-director of the laboratory.

Although I had extracurricular activities in the community and spent time as a civic-oriented person, my volunteer work in the community of Filipino Americans in San Diego was conducted after working hours. It neither disrupted my routine practice nor resulted in neglecting my objectives in the practice of pathology. My American colleagues appreciated my services, and I never felt any discrimination. In April 1981, I participated in the Second International Lymphoma Conference in Athens, Greece, at the University of Athens, School of Medicine. My wife and I joined a guided tour of Athens city where we enjoyed sightseeing, exploring and visiting the principal and classical sites. We embarked on a cruise of Aegina, Poros, and Hydra, the fascinating Greek Islands.

To continue my story at the height of my professional career, I felt profoundly gratified as a partner of the San Diego Pathologist Medical Group. (SDPMG). We were uniquely united, cohesive, harmonious, and friendly, with much camaraderie.

I served as secretary and later as vice president of the San Diego Pathologists Medical Group, Inc. Having been a dreamer for so many years, my unimaginable and modest achievements were products of this American Dream.

In the late '90s Mercy Hospital and Medical Center became Scripps Mercy with California campuses in San Diego and Chula Vista. Our group doubled in number, with two of us retired in late 1998. I worked part time for an additional two years.

CHAPTER EIGHT

MY LIFE

"In three words I can sum up everything I've learned
about life: it goes on."

— ROBERT FROST

EARLY LIFE

Dateline, January 2011

LET ME TELL YOU how I got here today. I have always believed that life is a series of adventures. In adventures we discover our beliefs and dreams and come to understand ourselves. In adventures we explore the possibilities of our life's pursuits. My modest achievements reflect how I played my part. But before accepting the reality of a life that has given me such pride and respect, the truth must come out.

Discovery of truth is the sole purpose of philosophy, and it will likely exist to the end of time. As I suspected, it was very difficult to write about anyone but yourself. It is necessary to dig deep in one's story to find the truth.

One of my favorite sayings goes like this: "Digging underneath the story is where the stunning truth is often hiding. Whether it's told in a straightforward language, a secret letter, or even a list, the nonfiction should be an honest, evocative, and unique experience."

Only you can tell this story because your life counts; what you leave behind is the evidence of the life you have lived. Why not tell it your way.

I considered myself to be one of those individuals who nursed a secret passion and heeded its irresistible call in spite of uncertainties, fears, discouragements and daunting odds. Ultimately, I went on to do what I felt was right and good for others and myself. Things begin to happen when you start something. Even a small action produces consequences and leads to more actions. The mere act of starting will get your momentum going, reinforce your beliefs, and push your fears away. As much as I can remember, I worked hard and persevered. Dedicating and committing myself to hard work was challenging. I did whatever it takes without compromising my values to realize my dreams. I was true to my glorious quest-- followed that guiding star!

I have faced every difficulty I encountered in my career through determination, perseverance, hard work, and confidence. Although the path towards success is to some extent tough, one must have determination and perseverance in order to conquer the challenge, which is the main message.

I have touched my dream. I achieved my destiny!

THE PLACE OF MY BIRTH

Dateline, January 2011

I WAS BORN ON August 31,1933 in the home of my parents near the market place in a small town of Pandan, province of Antique, Philippines, across the street of my mom's friend, aunt Elena, the wife of the former Governor of Antique, Calixto O. Zaldivar. My mother told me that there was a choice of naming me either Augustus Caesar or Julius Caesar. Born on the last day of August made this consideration by my parents. Growing older, I have not used Augustus. I was more interested being called Julius Caesar. The latter was more attractive, a Roman general and statesman, who became a dictator of the Roman Empire. He was slain by Brutus at age fifty-five because of ambition. To me, plain Cesar is a lucky name.

Was it a lucky year to be born in 1933 in the Philippines? Franklin D. Roosevelt was inaugurated as the thirty-second president of the United States on that year pledging to lead the country out of the Great Depression—and he did. In 1973, the United States of America became my second homeland. I became a U.S. citizen.

My birth was humble. There was no doctor or nurses in town to assist during my birth. I was born in the moonlight with a clear sky before midnight. I was told that my mom's birthing was uneventful, assisted by old folks in town. My parents were poor, but they raised my siblings and me with care in this impecunious town, Pandan. The province of Antique is located in the island of Panay of the Philippine Archipelago (Visayan region).

According to legend the name Pandan came from a byword during the Spanish time--it means "bread on the table". The word "pan" in Spanish means "bread" and "dan" in our dialect means "that". Therefore, the word Pandan means the daily bread on the table.

My mother Fulgencia Condez Dioso was also a hardworking schoolteacher. They were loving parents and before I was born, my mama left her teaching position to raise us. I was one of six siblings who were taught respect and care for others; our education was a top priority in my household.

We lived in a property compound of the Candari clan in the middle part of a small town. It was in 1938 when my parents built a fairly comfortable home built near my grandmother's house.

I wish to inform my children and grandchildren and the future generations so they know about my life and of my unfinished family tree. Our town Pandan, poor as it was, has produced some prominent people in government of which there is much to be cherished. My agnate great-great-grandfather, Vicente Rendon Gella (24 June 1856 – 24 April 1926), was a teacher, school director, lawyer and governor of the Province of Antique in the early 1900s. For his college education he was sent to Colegio de San Juan de Letran where he graduated with a Bachelor of Arts. He studied law later on at the University of Santo Tomas and finished the course in 1885. He was born in Pandan, Antique, to Bonifacio Gella and Juana Rendon, who owned parcels of land and fishponds in the municipality. He was a maternal great-granduncle of Senator Loren Legarda (as of this writing she is a candidate for vice-president of the Philippines); by paternal genealogy, Senator Legarda is my third degree cousin

Bonifacio Gella, his musician father, was elected Capitan municipal (municipal captain) during the Spanish Period.

Internet information stated Vicente, maintained a close friendship with Jose Rizal during his college years. When Rizal left the Philippines on May 3, 1882, he was part of the party who sent Rizal off aboard the Salvadora. He accompanied Antonio Rivera, father of Leonor Rivera and Mateo Evangelista.

He communicated with Rizal even when Rizal was already overseas. Evidence of this can be found with the letter he sent to Rizal dated 30 June 1882. Part of the letter read as follows:

> *"If the absence of a son from the bosom of his*
> *esteemed family is sad, no less will be that of a*
> *friend who, being very dear to all of us who has*
> *had the honor of being called his friends and*
> *comrades, now is away; from us seeking the*
> *welfare that we all desire. Had it not been for*
> *that, the separation would have been more*
> *painful for the distance that separates us. May*
> *God help you for the good that you do to you*
> *fellow countrymen."*

One year after graduating from the University of Santo Tomas in 1886, he returned to Pandan. He was the only registered lawyer in the whole province of Antique in 1890, and he practiced law even while teaching in his school in San Jose, the capital of the province of Antique. In time he was appointed justice of peace and for a few years even became the acting judge of first instance.

During the American occupation, he was appointed as fiscal for Antique on 13 April 1901. He held the position until January 1913, and then served as governor of the province from 1919 to 1922—but he refused to run for another term.

MIDDLE CHILDHOOD

Dateline, February 2011

THE SECOND WORLD WAR disrupted my first year of learning at the Pandan Elementary School. I was then eight years old. As defined, middle childhood begins at around age seven or eight, approximating primary school age.

On December 7, 1941, Pearl Harbor was bomb by the Japanese forces. Ten hours later the Japanese invaded the Philippines. This was the start of the Second World War. From 1942-1945, we left our house to evacuate to the mountains and finally, our town was totally burned, not by the Japanese but by Filipino guerillas, the reasons unknown.

I vividly recall the brutal atrocities of the Japanese Kempetai – Japan's dreaded military police during the Occupation. Japanese airplanes bombed our town. During a four-year period my family was forced to flee from one mountain to another. We fled to the farthest and most remote places to escape annihilation. For four miserable years we suffered the sadism of the Japanese military rule with plundering of villages. You could fill many books with the full account of the massacre of Filipinos by the Japanese troops. Torture, famine and death were the order of the day for my countrymen and us. With trepidation we went into hiding from the Japanese who took over the control of our town. They slaughtered the helpless civilians who were bayoneted and beheaded. My uncle Ted Gabor, a civilian, husband of my aunt Pastora Candari, was captured, then bayoneted, stabbed twelve times and he pretended to be dead. He survived. The Candari name being identified as the leader of our town during those years were clearly important and sought for by the Japanese forces. My uncle Francisco Candari, the mayor, at one time, surrendered to the Japanese in order for the people of Pandan harvest rice and saved from being slaughtered. It was a temporary surrender and the people hid back to the mountains.

It was in the earlier part of the war that all the Candari families were put out of sight together in the high mountain of barrio Sta. Cruz where uncle Paco (short name for Francisco) chosed to hide. For the very first time in my childhood, I had a meal of fried frog legs caught in the ricefields and creeks around our hiding place. Of course no one among relatives knew it will be a delicacy in Swikee restaurant places in around the world. In Hotel Casino Bufffet in Las Vegas, frog legs reminds me of Sta. Cruz *bukid* (mountain).

My uncle became sick of pulmonary tuberculosis, an ailment untreatable in those years and passed away in late 1943, one year before General McArthur landed in Leyte for the eventual liberation of the Philippines.

The remote places we hid were forested high mountains and jungles from south to the north part of town. I had to carry sacs of rice on my shoulder during this constant escape from the Japanese, moving from place to place, day and night. I grew and became strong, in other words I grew physically; I was not weak or frail. In the barrio of Duyong, we stayed for a long time in the mountain of Batobato where rocks and huge boulders taller than two-story buildings beautified the hills. My father built a nipa hut along a river creek where a rivulet of crystal clear water flows. My godmother Gauden Tayco and her family with five girls (I refer to them as my sisters; one of them is Fleur de Liz Tayco Mutuc, now residing in Los Angeles) isolated themselves in a tiny sitio (barrio) Lumangug, overgrown with ancient large trees called 'lunok' believed to be where the *encantos* (fairies) dwell. These *encantos* are similar to Western fairies or nymphs, possessing supernatural powers.

It was in Batobato where my parents mastered the homemaking of soap for cleaning and soap bars made from coconut dry leaves and coconut oil. Our water for drinking came from a small hand dug water well in the side the creek. Despite these hardships, we survived and did not get sick. Such memories I can never forget.

This furnace of war and the constant danger to our lives likely strengthened my mettle. In late 1944, our town stood as the beachhead of freedom when the Americans landed in their submarines with all the war supplies of arms (carbines, Thomson submachine guns, hand grenades and bullet supplies in enormous number given to everyone identified as people of Pandan. The people became automatically as Filipino guerrilla - indigenous military or paramilitary unit operating in small bands. Every adult civilian had to be trained how to pull the trigger of guns. I was always there not too far behind the firing training ground facing the beach at barrio Duyong of Pandan. By then the Japanese left the province of Antique and concentrated themselves in the City of Iloilo, 300 kilometers away.

In 1945, after the liberation of the Philippines, my father was back to his work as a schoolteacher. I grew up and was transformed from a shy boy to a school achiever.

I passed through the usual stages of physical development, learning to walk, talk, play, work and journeyed in miserable living condition. My growth and development is perfectly natural. It's like any other child. I lived a normal Filipino boy's life in an ordinary small town. I grew and matured from infancy through boyhood to manhood.

My parents built a small bamboo/nipa house in the outskirt of town in a small farmland that my dad's family owned. I was twelve years old. On my third grade we moved back to our original place in town.

Consequently, a new home was built in the same place where our former house was burnt. Once again, my parents could not afford to build a bungalow, however, we were happy in our little ménage. Our next-door neighbor Tito Varua became my close friend and classmate. I remember Tito (we call him Totong) to be very friendly, amiable and auspicious boy and yet would simply retaliate back when goaded. I saw him having a fistfight with my cousin Manuel Dionela, another impish boy. When I was on my third grade in the elementary school, one accident that I can never forget was when Tito and I were playing on an asphalt road roller-non-vehicular-compactor when my left thumb was run over. It was smashed flat and his mother, a nurse, Tia Feliz, took care of me. Today my left thumb is deformed with a scar, yet functionally normal. Funny, every thumbs-up, reminded me of the accident.

During my secondary schooling at the Pandan Bay Institute, I pursued my studies with serious zest. I was not afraid of failures, knowing that every failure nurtured the seed of equivalent success. It was at this time that I believed I started to project my future and dream in life lodged in my mind and charge them with intense desire and emotions. I imagined my ambitions, thought of it repeatedly and almost daily. Was I learning how to use the power of imagination to achieve my desires? I was dreaming.

It was in my third year in high school, when I was selected to represent Pandan Bay Institute in an oratory contest between high schools in the province of Antique. I accepted the challenge and approached Mr. Hilario Mantac, my schoolteacher in the 6th grade , an excellent, sagacious writer, to draft me an oration about liberty, freedom and democracy. The introduction went like this:

> *"When man in the pre-historic days was threatened with*
> *death by the freezing cold nights, he discovered*
> *methods to build fires. When fire was used by Magellan to*
> *burn the homes of our forefathers in Mactan, Lapu-Lapu*
> *rose up and killed Magellan and his men along the shores of*
> *Mactan Island. When arms were used by the bandits of*
> *Europe in plundering villages and the palaces of kings, the*
> *Lords invented cannons and bullets and wiped those*
> *plunderers out. When those cannons and bullets were used*
> *by Japan to subjugate the people of the Far East, the United*
> *States of America invented the atomic bomb and reduced*
> *much of Japan into ashes..."*

I delivered this oration in a semblance of having a prompter and now I wonder how at my age of seventy-eight, I can still recite the beginning of the speech word for word. Manolo, my colleague and friend said, "how are you able to remember at your present age?" An adage goes: "There is only one thing age can give you--and that is wisdom."

How my speech got imprinted in my mind until today is absolutely amazing. The introduction of my short oration—that oddity of events about freedom and liberty inherent in every human being—is truthful and factual. I tried my best to deliver it with eloquence. Words, especially great words, often have the capacity to convey to an audience "what could be" and inspire them in a way that might help transform their dreams into reality. I had never considered myself a gifted or studious student. Yet, if a god or goddess of speech ever existed, they would have been present on the day I first saw the light. Even as a young lad I displayed a flair for words.

I represented my school in oratorical contests and easily wooed the judges to my side. I might have gained an incredible latent talent to imitate good speakers and impressed not only the teachers who were convinced that I was a top student, but also those in town who saluted me as a gifted speaker. I utilized this skill and became a permanent competitor for Pandan Bay Institute in any oratorical contests. I was a well-recognized orator according to my town mates. I am very grateful to the late Mr. Mantac for his desire to help me dream and establish my goal in life. His avuncular statement has stayed with me for a very long time: "...Opportunities abound. They may be created through other people's problems and needs. If you cannot find opportunities, create them and let them work for you." With these words, I developed the right attitude. When you think, talk and take actions all day that will surely lead to your desires. Avoid thinking about doubts, fears, and negativity. When you continually think about what you want, you attract the people and the situations.

DREAMING FIELD

Dateline, February 2011

I GRADUATED VALEDICTORIAN of my high school in 1952--a milestone! I prepared my own valedictory address. I felt I didn't have to be the best writer to prepare and deliver one. It must be powerful, yet simple and touching enough to be remembered by my classmates over the ensuing years. I created my speech in a manner that would embody my class and at the same time reflect my own leanings, beliefs and dreams. I requested *Minong* (respectful address to an elder person) Daniel (Dr. Dioso) to review my draft for corrections. My classmates very much enjoyed the short valedictory speech, entitled "A Dream Comes True". My theme: Believe in your dreams. The power of the mind can draw in the things, circumstances and people necessary to make our dream come true. A beautiful quote from Cahill Gibran, "Trust in dreams, for in them is hidden the gate to eternity."

Henry David Thoreau said: "Dreams are the touchstones of our characters . . . that if one advances confidently in the direction of his dreams and endeavors to live the life which he has imagined, he will meet with a success unexpected in common hours." Am I right to emote my desires? Was it correct to project my future achievement and dream about life in my mind and charge them with intense desire and emotions? I was imagining my ambitions.

As far as I can remember, my mother was chronically sick, yet she taught us—and me in particular during my elementary school days-- diligently. We were not aware she was suffering from a rheumatic heart disease until our relative Dr. Daniel Dioso, the only practicing physician in town at that time, diagnosed her when I was in high school. My close attachment to my mother inspired my young heart with the desire to become a doctor, so that I might treat her for this debilitating illness. Medical doctors were my childhood heroes and greatest role models. I firmly believe that health is the most valuable blessing one can receive, enabling us to enjoy our surroundings and find satisfaction in our accomplishments.

And one day—yes, one day I would build a house for her where we would all live comfortably like other successful families in our town. A relative doctor, who treated my mother generously, also inspired my desire to be a physician. This was my first consuming desire. It was a starting point to decide what is it that I want and what my burning desire means to me—and I stuck to those thoughts. Did I feel lost and unsure; push myself to think about my goals and aspirations? The answer was no. It was my commitment that came only after I have seen my mother's unbearable ailment.

My teacher once told me that my persuasive speaking ability was undeniably excellent. When I graduated from high school, my relatives, especially *Lola* (grandmother) Paisa who was Dr. Dioso's mother, tried to convince me to become a priest. No offense to such a sacred vocation, but it was not for me: I was meant to be a doctor!

As high school valedictorian I received a scholarship for one year of pre-medical studies at San Agustin University in Iloilo City, 230 kilometers away from home. I completed my first year in college with a scholarship grant but with great financial difficulty. I stayed in a boarding house of my town mate in Iloilo City together with my girl friend Alice. Unfortunately, in my second year my parents had to make the painful decision for me to quit school. Our family income was scarcely enough to support the family even though my oldest sister Eden was a schoolteacher and helping with financial expenses. The burden was accentuated by the schooling of my older sister Loida, who was studying nursing in Bacolod City, Negros Occidental, and by my older brother Marcelo, who was taking up education in the town of Kalibo, Aklan. Sacrifices were necessary, and I had to stop my own schooling. I felt sad and hurt but abided as the obedient son.

TOUGH TIMES NEVER LAST, BUT TOUGH PEOPLE DO

Dateline, February 2011

WITH GREAT DISCOURAGEMENT and sadness, I closed my eyes to a sore truth—the reality of life—that no matter how much my parents wanted to give all six of their children a good education, they would never afford to send me to medical school. Despite the apparent adversity I did not fail to nurture my dream. A real dreamer! Day in day out I continued to keep the torch aflame. I learned to savor the joys and learn from the pains in life. During moments of despair and disappointments I never quit; rather, I relied on the saying, "Tough times never last, but tough people do."

In my small, quiet and poor town, work opportunities for young men were virtually non-existent. There was no government sponsored student loan program. Feeling abased with what poverty could bring, I felt ashamed and frustrated by being out of school and unable to chase my dream. Nevertheless, I continued to believe in my dreams. The power of the mind can draw to us the things, the circumstances and the people necessary to make our dream come true.

Occurrences in odd times: My despair grew when my town mate girlfriend severed our relationship while she was in college in Manila and I was out of school in Pandan. I considered her the prettiest girl in town. Paranoia developed and bothered me for being a paltry man without a future, and possibly the principal reason why she broke off our relationship. George Bernard Shaw stated: " First love is a little foolishness and a lot of curiosity." I made a resolved to stick to my goals regardless of the challenges and obstacles that showed up. I was left in town with nothing to do but enjoy the company of my *barked* (buddies) where every late afternoon we were in our usual gathering place- our 'watering hole' to relish our local *tuba* or palm toddy from a coconut palm tree. I was nineteen years old.

A year passed. Did I abandon my dream?

My cheerfulness reappeared when my parents allowed me to continue my pre-med studies at San Agustin University. Despite of greater financial difficulty, I finally obtained an Associate in Arts Degree - a pre-medical degree.

In 1954, I had a college degree and prayed hard for a place in a medical school in Manila. My spirit began to soar, only to be crushed when I learned I could not enroll due to my family running out of money. Whatever small pieces of farmland my parents had were all sold or mortgaged. I realized and understood that problems were an integral, educational and on-going part of human life. I learned to look for the positive side of the issue even in bad situations. There were people in my hometown that wondered what I was aiming for in spite of my parent's financial difficulty. A brilliant quotation by Mark twain, "Keep away from people who try to belittle your ambitions. Small people always do that, but the really great ones make you feel that you, too, can become great."

Having a college degree in Associate in Arts (AA) and with a burning desire for higher education, but because I had no job, I was left feeling disappointed and frustrated—a chapter in my life that haunted me to this day. My pride was wounded; I felt bitter and ashamed that I had been forced to stop my schooling again. Nevertheless, I learned to view things in proper perspective. I avoided the trap of self-pity and placed the idea of having money into its proper perspective. I looked at every event in life as a process--a continuing process. While spending a year in my hometown with little to do, I thought of going to Manila to search for employment. I wrote a letter to join the U.S. Navy to no response. I was 21 years old then. I dated a number of girls. Would getting married to a rich woman lead me to a path of becoming a doctor? The whole situation almost seemed comical. Napoleon Bonaparte said, "We must laugh at a man to avoid crying for him." How true.

My younger sister Rhodora had a very attractive friend and a distant relative became my girlfriend. She is a *mestiza* (Filipino/Spanish blood). Her influential parents, both schoolteachers in the elementary school, were kind to me. My thoughts, filled with vibrating energy, came in a positive fashion. To get married was out of my way.

The Possibility Thinker's Creed states: "When faced with a mountain, I will not quit! I will keep on striving until I climb over, find a pass through tunnel underneath, or simply stay, and turn the mountain into a gold mine—with God's help." For that reason I stuck to my dream, for I had goals in mind. Dreams and goals in life are like stars. There is an adage that has been popularly accepted as truth: "Like a seafaring man in a desert of water, follow the stars, and having followed them, you will reach your destiny." At the touch of one's goal, everyone becomes a dreamer.

Finally, my older sister Loida graduated from nursing and worked at the Antique Provincial Hospital. Marcelo, whose dream was to eventually become a dentist, obtained a position as a school dental assistant in the province of Antique. With all the family's income and resources combined, supporting each other, I went to the nation's capital city, Manila, to further my education. My parents recommended me to take up a degree in chemistry. It was cheaper than a medical education. I accepted their wishes, though my secret desire to become a doctor remained in my heart.

STUDENT OF MEDICINE
A STRUGGLE

Dateline, 2009

IN 1956 I ENROLLED first at the University of the East Medical School (I could have been the first Medical Graduate of the Institution). Truly for no significant reason, I switched to enroll at the Far Eastern University Institute of Medicine without my parent's knowledge. I have long been a very determined person and my dream of becoming a doctor has been my central driving force — but I paid a severe price. Because of the higher tuition fees I could not afford to buy the required textbooks. But I was a serious medical student and focused on my dream to come true. After a few weeks I told my parents the truth that I enrolled in medical school. They could not do anything but let me pursue my heart. The philosopher William Jennings Bryan said: "Destiny is not a matter of chance, it is a matter of choice; it is not a thing to be waited for, it is a thing to be achieved." I considered myself to be an achiever — the future belongs to those who keep their passion alive!

The start of my freshman year at the Institute of Medicine was exciting, albeit full of questions. Could I afford the required reading? Do I have the money to buy for myself the books and more books? I tried to solve my problems only to realize that becoming a physician was an uphill task — a destiny difficult to reach. I was a serious student, full of the dreamer's devotion who wants only to pass the final exams.

I seriously focused on my goals and maintained the disciplines of diligently studying, learning and to pass the examinations. By focusing on my goals I pushed myself to develop the disciplines to do the things even if I do not feel like doing them.

No one in my class knew about my financial predicaments, including my three closest friends, Manuel Catalan, Gerry Delfin and Bonifacio Gamo who were also my board mates. I relied heavily on reading the books at the library, borrowing them from my classmates and board mates, and taking copious lecture notes during class. I am a human being and have the power of choice. I will never leave my destiny to chance; rather, it is a thing to be achieved.

Manila city was not totally a safe place to live in. Tito Varua and I were together in a boarding house. Tito was not only a friend but also a compassionate, loyal and trustworthy young man. He was our leader in many of our social activities. He had a job and money and represented us as our security person in this city. He was licensed to carry a side arm, employed as special assistant to Honorable Congressman Tobias Fornier of Antique. We felt safe around him. There were groups of thugs in our neighborhood at Sampaloc, Manila. I worried for Tito when he gets mad at the "gangs" roaming the streets. At one instance, a hilarious yet blatantly dangerous encounter when he brandished his forty-five caliber automatic pistol, raised up in the air, easily seen by these hoodlums and they all run away. I was standing behind him when this happened.

The FEU Institute of Medicine was close to the boarding house I was staying. I was so concerned of my safety in Sampaloc for I have to walk to school in Morayta everyday.

I was never known in my class other than a serious student of medicine. Our medical school had high standards and the discipline required was higher still. I had neither the time nor the inclination to be a student politician. As a result I did not join the fraternities, Beta Sigma or Sigma Mu Sigma, the Student PMA or other associations including Student Council. I was satisfied to be hidden in the 'shadows'.

On many occasions the money sent by my parents for tuition fees, board and lodging, personal expenses were delayed. Non-payment of fees would prevent my taking the class exams, and it always worried me that such delays could jeopardize my dream. Pursuing that dream was a great adventure; in such adventures, people succeed in discovering who and what they really are.

When money to pay my tuition was not at hand, I would find myself in the office of our Dean, Dr. Lauro Panganiban, pleading for permission to take the examination. My earlier training in convincing people to come to my side paid off, for I won his sympathy without exception- man of compassion, magnanimous, supportive Dean, and with inspiring encouragement to keep on studying.

Incredible event happened. In 1958, during my second year in medical school, my oldest sister Eden immigrated to the United States. She married a U.S. citizen and found a job as a medical secretary in a small hospital in Santa Monica, California. My intense desire to make my dream come true created a situation in my life and the lives of those around me to move in a certain direction. As a close family we became each other's business. We were each other's magnitude and bond. We were a family whose member loves each other as a model of how humanity can live together in harmony. It is my sincere conviction that an individual must live for the family, the family, for the people, the people for the world, and the world for God.

With better income overseas my sister's support assured me that my medical studies would be realized.

In 1959, just when my studies leaped forward in my third year of studies, my beloved mother passed away of congestive heart failure. Her death was my greatest loss, extremely devastating. Life was indeed a beautiful rose with sharp thorns. I felt as if someone had reached inside my chest and ripped out my heart. Of course there was emptiness and sadness and maybe even anger at death, but in many ways, the gift of my mother's life is still here with me. The world is such a random, arbitrary place--pain and joy are both facts of life. We all encounter personal loss and sadness. Animals, creatures, and humans all suffer calamities of emotional feelings and physical pain during their lives. She lives on in my memories and stories. The pain was even greater due to her lingering poor health. Indeed, this inspired me more to be a doctor. The thought that I lost my goal to treat her personally devastated me. But I took consolation in the words of the philosopher Norman Cousins: "Death is not the greatest loss in life. The greatest loss is what dies inside us while we live."

My buddy, classmate and board mate Gerry Delfin provided the emergency transportation expenses to be with my mother's farewell funeral services. For the first time, my brother Marcelo and I took the transportation by plane to Kalibo, Aklan and drove fifty kilometers to Pandan. All of my three sisters were present. A vigil services (wake) were held in our small home. This is a traditional venue of services in our impoverished town. No funeral parlor or mortuary facilities were available.

The call of death for my mother was a call for my deeper understanding of life. My mother taught me life is so much easier when one lives as the person they truly are; living life openly and honestly saves time, energy, heartache, and misunderstandings in situations and relationships. For me it became a great eternal form of life and transformation. In moments of grief I remember my dream and efforts to realize my vision. Although my mother was sickly, she toiled with my father so that my sisters, my brother and I could acquire a good education. Through my parents' inspirations, our family became a close bond helping one another with the grace of God Almighty. My mother was a very religious woman, and we were blessed as a pious Catholic family. I am greatly indebted to my mother's foresight and persistence in instilling the importance of education; without it, I would not have achieved what I am today. At its essence my mother taught me a thing of great value: discipline, that is, helping one to achieve competence, self-control, and self-direction. Successful discipline promotes age appropriate behavior that is socially acceptable and promotes respect for others as well. Discipline involves obedience.

Life went on. On April 8, 1961, I graduated from the medical school.

GRADUATION

Dr. Cesar D. Candari, 1961

Dateline, 2009

MY GRADUATION WAS a momentous relief not because I would be relieved of attending class daily but instead because it was a reprieve from my financial difficulties. During this time my father had retired and our family lived in Manila. My sister Eden in California was supporting us along with my sister Loida, a nurse employed in Antique Provincial hospital. We lived a frugal lifestyle. Did I receive a graduation party? Sadly, no. When I passed the Philippine medical board examination, did we celebrate? No, it was never important to me. I dreamed of going home to my hometown. My vision was to be a positive influence and force in society by improving the quality of health care in my community. I had been diligent in my pursuit of medicine as a career because I was convinced that medicine offers me the opportunity to live a fulfilling life dedicated to helping others. It was my thirst for the knowledge to help my fellow human beings.

But there were also regrets—especially that my dear mother never had a chance to witness my graduation. With great fortitude and courage that resulted to reach the unreachable star, I had cruised the dream field for a heavenly cause with my mom's blessings. Her inspirations gave me the ultimate reason why practicing medicine will be such a great joy, the privilege of returning a sick person to health, restoring the happiness that has been lost to illness, giving someone additional time to share with loved ones. I never had the chance to treat my mother.

Immediately after passing the Philippine medical board examination, I volunteered my services at the Kamuning Quezon City Community Health Center.

It was a complex postgraduate life. Was I looking at the future with anticipation? You bet. It was all about my dreams and desires to establish a private practice, get married, and help my family enjoy life with the tang of prosperity.

My graduation as a doctor was a time filled with happy moments and the excitement for change. This reality compelled me to include those moments of distress and sadness in my story. In doing so, the contrast to my moments of happiness, if not ecstasy, could have greater meaning and relevance. Dreams really do come true.

Who would ever think in my hometown that I would become a doctor? I would hear this all of the time by the old folks in Pandan whenever I visited home.

I spoke with an organization of the Youth in Pandan, my hometown and narrated my short story of my life on how I became a doctor.

In my introspective analysis of what I had gone through in my early life, I shared my experiences, the trials and tribulations as a guide for their personal growth from having dreams, goals and desire in their life. My message was to keep on dreaming, even if it seems an impossible dream. They do come true. Believe in them. Count your garden by the flowers but never by the leaves that fall. Count your days by golden hours.

I continued to emphasize of what I have gone through in my youth time. These were points to ponder. Somehow, in retrospect, I had followed these simple disciplines relentlessly.

I said, first of all, you must have a consuming desire. The starting point is to decide what is it that you want and what your burning desire means to you and stick to that thought. When you feel lost and unsure, push yourself to think about your goals and aspirations. Commitment comes when you have clear goals.

Further, I stated, get started. Things begin to happen when you start something. Even a small action produces consequences and leads to more actions. The mere act of starting will get your momentum going, will reinforce your beliefs and push your fears away. Emotionalize your desires.

Finally, I encouraged them to work hard at it and persevere. Dedicate and commit yourself to hard work. Get yourself busy and give your best. Be hard on yourself and keep trying until you actualize your aspirations. Don't wait for the right time. Resolve to stick to your goals regardless of the challenges and obstacles that show up. Do whatever it takes, without compromising your values, to realize your dreams. Be true to your glorious quest- follow that star!

Pamela V. Stern said, "Reach high, for stars lie hidden in your soul-- Dream deep for every dream precedes the goal."

CHAPTER NINE

MY ADOPTED COUNTRY
AMERICA

A BRIEF NARRATIVE - FILIPINO MIGRATION

America is a tune. It must be sung together.

- GERALD STANLEY LEE

Dateline, March 2011

NOTHWITHSTANDING THE FACT that I became a doctor ready to pass my life and practice my art, I had this desire to 'even the score'. I do not mean to get revenge on someone who has cheated or done harm on me...it was a feeling of retribution on the early departure of my dear mother at age fifty-eight. My mother lost her brave and courageous fight against rheumatic heart disease. My mother's death nonetheless inspired me more to become a specialist. To achieve this dream, I would again have to undergo postgraduate medical training in the United States, the highest center for medical education. I swear to uphold and exceed all that is expected of a future physician while promoting the progress of medicine and humanity.

I was twenty-eight years old when I graduated from medical school. Finally, I was a doctor—and yet I never knew that my graduation was a big step toward a bigger dream—the American Dream. I was almost ready to get married to my fiancée and classmate Shirley, however, things did not materialize. She graduated as an "Octoberian". I agreed to wait for her in America.

By the way, my girl friend Nettie in my hometown who gave me her photo with an autograph, "Forget me not" became a teacher in the elementary school in my hometown. Her brother, a priest, told me later that their father relentlessly was convincing her to follow me to America.

The story of how I came to America is similar to the other 22,000 Filipino American doctors who practiced in this country. By the same token, Filipino professionals - lawyers, engineers, nurses, dentists and others - came the same way.

I came to the U.S. under the Educational Council for Foreign Medical Graduates (ECFMG) sponsored by the Association of American Medical Colleges, American Hospital Association, American Medical Association, and Federation of State Medical Boards of the United States.

It was at its providential time that I graduated in 1961 with such opportunity at hand - the easiest way to come to America for postgraduate training.

The influx of foreign physicians into America house staff positions began in 1950s, and has continued unabated through the 1970s. This influx started when the postwar prosperity boom spawned many new hospitals and created a huge demand for physician as well as non-physician medical personnel that could not be adequately met by American medical schools. An amendment to the Smith-Mundt Act in 1965 required all persons to have come to the United States on an exchange visitor visa to be absent from the country for two years before receiving an adjustment to permanent residency status. We were limited to not more than five years in internship and residency training and thereafter must go back to the Philippines. Neither of these rulings had affected most of FMGs and I did not return home to the Philippines.

In reviewing this particular subject, I believe it will be of significant interest to relate the olden times to everyone, in particular to our American-born children, the younger generations of Filipino descent of how Filipinos migrated to America. As Filipino Americans, we need to tell our story and when it all began. I realize that I must delve into the history of Filipino migrations to America and, therefore, this subject is away from my personal life story. However, it is an opening of how I came to America, a nearly identical story to thousands of Filipino doctors and other professionals.

FILIPINO MIGRATION: It was the American colonization of the Philippines which paved the way for an exodus of Filipinos to the United States. There were two types of Filipinos who went to the United States. One type was comprised of the educated and, initially, middle class Filipinos who came as *pensionados*, or government scholars, for the purpose of furthering their education and training in the U.S. The second type were poor Filipinos who came as a cheap migrating labor supply for Hawaii plantations, California farms, and the Alaska fishing industry. These constitute the early history of the Filipino Americans, and they occupy a significant niche in the history of Filipino diaspora.

Mass migration, however, began at the beginning of the 20th century when the demand for labor in the plantations of Hawaii and farmlands of California attracted thousands of mostly male laborers. The movement of agricultural workers later expanded to California and to Washington and Alaska to work in fish canneries. This migration was reduced to 50 persons a year following the Tydings-McDuffie Act of 1934. Its main purpose was to exclude Filipinos because they were perceived as a social problem, disease carriers, and an economical threat. The American attitude toward Filipinos changed with the onset of World War II. It was offset by the United States Navy's recruitment of Filipinos who were exempt from the aforementioned quota.

Successive waves of Filipino migrants followed in the 1960s, which were largely professional workers. They were Filipino nurses, doctors, lawyers, dentists, medical technicians and others, who filled in the skill gaps in the United States.

The earliest permanent Filipino Americans to arrive in the New World landed in 1763 and made their first permanent settlement in the bayous and marshes of Louisiana. As sailors and navigators on board the Spanish galleons, Filipinos--also known as "Manilamen", or Spanish-speaking Filipinos--jumped ship to escape the brutality of their Spanish masters.

It is evident that with the passage of time, the different kinds of Filipinos coming to North America changed. Different classes of Filipinos arrived in the U.S., each having their own sets of goals and objectives. The one common denominator that drew these people here was the demand for Filipino labor supply. It was this factor that bound the early Filipinos who were called the "Manilamen", the "pensionados" (with pension grants from the Philippine government), and the "manongs" (Filipino men in their senior years), and later on the two other distinct groups of Filipino recruits: those in the U.S Navy and Filipino medical graduates and other professionals.

MANILAMEN - THE FIRST WAVE: To trace back before the 1900s, there were earlier Spanish-speaking Filipinos who were not truly immigrants but instead transplanted to America by accident and appropriately called "accident immigrants" i.e., not to serve for the labor demands of America but for Spain. It was not until 1898, when the U.S. acquired the Philippine territory at the end of the Spanish-American regime, when true immigration to the United States began.

Filipinos had settled in North America before the American Revolution. In 1565, the Spanish galleons left the port of Cebu, Philippines, bound for Acapulco, Mexico, which created the Manila-Acapulco trade route. Among the crewmembers of the Philippine-made Spanish galleons were Spanish-speaking Filipinos, the Manilamen. Many of the sailors were subjected to hard labor for the galleon service. While their ships were in port in Hawaii, Guam, Acapulco, and New Orleans, a few managed to escape the brutal conditions imposed by their Spanish masters.

Some of the Manilamen eventually settled in the French Louisiana territory where they began to build settlements. They created settlements such as Saint Malo, Louisiana and Manila Village in Barataria Bay. The Saint Malo settlement was established, by some accounts, as early as 1763 by Filipinos who deserted from Spanish ships during the Manila Galleon Trade. Other accounts suggest that the community was established sometime after 1812.

Other settlements like St. Malo sprouted in other areas. In the early 1900s a Filipino community leader revealed there were over two thousand Manilamen in the New Orleans community alone, and the Louisiana area outside of New Orleans was home to several hundred more Filipinos. During the War of 1812 Filipinos from Manila Village (near New Orleans) were among the "Batarians" who fought against the British with Jean Lafitte in the Battle of New Orleans.

PENSIONADOS AND MANONGS - THE SECOND WAVE: From 1900-1940 the Second Wave of immigrants showed up on American shores. These were the pensionados, the sons and daughters of rich, influential families who came to the U.S. specifically for a college education. They were given Philippine government grants and fellowships, known as government pensions, hence the term *"pensionados"*. They were to return to the Philippines after completing their academic work. Because of their small number on American campuses and were in the U.S. temporarily, they did not pose a threat to the majority of white Americans. A writer described the white Americans' attitude regarding the early pensionados as benign.

Beginning in the early 1900's, pensionados portrayed that identification with an image of being well mannered, well groomed, and knowledgeable of white American etiquette. Since the early pensionados did not experience much prejudice and discrimination, they returned to the Philippines with glowing reports and unrealistic views of mainstream American culture. These impressions gave false hopes and expectations to another second group of immigrant laborers, the *"manongs"* (old timers).

Not all Filipino students in the United States were *pensionados*. In the 1920s, most of them were sent by their wealthy parents for schooling. In the late 1920's, my wife's two uncles, older brothers of her dad, were fortunate enough to belong to an affluent Filipino family. His uncle Festo Asprec a graduate of Conservatory of Music (violinist) in the University of the Philippines became a *pensionado* for postgraduate studies in the U.S. Pepito Asprec, the younger brother who was a graduate schoolteacher, followed him. They were both single. They were under family financial support- not governmental pension grants. Sadly, her uncle Festo had a car accident and died. Pepito on the other hand passed away of a natural cause. Because they were pensionados with financial means, the two brothers were buried back in Agoo, La Union. They would have stayed in America for an unlimited time unlike the government sponsored students.

In 1907, there was an agreement between the United States and Japan to limit the number of Japanese as immigrants to the U.S. The Exclusion Act of 1924 barred the Japanese from further immigration. These actions led to a labor supply crisis for the sugar cane and pineapple plantations in Hawaii as well as the farms in the mainland. Agents for labor started a recruitment program to bring Filipinos to the United States. Steamship companies were instrumental in transporting these immigrants.

Besides the economic condition of the Philippines, other factors influenced the Filipino migration. The American public schools also played an important factor. The American virtues set forth in the American textbooks used in the Philippines made some boys dissatisfied with the economic condition in their country; they became desirous to go to America.

The first labor immigrants were sending money back to their families with glowing reports that work was easy to find in the U.S. The early pensionados also sent word home of a positive life, which resulted in turning the Second Wave of immigrants where a trickle of a few hundred men became a migration of thousands arriving each year in the 1920's. Many Filipinos saw their fellow countrymen who had left for the United States, mostly by joining the United States military, return to their hometowns to retire after working for several years. They came back as heroes with money in their pockets and an elevated status in their community. Combined with the glowing reports of the early immigrants, this impression led to the prevailing attitude of prospective immigrants that they were going to America and return as heroes.

Mass migration began at the beginning of the 20th century when the demand for labor in the plantations of Hawaii and farmlands of California attracted thousands of mostly male laborers.

The Filipino immigrants were unlike the two earlier Asian groups, the Chinese and Japanese. Although most of the early Asians came as laborers, the most striking difference was that the Chinese and Japanese stayed as a cohesive group and settled in specific areas, whereas the Filipinos were transients, moving from city to city and from farm to farm. The reason that Filipinos never settled into specific areas was that they considered their immigration to the U.S. to be only temporary. Since the Philippines were a United States territory at the time, there was no need for a passport or immigration papers. The only thing necessary was enough money to buy a ticket. Between 1920 and 1930, eighty percent of those entering the U.S. were between sixteen and thirty years old, seventy-seven percent of them unmarried. Because they believed that they were going back to the Philippines, they saw no need to transplant their culture and build communities.

Upon arriving, the new immigrant was shocked by the reality of American life. He faced prejudice and discrimination for the first time, something that he rarely experienced back home. He also found that the low wages were not what he expected, and the cost of living ate up much of what he earned.

At first, the new arrivals tried to find jobs as soon as possible, which meant working in the fields. Filipinos were known to specialize in stoop labor like cutting asparagus. For instance, the lettuce industry in the Watsonville district of California was created largely by Filipino labor.

Not all Filipino immigrants came in search of money. Others dreamt of completing their education in the U.S., hoping to find work and attend schools at the same time. Unfortunately, unlike the pensionados, these immigrants were unprepared for the education system in America. Some lacked the basic skills to enter a university and became discouraged, while others simply lacked the money.

Dr. Roberto Vallanga described what happened to many of them:

"As the years passed, their dreams of completing their education were thwarted; finding employment to support themselves became the only objective. They were drawn into a lifestyle out of necessity, against their will. Their lives were molded not by laziness or an unwillingness to better themselves, but instead by social and economic conditions in America. Some were able to finish a university education.

For example, Camilo V. was able to obtain an MBA degree from the University of Southern California (U.S.C.) in the 1930's, but because of the well of prejudice, he was only able to get a job as chauffer. But as a happy ending, when his employer passed away he willed his car to Camilo."

The Second Wave of Filipinos who intended to work temporarily in the U.S. discovered the harsh truth of reality. Like the other previous immigrants, they also fell for the "American Dream" trap. Some were able to return to the Philippines as heroes, but the vast majority could not bear to return home as failures.

THE FILIPINOS NAVY MEN - THE THIRD WAVE: The *manongs* came mostly between 1900 thru 1940 while the professional class did not arrive until the end of the 1950's. When the Philippines became a U.S. territory, Filipinos had constantly been members of the U.S. military and the merchant marines. Article 27 of the Base Agreement, signed after the Philippines obtained independence, allowed provisions for "special relations" between the U.S. Navy and Philippine nationals. The U.S. had no other agreement like this with any other country in the world. The provisions were mutually independent. The U.S. military bases in the Philippines were neither required to recruit Filipinos nor were the Filipinos required to serve in the U.S. military in order for the bases to continue to exist.

The economic pressures in the Philippines drove the men into the Navy. This began the Third Wave of Filipino immigration (1945-1965). Filipinos from the Philippines joined the U.S. Navy to fight against the Japanese. Filipinos were allowed to join the Navy because they were so-called "nationals". They were neither U.S. citizens nor were they illegal aliens. Ramon J. Farolan wrote on this topic in From Stewards to Admirals: Filipinos in the U.S. Navy published in Asian Journal, on Jul 21, 2003:

I truly praised the Filipino Navy men. In the Navy, many Filipinos were given the label "stewards man". As stewards, Filipinos in the U.S. Navy cooked, cleaned, shined shoes, washed and swabbed the decks of naval ships and naval bases across America and the entire world. Despite their status, Filipinos fought side-by-side with the American soldiers for freedom against the Japanese."

The restrictions for higher positions for Filipino Navys were lifted in the '70s, and they could become officers of the U.S. Navy up to the highest rank position. In 1985 Commander Tem E. Bugarin became the first Filipino to command a surface ship of the line when he assumed command of the USS Saginaw, LST1188. There are now hundreds of Filipino officers in the U.S. Navy. The Navy immigrants were a more cohesive group than the early manongs.

Before the Philippines got its independence, those who joined the Navy had the original intent to return to the Philippines. However, after the Philippines' independence, many of them had the new attitude of permanently emigrating to the U.S. They felt that they had better advantages if they remained here since the U.S. Navy treated Filipino retirees better in the States than in the Philippines. The U.S. Navy's recruitment of Filipinos, who were exempted from the established quota, brought a heavy wave of immigrants to the U.S. Thus, Filipino American communities developed around United States Navy bases whose impact still can be seen today.

MEDICAL GRADUATES/OTHER PROFESSIONALS - THE FOURTH WAVE: The Fourth Wave of Filipino immigration began after the passing of the Immigration Act of 1965 and continues to the present day. This allowed the entry of as many as 20,000 immigrants annually. One of the most identifiable groups in this wave of immigrants represented the medical profession. During the late 1950's and early 1960's the U.S. was in critical supply of technical people, especially in the medical services. Filipinos were again heavily recruited to fill the labor demands of the U.S. Other groups of Filipino immigrants during these years were from the professional class: doctors, nurses, engineers, lawyers, and Navy men. The United States opened its doors to professionals under the "third preference" status.

Have you heard of "brain drain?" The Fourth Wave had this impact on the Philippines with the exodus of professionals leaving the country to come to the United States. These professional immigrants were very similar to the *manongs* who had come seventy years earlier. They were mostly single, young, and were scattered throughout the U.S. moving to a job first and subsequently forming a Filipino community. The main difference is that after 1962's change in immigration guidelines they knew they were here to stay.

THE FILIPINO AND AMERICAN IN ME

Dateline, June 2012

NOW IT IS A FACT that Filipinos have been in America for quite some time. Yet one might persistently ask, who are the Filipino Americans? What makes them appear different, yet one and the same?

My son Roy admits that he is a second generation Filipino. He has an interesting point of view in fact: "Of course being American-born, I am more biased towards the American culture. But as to which of the two cultures I truly belong to, I claim neither one. As a Filipino, I am the first son of a successful doctor who holds much respect within the Filipino community. I am proud to be a Filipino American..." I assume he is linking his public persona to being an American and his private feeling of identification to being a Filipino.

It is unfortunate that many American-born children of Filipinos do not see themselves in the American mainstream or in the Filipino community because of this "invisibility." They lack a certain voice reminding them that they, too, are Filipino. This may be one of the reasons they act more American than Filipino.

The United States is a country where all men are created equal and where there exists the fundamental inalienable rights for freedom and justice. In the early years Filipinos were called the "forgotten Asian Americans". In the 1950s and 60s, Filipinos were invisible to mainstream society. How often in those days did you find Filipinos in books magazines, television, or radio?

The history of how they came to the U.S. was never kept alive among the Filipino Americans of today. What appears to be some underlying confusion actually underscores the fact that so little is known about the history of Filipinos in America.

There has been a significant change in the lives of the last wave of Filipino immigrants in this country. The Filipino American community is the second largest Asian American group in the United States. Filipino Americans are also the largest subgroup of overseas Filipinos. The American Dream is very much alive. I am a Filipino and an American citizen. My heart isn't devided; it has grown larger.

My family resided in San Diego County for thirty years. There are now 200,000 Filipino Americans living in San Diego County. It is stated that Filipinos in the State of California are about 2 million making it the second largest minority group. Yet in the past, as Filipino Americans, we remained invisible to mainstream society.

Yes, indeed, now there are changes in Filipino Diaspora. Filipino newspapers are everywhere, writers are in abundance, and thousands of articles about Philippines and Filipinos are written. I continued to write as editorial contributor in Philippine newspapers. I became a columnist in weekly newspaper, Philippine Times Southern Nevada since 2011. Indeed, as Filipino Americans, we need to tell our story and be recognized and respected in mainstream society.

ASSOCIATION OF PHILIPPINE PHYSICIANS IN AMERICA

*"A man only learns in two ways, one by reading,
and the other by association with smarter people*

- WILL ROGERS

THE POLITICAL PRAXIS circulating in my veins were evident when I participated in the political system of the Association of Philippine Physicians in America (APPA).

Speaking of my dream, desire and aspiration to participate in the leadership of Filipino American doctors in America, I analyzed and evaluated my affectivity on this journey. I joined the APPA in 1975.

I am aware great leaders keep the members focused on moving the organization towards its ideal future, motivating them to overcome whatever obstacles lie in the way. I do not say I am a great leader, but I know that effective managers, administrators, top executives are not necessarily true leaders. They execute their responsibilities successfully without being great leaders. True leadership includes effectively orchestrating important change, setting the direction and creating a vision for the organization. Great leaders keep the members focused on moving the organization towards its ideal future, motivating them to overcome whatever obstacles lie in the way. We need leaders. Leaders inspire us. Leaders bring out the best in others. Leaders change the world and keep us moving forward. True leadership includes effectively orchestrating important change, setting the direction and creating a vision for the organization. Broadly speaking, the chief reason wherefore leaders are important, is to succeed to a mutual goal among a group of people.

I do realize, however, that there are organizational politics in the Fil-Am organizations, such as the Association of Philippine Physicians in America (APPA). Hence, I was disturbed about the organization when deciding to be an active participant.

I continued to attend the annual convention and scientific meetings of the Association of Philippine Physicians in America (APPA) and served as a member of the board of governors from 1976 to 1978. I was re-elected to the same position in 1978.

It was in 1977 that I became a member of the board of directors of the APPA Education Research Foundation Inc. (ERF) with Dr. Manuel A. Sison as chairman. It was also this year that Dr. Sison was president of APPA. The specific and primary purpose was "to operate as a non-profit charitable corporation, to guarantee loans to disadvantaged and deserving medical students of Pacific Asian lineage and other disadvantaged and deserving medical students to enable those individuals who receive said loans to obtain a medical education and do research." Fundraising activities by ERF were a profound success.

In 1982, I was appointed as special counsel to the president Dr. Noli Zosa. I served as a member of the House of Delegates representing the Philippine Medical Association of San Diego.

From 1985-1992, my activities in the National Filipino Doctors Association, the Association of Philippine Physicians in America, were at its pinnacle. I was elected for three consecutive terms as board of governor, Secretary of the House of Delegates (2 terms) , Speaker of the House Aseembly.

Somewhat disconcerting, like any other Fil-American organizations in the country, problems, discord and relentless disunity were blatantly apparent in this largest organization of Filipino professionals in America. I am not going to name names to protect the privacy of certain fraudulent and corrupt individuals. My intent here is not to pour scorn on the previous leadership of the Association but rather to look back and learn from the experience.

There was a libel suit filed, counter accusations, intramural rifts between "factions," and hotly contested elections punctuated by highly acrimonious pre-election campaigning.

Organizational politics was apparent. It was a struggle for resources, personal conflicts, competition of power and leadership, and tactical influence executed by individuals and groups to attain power, thereby building personal stature and controlling the organization.

As a member of the House of Delegates, I was appointed chairman of the constitution and bylaws committee. I was not overly ambitious to become an officer, yet was remarkably active in my committee position.

There seemed to be a pervading mistrust all around...

FIL-AM IMAGE had this to report: "The hotly contested position of Speaker of the HOD in a lopsided result when Dr. Cesar D. Candari (FEU'61) of San Diego, California, won the election running against the incumbent Dr. Manuel Pinzon (UP '63) of Flushing, New York." FILIPINO REPORTER of New York headline stated: 'Candari Pulls Upset Victory." MABUHAY TIMES of San Diego, California, had another headline: "Dr. Cesar D. Candari trounced his opponent for Speaker of the House of Delegates position.

THE HOUSE THAT NEVER WAS

Dateline, August 1988

In 1988, I wrote a critique of the proceedings of the House of Delegates assembly, Association of Philippine Physicians in America (APPA).

THE RECENT CONVENTION of APPA at the Hyatt Regency Hotel in Long Beach, California, was a resounding success in every aspect. However, as the annual regular session of the House of Delegates convened, opinions were expressed that the body suffered a serious flaw. This flaw happened at the time when the House acquired the very historic legacy of being called the "supreme policy-making body of the Association." It was precisely for this reason that the body should have acted responsibly and not be involved in too much politics. The result was that precious time was being eaten up by internecine confrontations.

To the dismay of many, not one resolution was introduced to the House for deliberation and action.

The question to ask now is this: Did the House scrutinize and define the present and future course for the organization at this annual regular session? Could our actions be equated to responsible leadership? I fear the answers to both questions are no. This is not to say that the debates were irrelevant, however, as someone described them as no less than the imbroglio of the convention.

If the House has to take charge of promulgating the policies of this organization, it must correct itself of these irregular actions. If this sounds depressing, you are darn right! But let us look at the brighter side. The House of Delegates is composed of highly motivated members seriously committed to the responsibility vested upon them. There are excellent and articulate speakers within the ranks who are also visionary and intelligent leaders of their respective component societies. Let us harness that leadership in bringing unity and harmony among ourselves. And let us not waste our time caught in the web of cynicism and in chaotic and cacophonous sessions.

I am neither writing this to blame anyone, nor do I intend to discredit the leadership of the House. It is my intention, instead to open one's eyes so that in the future we can better exercise responsible acts and adhere to the rules and decorum of the House. By so doing, we bring about the making of the House of Delegates as one of action. It will be a House that acts with compassion and fairness in its deliberations. It must be objective, dispassionate, and devoid of factionalism and a real policy-making body of the association. All of these virtues are for the good of the APPA.

A HOUSE UNRAVELED - A DÉJÀ VU

Dateline, August 1989

In 1989 the House of Delegates convention was held at the St. Louis Union Station Omni Hotel in St. Louis, Missouri. I described the House of Delegates session in my editorial, a critique of a sequel to 1988 imbroglio.

WE WERE TEN minutes into the House of Delegates session at the St. Louis Union Station Omni International Hotel last October 29, 1988, when BOOM! The HOD meeting was interrupted and later terminated, like a runaway locomotive crashing into Union Station.

Two things happened simultaneously. First, there was an urgent request by the Executive Council for the members of the HOD to attend a key report in the Council session in another chamber. Second, a raucous, furious and acrimonious assembly of the HOD vehemently disagreed and questioned the veracity and motive of the presentation by the legal counsel, who was invited to the House of Delegates. Some members were stunned the meeting opened with what first appeared to be a presentation by the lawyer on a primer of parliamentary procedures, duties and rights of the HOD; it turned out to be a discourse on micro-dissection of the intricacies of the constitution and by-laws of APPA as it relates to the Executive Council and the president. Enumerated were the ambiguities, shortcomings and inadequacies of the by-laws; items such as the start of the term of office of the president; the overpowering posture of the House of Delegates; the impeachment process as a function of the Electoral College and the difficulty of its implementation; and need for a parliamentarian in the House sessions. A delegate from Illinois questioned the lawyer for sowing seeds of dissension and fueling fire to an already "burning bridge" across the room. The HOD meeting ended prematurely.

Thirty-five members of HOD attended with a purpose and mission. As delegates, they attended the sessions because they felt that the meetings were vital links in the conduit of information that flows between the component society and the national organization. The aforementioned conduit is important to achieve two major goals: first, that the component society be heard at the national level; second, to bring information back to the component State Society with insights gained from the House sessions regarding current views. They came to discuss issues affecting all of us, the perennial FMG problems, the practice of medicine and the shaping of the future of our profession. Included in the agenda was a draft of the Rules of the House for deliberation by the assembly and resolutions for introduction appealing for membership and other positions, all of which would support us, protecting our interests from the legal carnage on our practice of medicine in this country. More importantly, there was an outcry to examine critically the Constitution and Bylaws of APPA related to the pressing problems and intramural turmoil. These were the reasons they came to the meeting; to their dismay, it did not happen.

I am sure we agree that these are critical times for our group, and we must address this crisis. Let us regroup and cool our heads. Sartorial splendor and oratorical glibness in the House sessions are welcome, but the intramural turmoil must stop--it is a threat that will irrevocably end the unity of the House..."

Editorializing again an event such as this that is characterized by unnecessary embarrassment hurts all members of the House of Delegates. However, silence, passivity, meekness, and inactivity will drag us down until we teeter on the precipice of doom.

It would be foolish to give up and drop everything even though a solid foundation for the association had been laid down before us. We are gaining ground despite these impediments. Let us forge ahead. General McArthur and Eisenhower, when pursuing the retreating enemy, found that a point of turning could be disastrous. If we retreat from these problems, if we yield to these agonizing protracted pangs of pain, we can only expect our own extinction. Let us launch an offensive against those that introduce discord. Dissension and rift divide the House--and a House divided will surely fall.

A CRUCIAL MOMENT IN THE APPA

Dateline, fall 1990

THE RECENT ANNUAL meeting of the House of Delegates of the Association of Philippine Physicians in America (APPA) in the Grand Hyatt Hotel, Washington, D.C., was **déjà vu** all over again. It was embroiled in the credentialing question. There were a charade of questions and disagreements regarding the legality of the credentialed delegates, the legality of the appointed Interim Executive Director as well as the relocation of the Executive Office. Filibuster appeared to be the order of the day. There was a clamor to declare the credentialing process illegal; therefore, null and void. A postponement of the election was in the minds of many partisan delegates. We had the same situation before. Now, for the third consecutive year, the assembly was stalled by the same problem. Why?

Clearly, it showed that for as long as the delegate count was tied up with a vote especially in a partisan election, there would always be questions about the credentialing process. There seemed to be a pervading mistrust all around.

The main problem that persists was the questions emanating from credentialing of Delegates.

"Pure and simple," declared one delegate." Follow to the letter the Constitution and Bylaws of APPA and the Rules of the House of Delegates." It was also time to re-evaluate the voting function of the delegates for the officers of the association (President-Elect), a hotly coveted post that somehow brought factionalism among its leaders (members of Electoral college).

Solution: Let the general members elect the **main officers** of the association!

The principle of "one-person-one vote" started to be considered. I certainly agreed and endorsed this proposal without realizing that a certain "manipulator" of votes had already designed a fraudulent way of winning an election. It was believed that if the Electoral College were to be dissolved, this would certainly remove cliques and factions. It would also finally end the question regarding the unwieldy credentialing procedure of delegates, a problem that haunted the House assembly year-end and year out and hindered its functions.

Once again, the House of Delegates in this annual meeting failed to perform many other important functions.

In the final analysis, APPA had escaped the jaws of death not once, but twice. A postponement would have destroyed everyone's faith, and not just those of the APPA members. Technical disqualifications of delegates would have been the last straw that would have drawn us to the day of doom.

In the end it appeared that all was well in the APPA. Dr. Amante Legaspi, the President of the Association, had this theme at the first Executive Council meeting of his administration, "Working Together Works"... "Because when all is said and done, working together doesn't only bring out the best in all of us; it also brings out the best in each of us."

If there was anyone to be given credit to in the resolution of the "crises in crucial moments," the delegates with cooler heads deserved the honor. They were fair and resolute. They saw both sides of the issues and maintained popular, unbiased judgments and decisions. It was the House of Delegates that prevailed. To one and all, we had learned our lesson. It should never happen again.

Once and for all I shall make this appeal. Let us not make the past dominate the future of APPA. Let us nourish the desire for a new spirit within us – the spirit of community, compassion and reconciliation in this association. Give us a chance to start all over again in this new administration.

SPARE ME THE AGONY OF...

Dateline, July 1991

Campaign Speech for Speaker of the House of Delegates, Association of Philippine Physicians in America (APPA)

...YOU AND I know there is a problem in the APPA today. Problems or not, this House of Delegates must listen to the call of change for progress. If elected as Speaker of the Assembly, I pledge to lead the House to achieve its potential and assert our authority as the policy-making body of this organization. I FIRMLY BELIEVE the Speaker must lead the House to consider policies reflecting the needs and wishes of the members to ensure a strong and effective APPA leadership. I FIRMLY BELEIVE the Speaker must take the initiative to continue to seek and listen to the views of everyone and to continue to inspire the members of the House to exercise their responsibilities as the makers of the policies of this organization. I ALSO FIRMLY BELIEVE the Speaker must have a thorough knowledge of the operations of the HOD and Rules of the House in order to be an effective leader in this assembly. VOTE FOR CANDARI! TOGETHER, WE SHALL MAKE THE DIFFERENCE.

Friends, in this difficult time and trying year for the APPA, I am seeking the highest position in the House of Delegates as Speaker of this assembly. I believe I am well qualified for this position, and today we are here to make a choice, one that is very important and sometimes a difficult one. However, if you my friends use the yardstick of service to this association, you will make the right choice. I have served in various capacities in the APPA in the past ten years. I have been a member of the HOD for seven years. I am confident my long experience in the House of Delegates has given me the expertise and leadership skills to effectively guide the affairs of this assembly. I am a devoted worker in the House of Delegates. I have compiled and drafted, along with my members of the committee, and completed the RULES OF THE HOUSE for your easy reference House manual.

I strongly support the goals and objectives of the past and present administrations. However, before these goals and objectives can be achieved, first and foremost, let us go back to basics – UNITY. Yes, unity, which we will use to resolve the controversies pervading in the APPA hierarchy. Please, my friends, no more of the "hard-ball politics" that undermines leadership. Let us have more harmony, away with personal ambition and partisan mentality. Crucial as it is, what we need in the APPA today is to relearn the true meaning of BAYANIHAN (working together), the embodiment of what a true Filipino like you and I should be, doctors in this foreign land and not really politicians in the true sense of the word. I appeal to your sense of fellowship and to your kind hearts to share with us the spirit, your spirit of PAGKAKAISA or UNITY to build a solid and stronger APPA.

There is an inherent spirit of man to rise above hostility and arrogance, to survive over potential annihilation and destruction. The analogy in the APPA is this organization is threatened to the brink of collapse. However, I can assure you that we, the champions and defenders of unity and democratic principles, shall rise to the occasion with the courage and wisdom of Lapu-Lapu. We shall rise with a resolve to restore and preserve harmony, camaraderie, friendship, and comity of people the old spirit of this organization for the survival, growth and progress of the APPA.

Lastly my friends, I want you to know that during my long and active participation in the APPA, like I stated before, I am not overly ambitious for senior positions. When Brutus killed Julius Caesar due to ambition, I am Caesar, please spare me the agony.

MESSAGE
SPEAKER HOD

Dateline, 1991

THIS IS AN unprecedented 20th anniversary of APPA for the HOUSE OF DELEGATES (HOD) to come at a landmark decision 'one man one vote,' full and unrestricted rights and direct participation in the election of the APPA officers by the general membership including those not attending the convention. Indeed, these are the clamors and wishes of the members who are demanding greater involvement and participatory leadership. For a long time the members have been increasingly apathetic. They are outright negative and 'turned off' towards participating in any manner while the APPA is engulfed in discord. The onerous provisions in the Constitution and Bylaws somehow impair the development of leadership at the membership base. It is perceived that the elections of the officers of the Executive Council may not be an accurate reflection of the prevailing sentiments of the members. Some felt that a small hard core of old guards are unwilling to relinquish control over the APPA affairs. We contend that these negative scenarios belong in the past, and the power to select the officers rests with the general membership where it rightfully belongs.

Now we needed to increase our membership base. I have written about this subject before and I'm doing it again. For $50 membership dues annually, a Filipino physician in this country can be a participant to organized medicine. Simply stated, thirteen cents a day will help preserve the freedoms of our profession in this country. Realistically speaking, organized medicine within our group of Filipino physicians is a real bargain.

It is lamentable to know that Filipino doctors practicing in the US and not members of the APPA are benefiting from the accomplishments promoted by a small group of their colleagues who are protecting our principles. Do not shy away from the mainstream of organized medicine.

We need every Filipino physician practicing in America to actively support our cause. We must have that support if we are to continue to protect and defend our profession and the future, including our children who follow our lead.

If in the perception of many the HOD has been relegated to a second-class status throughout the years in the archives of APPA, now it will be changed. Through this Bulletin, we urge the delegates to take up the light and keep the mill rolling. Keep those resolutions coming. Get the House on track. Start tilting the balance now!

Filipino Reporter, a New York newspaper, had this to say:

"The Physicians' association has been acrimoniously split between two major factions – the Leadership Alliance for APPA Reforms and Progress headed by Candari, and Cueto's National Coalition For the Advancement of APPA. Just a few days away from election time, politicking in Orlando is heating up, already marred by some earlier charges of unethical tactics, mudslinging and even ballot abuse.... as of this writing, eleven of the sixteen APPA past presidents have openly endorsed Candari in what may well be the most crucial election in the history of the association."

VISION FOR APPA

A Campaign Speech delivered to different PMAs in the U.S.

Dateline, July 1992

... YOU MAY ASK the fundamental question. What is APPA for and what has it done for the Filipino doctors in America?

First, allow me to briefly mention in perspective a significant historical background on why we are here in this foreign land and how THE ASSOCIATION OF PHILIPPINE PHYSICIANS IN AMERICA (APPA) has evolved. At a time when there was a dire shortage of physicians in America three decades ago, Foreign Medical Graduates (FMGs) were swayed into coming to this country, including many of you in this room tonight. But due to the ever-increasing number of U.S.-trained foreign medical graduates (FMGs), we became less welcomed. To put it bluntly, this is due to the competition that we FMGs impose upon our native colleagues for the "green bucks." I know that we FMGs contribute high quality and standard care to the health care system in this country that is on par, if not better, with our native colleagues. Stringent and discriminatory laws were imposed upon us. It was and still is complicated, if not impossible, to take a state licensure examination of transfer to another state to relocate our practice at any time. Subtle as it may be, everyone has felt such discrimination.

Formed many years ago by the founding fathers of the APPA under the leadership of Dr. Lucito Gamboa, this association of twenty-one years has the basic concept of promoting the image and unity of the Filipino physicians in this country. Additionally, its emphasis is to protect the rights of the FMG and to fight any acts of injustice that are being thrust against us.

Over the years, the APPA has slowly attracted members and component societies from different cities and regions of this nation. It has demonstrated a strong display of unity and camaraderie, friendship and reunion. It became a social vehicle for many of us for our families and children who, in turn, became conscious and proud of our Filipino heritage. The humanitarian projects in the form of medical missions have been active the last 10 years in helping the poor people in our country. Excellent CME programs have been organized at annual conventions. Our publications in the Philippine Physician have been an excellent medium of information for all readers. There is a sense of urgency in restoring the faith of the APPA members.

So we see the APPA has not been dormant all these years; rather, it has accomplished a number of goals and objectives. However, it has been slow in achieving its important priority--the total unification of the Filipino doctors in this country. It lacks more aggressive, well-defined, and coordinated efforts through its lobbying arm--the Political Action Committee--in protecting the rights of the Filipino doctors in this country....

Our Political Action Committee was never the focal point of our thrust. The PMA of San Diego during my presidency of that society back in April 1987 was instrumental in getting the sympathetic pioneering stand of Congressman Jim Bates of California in introducing the first anti-discriminatory bill in Congress, the HR 3241-Equal Opportunity for Medical Licensure and Reciprocity Bill. It had caught the eyes of other politicians, and the Filipino doctors in general have made friends in U.S. Congress. Congressman Solarz of New York, Senator Paul Simon of Illinois, Senator Moynihan of New York, and others introduced similar bills.

We appreciated the work of members of the APPA FMG committee chaired by Dr. Andres Botuyan, Dr. Antonio Donesa of the ACIP, Dr. Cosme Cagas and others who have put their time and efforts along these endeavors. Many hurdles had to be surmounted. Letters of support and monetary political contributions to politicians from our members came in slowly. Documented discrimination of FMGs had been difficult to gather. Although AMA seemed sympathetic to our flight and denied any adversarial stance, many of us perceived that it was the reason behind our difficulties. The FMG alliance and the APPA also played a part in it.

For many years the APPA became a participant in the lobbying efforts with International Association of American Physicians and became watchdog in the capital for all FMGs. The APPA contributed monies to the IAAP. In April of 1990, the General Accounting Office (GAO) had a favorable assessment of the problems encountered by the FMGs declaring that a double standard of treatment existed between U.S. and FMGs. In the most recent month, the U S House of Representatives favorably acted on HR-3508 that would establish a national advisory council so that the IMGs would have a voice in the licensure issue. This was a significant victory for IMGs. We can be proud that we are part of this initial victory, but for APPA, a participant in the International Association of American Physicians, the war was not over yet.

In essence, the APPA must take a new direction and should focus its energy and priority on the protection, promotion, and enhancement of the image of the Filipino doctors in America.

As some of you know, I had been very active in the APPA for seventeen years. I have served in various capacities in this organization as a delegate member, as a member of the board of governors, special counsel to the President, as Secretary of the House of Delegates for two terms, as a member of the Editorial Board, and currently as Speaker of the House of Delegates. I was co-chairman of two APPA conventions in California. I have served in various committees and have been instrumental in the drafting of the rules of the House of Delegates and as chairman of the constitution and bylaws committee two years ago. I initially drafted the amendments to the constitution and bylaws for the general-popular elections of its officers, addressing the clamor by the members that was long overdue. When I ran for speaker of the HOD last year, I spoke of my firm belief that I must lead the House to consider policies reflecting the needs and wishes of the members to ensure a strong and effective APPA leadership. I also spoke of my sincere and fundamental principle that as Speaker, I will continue to seek the views of everyone and continue to inspire the members of the HOD to exercise their responsibilities as policy makers of the APPA.

My friends, I believe that my years of service in the APPA have given me a clear idea of what our association truly stands for and a vision that details in no uncertain terms what APPA must have in this decade and beyond. Now we are all at the crossroads where the destiny of the APPA and its future will veritably evolve. I do not offer any miracles or quick fixes, but with the programs I envision and together with those who share my dreams of what APPA should be, I will do it. I am confident that I will steer APPA in the right direction. I am soliciting your support and ask you to join me in this task of renaissance...

A CRUSADE FOR CHANGE
Campaign Speech for President of APPA

Dateline, July 1992

...YOU AND I come to this convention full of enthusiasm, excitement and expectations for a happy reunion with friends and classmates and to enjoy this social function. This is the old spirit of the organization--and we must preserve it. I come as a candidate with great pride and optimism, even if there are still a number of problems in the APPA today.

My friends, in this election you will make a difficult and crucial decision. APPA is now at the crossroads where its destiny and future depend on what we can deliver as the best, the most effective, honest and credible leadership. YOU ARE THE ELECTORATE, and APPA's destiny lies in your hands.

Despite our persistent and tiresome call for unity, reconciliation and compassion, conflicts still exist in our leadership because there is a cycle of crisis in leadership emanating from a call for change by a group of well-meaning leaders versus a STRONGHOLD MENTATLITY by others. Ladies and gentlemen, this problem threatens the very existence and soul of our Association.

It is therefore in this context and for our love of this association that the Association of Philippine Physicians in America must continue to grow and listen to the call of change for progress. These are the very problems that compel me to seek the position of President Elect so that I can continue to work within and effect important changes. In all these years, I have been a strong advocate of change for harmony, unity and removal of the "fires of politics" in the organization, to which my editorial writings can attest. If elected as your president, I pledge to institute reforms that will restore our image and credibility in this society.

Friends, what we need are leaders with the courage and wisdom to carry on these reforms. To lead by the RULES is most basic and fundamental to me.

True there is a certain kind of gloom hovering over us. I too see the dark heavy clouds of dissension and distrust. There is even a despicable enmity. I am sorry to say, my friends that we are in the deep morass of politicking. WE CERTAINLY HAVE MORE THAN ENOUGH OF MUTUAL RECRIMINATIONS. MUCH TO MY DESIRE NOT TO PARTICIPATE IN THIS NEGATIVE EXERCISE, I MUST ANSWER AN ALLEGATION THAT I HAVE TESTIFIED AGAINST THE APPA. I DID NOT TESTIFY AGAINST THE APPA. I TESTIFIED AGAINST THE STATEMENT OF OUR OFFICERS UNDER OATH STATING THAT THERE IS NO RULES OF THE HOD IN THE APPA.

These recent unfortunate events that we know should teach us all a lesson. Another breakdown of our rules will mean the final breakdown of our association. Such a breakdown will be a significant negative impact not only to the members of the APPA but also to the entire Filipino doctors, community, and especially our children. What legacy shall we leave for our children and the Filipino community of tomorrow in this country?

It is my fervent hope that all these problems and conflicts will come to pass soon. That when we meet again, it will be a new beginning, a new and vibrant summertime for all of us, for our lives, and for our hopes in the APPA...

...We must restructure our basic empowerment to assure a clear definition of our roles and responsibilities. Above all, it must be a leadership that reaches out to all of us, the rank and file, and not a cultivation of a vacuous posturing of an elitist cocoon. I envision a leadership that heals, soothes and pacifies the troubled waters and gusting winds but also a leadership that will inspire interest, involvement and renewal.

Deep as we are in the quagmire of politicking, survival dictates that we rise up to a level of health where positive accommodation and understanding will prevail. Thus, our initial post election agenda will be to call a moratorium on hostilities. I will call for a meeting of the minds and hearts to try to resolve what could be resolvable. Beyond that, we will allow due process to rule. Healers that we are, let us all lay a healing hand on our beloved association.

I HAVE AN APPEAL from the bottom of my heart: please, let us leave behind what is petty, narrow and selfish and instead enter a better orientation—one of magnanimity, and generosity, worthiness. Let us rise together to work, change, and be steadfast. For all the pains that we suffer through these days, let us forget them and work for a better tomorrow. APPA must move forward beyond any odds of power politics.... Only then can we regain the faith and confidence of our members and the community.

Finally, my friends, in this unseemly twilight, as we observe the quintessential discovery of America, let me enjoin you to rediscover our compromised pride and our compromised honor. Let us set forth on a new direction from hereon--a **Renaissance--a resolve as never before that this association, 'under God, shall have a new birth of freedom and shall not perish from the earth.** Thank you.

IT'S ALL POLITICS

Dateline, December 15, 2011

IN THE RECENT issue of PMAC News, October 2011, I read the astounding story of Dr. Ulysses Carbajal and the mysterious ways he experienced the grace of God. In one part, he discussed wanting to help the Association of Philippine Physicians in America (APPA) in 1993 and decided to run for president of this association. How could such a righteous, brilliant, experienced, and former PMA President (Philippines) lose? According to Carbajal, "Flagrant election irregularities, typewritten ballots, proxy voting, led to my defeat."

I would be dishonest to admit I was not annoyed to hear such things.

It was neither an embarrassment nor the will of God for Dr. Carbajal to lose in the election; rather, it was the farcical election in a premier APPA. Was it a reflection of the Philippine style of elections?

My friend Uly knew my story. I had also run for president of the APPA in 1992, a year before his presidential defeat. You may call this as my exposé. It is important to post this story so that every Filipino American physician can understand these shameful political shenanigans. My story was to show the readers what I tried to do to streamline the Constitution and By-Laws of the APPA and the Rules of the House of Delegates in order to make the association a premier among ethnic medical organizations.

Before I joined the APPA, I evaluated my participation. Great leaders keep the members focused on moving the organization towards its ideal future, motivating them to overcome obstacles. Leaders are made, not born. Such organizational politics can be described as self-serving and manipulative in promoting their self-interests at the expense of others. Hence, I was concerned about the organization when I decided to be an active participant.

From the early part of 1989 to 1992, I witnessed the storm of gushing winds had developed; yet no "Winds of Change" were eminent. The problems that beset the association despite relentless calls for unity and reconciliation grew worse.

They evolved in the aftermath of every election. There was a long and simmering conflict between the contending factions, a usual pattern of actions in Filipino American organizations.

From being a member of the board of governors, delegate, and secretary and then speaker of the House of Delegates (HOD), I was very active for seventeen years in the association. APPA's growth was thwarted, its very foundation shaken by vindictive behavior, intolerance of personality differences, and petty politics of past and present leaders. Organizational politics was a struggle for resources, personal conflicts, competition of power and leadership, and tactical influence executed by individuals and groups to attain power. There were many who perverted integrity, the Constitution and bylaws of the association for their selfish political ends. Was it politics that is a reflection of the Filipino culture that doctor's political behavior mirrors innate particulars that are inherent in their culture?

I lost in the election.

Individual votes were being "bought" under the guise of dues payment. For instance, one Medical Society headed by a doctor running for secretary "allegedly paid APPA $3,000 for its fifty members' dues to bring them up to date with their voting credentials." And there were more of these.

I congratulated Dr. Cueto. I wished him luck in steering the organization in the right direction. I come out a wounded soldier; however, my wounds will heal and I will emerge as a stronger, wiser, and better person.

We must learn from our shortcomings in these elections. We all suffer setbacks in life and must learn the lesson of minimizing the impact of setback by accepting it with grace. How we face those setbacks defines our fitness to become leaders and role models. The House of Delegates, with its new and mandated powers, must be in the forefront in making sure these rules that we have labored so long to legislate must be followed. No organization can exist; much less prosper, without rules and the members' respect and adherence to them. For if we fail in our duties, I fear the day that our House rules will be supplanted by the law of a powerful few.

I did not return to APPA as I promised. Was I wrong not to return to APPA despite my promise? As I had confessed before, I am not overly ambitious politically. When Brutus murdered Julius Caesar because of his ambition, this time, I was not in AGONY despite having been a victim of a farcical election. With no sour grapes, I left the APPA with the hopes it would redeem itself and rediscover its compromised pride, honor and integrity, so that it would not perish from this earth. This is not to say Filipino Americans usually leave an organization after succumbing to the likes of a ludicrous and fraudulent fealty of the perverts in medical association.

While you and I have been a member of specialty organizations, state and the AMA, we do not see this ludicrous, 'Philippine political style' of fraud elections. This is a history of shame.

In all fairness things have since changed. I have heard APPA is in smooth and clear waters, and several of my friends are still active: Drs. Bofil, Jess Ho, and Vir Pilapil. Keep up the good work, gents.

Sorry if APPA now is snubbed. That isn't my intention - but this is a truthful history in the APPA.

CHAPTER ELEVEN

RUMINITIONS

The accent of one's birthplace remains in the
mind and in the heart as in one's speech.

- Francois de La Rochefoucauld

CHARLATANS IN THE PHILIPPINES

Dateline, July 13, 2011

WITH MY INADVERTENT meeting with a "faith healer, I become concerned of the practice of medicine in the Philippines by a "quack". They are considered as a "fraudulent or ignorant pretender to medical skill" or "a person who pretends, professionally or publicly, to have skill, knowledge, or qualifications he or she does not posses meaning, a charlatan." You may call it quackery. This is not "Holistic Medicine."

HOLISTIC MEDICINE: Before I describe the practice of quackery in the Philippines, I will define what is Holistic Medicine. The American Holistic Association, states that it is the art and science of healing that addresses care of the whole person - body, mind, and spirit. The practice of holistic medicine integrates conventional and complementary therapies to promote optimal health, and prevent and treat disease by addressing contributing factors. Furthermore, this approach is more complete and treats a patient like a whole person—not simply a piece of biological or organic machinery that needs to be fixed when its parts are broken or worn out. Such an approach offers treatments that target a person's physiology, psychology and spirituality.

In practice, this means that each person is seen as a unique individual, rather than an example of a particular disease. Disease is understood to be the result of physical, emotional, spiritual, social and environmental imbalance. Healing, therefore, takes place naturally when these aspects of life are brought into proper balance. The role of the practitioner is as a guide, mentor and role model; the patient must do the work - changing lifestyle, beliefs and old habits in order to facilitate healing. All appropriate methods may be used, from medication to meditation.

Of interest and acceptance, the Philippine Department of Health support and foster indigenous Philippine healing knowledge and herbal products. Heal and Wellness Alliance of the Philippines in partnership with the Department of Tourism, the Department of Health and the top medical institutions and wellness organizations are promoting overall, holistic health. Our department of health says there are healing modalities, knowledge and herbs outside of the US western medical paradigm. And we have laws protecting the rights and freedom of what you call "alternative" healing.

The World Heath Organization (WHO) of the United Nations had addressed Traditional medicine and has been discussed at several regional and sub regional meetings in recent years and was the subject of the technical briefing during the forty-ninth session of the WHO Regional Committee for the Western Pacific in 1998. Meetings of ministers of health of Pacific island countries in 1997, 1999 and 2001 discussed traditional medicine and made a number of recommendations designed to improve the practice of traditional medicine in Pacific island countries. It recommends that underdeveloped countries make use of their practice of traditional medicine to supplement the inadequacy of their health service programs. Even as of today, the so-called Western science-oriented societies now give recognition to some meritorious treatments through holistic medicine.

WHY FILIPINOS RESORT TO USE OF QUACKS: The practice of quackery among the Filipinos in spite of the advance in medical science still exists specially in the rural areas. In fact the uneducated rural folks believe more in the *herbolarios* (healers) than in the doctor. Our people in these areas adhere to some superstition and beliefs that no amount of coaxing can detract them and be led to the scientific know-how of real medical men.

To cure is to correct. To cure really means to care for and correct what is wrong. Disease is synonymous to distress, to not feeling at ease to pain. The sick need care and attention and the look for aid and love to all who can dispense it to them. And the charlatan all too often plays on the human motive, and frequently succeeds for more than the most skillful doctor. He asserts with fullest confidence and permits him to dominate his patients well. Since the earliest times, quacks of all sorts have preyed upon mankind and have been the source of trouble to qualified medical practitioners of all ages. Our era is no exception. It flourishes with quacks and quacks flourish through and inherent weakness in human nature.

The sick are petulant and prone to delusions. Like a drowning man, they seize anything that may readily relieve their distress of saving their lives. Since they need ease and comfort, they often find the charlatan and the most sympathetic to their plea.

Quackery: The antithesis of culture- The practicing of palpable frauds and financial extortions on our fellowmen by quacks and charlatans is surely the antithesis of the attainment of culture in our age.

Quacks are cunning and impudent. Because if their rash avariciousness, they tempt the sick to spend their money by means of false and deceptive publicity regarding their pills, herbs, and methods of cure which oftentimes is a poor imitations of a recent medical discovery. The promises of a quack rest on the sand, they bring just untold misery and useless expense and what is more tragic, the loss of life. In contradiction, medical men—the scientific doctor of today to whom experience and research have ultimately unveiled so many truths to announce to you, consider it their sacred duty to offer their scientific knowledge, experience and care, to this age of modern man with all its maladies. In the records of our medical societies we have numerous case histories too long to publish that emphasize the necessity for the laymen to make an early report of his sickness to the doctor, on the search of prevention or cure before it gets too late.

So long as there are fees to collect for service, and money at stake.... There will always be quacks and charlatans.

We could launch innumerable programs calculated to instill consciousness of modern medicine among the people but for as long as the faith healers and other varieties of herb doctors roam the country, these programs will not succeed. The thing to do is still to take to court the quack doctors whose practices seem to be flourishing even in such supposedly intelligent communities as Manila, where the Mecca of advance medicine from America is now available.

These vicious practices of quackery that infiltrated our people in the rural areas would be attributed to the following facts; they believed that there are cases of ailments, which cannot be cured by doctors but can be cured by a *Herbolario*. That these practices and beliefs still exist in our country is a reflection of the lack of adequate health education of the public.

How these impressions can be eradicated in the minds of our people is for the Department of Health to remedy before it can cause irreparable damage to lives of thousands of Filipinos. For no matter how superficially successful a quack doctor is, his luck will sooner or later run out, and he will then be nothing but a butcher capable only of harm to the community. It may be argued that we have licensed medical practitioners who are not any more competent than the herbolario. But this is again beside the point. For this law is on the side of even the mediocre medical school graduate. And this law is but wise, for surely, the health of the nation cannot be left in the hand of quack doctor. Otherwise witch-hunters will dominate the national health scene, and superstition and ignorance will continue to prevail.

ANTIQUE

Dateline, March 2011

I AM PROUD to be an Antiqueno. I was born and raised in the town of Pandan, the northernmost municipality of the province of Antique, which can be found on Panay Island in the Republic of the Philippines. Although I have been away from my hometown for many years, I still long for my simple, homespun pleasures, somewhere to spend the day lolling on sandy beaches or quiet brooks, unmolested by the noise and hustle of a nearby metropolis.

Antique is rich in history and legends, as it is beautiful with its white beaches and majestic peaks. One can experience nature's beauty at its best. With pristine waters the province is a temptation to both explorers and nature lovers. We have adapted gracefully to the various cultural climates, culling the best from each of these divergent cultures; as result, the Antiqueno genuine hospitality has been cultivated. We go out of our way to extend assistance to visitors and guests.

As a teen I often traveled during a two-year break from school. The trips were from Pandan to Iloilo City, past San Jose de Buenavista, the capital of Antique, and finally to Iloilo City. These trips were free since my uncle, Benjamin Candari, Sr., owned a passenger bus that made regular trips to Iloilo City. I would go to watch movies in Iloilo. You may wonder why I would go out of my way just to watch a few films. Well, a Milon Mayer's saying goes: "What can a man do who doesn't know what to do?" There were absolutely no jobs in my hometown for a college-educated person like me.

The trip from Pandan to Iloilo would take an entire day to travel a mere 124 miles. I would ride in an open passenger bus that frequently stopped to pick up and drop off passengers. The road was unpaved, rough, and gutted, making this dusty trip extremely unpleasant. In those days floods often destroyed the bridges in Antique, and passenger buses had to go through the water. The drivers had to carefully ensure they did not get stuck midway through and ensure the engine never stopped running. These were typical experiences of the 1950s that stay with me. All these trips left an imprint in my mind of not only the provincial town facades but also a beautiful picture of the surrounding mountains covered with lush forests of centuries-old trees, rich vegetation and diverse fauna. Extensive rice paddies, coconut trees, water systems that crisscross the roadways, major rivers, creeks, streams and beaches were frequently alongside the national road of Antique.

Presently the national roads of the province are fully paved and cemented into single-lane roadways provided in each direction.

With the advent of cyberspace, the Internet is loaded with online information about all places in the Philippines, our homeland. The province of Antique is one of them. An example:

"Allow yourself some enchantment and adventure. Visit Antique, historic land of the Binirayan festival, majestic mountains, cascading waterfalls, white beaches, rich fishing grounds and white water kayaking. Antique is a province of the Philippines located in the Western Visayas region. Its capital is San Jose and is located at the western portion of Panay Island, bordering Aklan, Capiz, and Iloilo to the east. Antique faces the Sulu Sea to the west."

Iloilo and Aklan are the gateways to Antique by land. It is also accessible from Palawan, Manila, Romblon, and Mindoro by sea. Buses and vans bound for San Jose and Libertad are stationed at the terminal in Molo District, Iloilo City. Transportation time from Iloilo City to the capital San Jose is 3 hours. To obtain more information on Antique, please visit http://google.com and search for Antique, Philippines.

I was astonished and little amused by the fact that some years ago, a few of my friends who are not Visayan still did not know where the province of Antique is, geographically speaking. And that is okay. One must realize that there are 7,100 Islands in the Philippines. In one of my speeches, I took advantage of mentioning the historical background of Antique and the special trait of an Antiqueno. They are ambitious, enterprising and hard working. They are proud of their heritage. A very flexible people, they have adopted gracefully to the various cultural climates to which they have been exposed and have culled and assimilated the best from each of this divergent cultures. They combine the leadership of Datu Puti from Borneo, the courage and wisdom of Marikudo, the system of laws by Sumakwel, the religious fervor of the Spaniards, and the sense of fair play and self-sufficiency of the Americans.

The national roads of the province are fully paved and cemented into single-lane roadways provided in each direction.

ANTIQUE SHAPED LIKE A SEAHORSE

Dateline, 2011

SIMILAR TO THE shape of a seahorse, the Antique province is a long stretch of narrow lowland. It nestles between the blue China Sea to the west and the tall mountain ranges to the east. The steep slopes and rugged long mountain ranges of Antique have kept it from the rest of Panay. If indeed it has the appearance of a seahorse, my hometown Pandan, anatomically speaking is situated at the neck of the marine fish. The absence of pulses in this area signifies death, but oh no, Pandan has normal regular strong pulses that Antique must never worry about. That's a joke. There is a saying by Woody Allen: "the structure of a joke is the juxtaposition of the trivial and the mundane... we have to reconcile the paradox of it all. The joke mirrors that paradox." Seahorses have no carotid arteries.

Antique is a second-class province composed of eighteen municipalities stretched along the coast of the South China Sea. The province of Aklan is in the north; Capiz, Iloilo, and Guimaras are in the south. There are eighteen municipalities and coastal towns endowed with nature's scenic exquisiteness. One can find many tourist destinations and attractions with an abundance of sumptuous delicacies and world-class products.

The rugged and varied land of Antique offers visitors a variety of outdoor activities. Diving and beach enthusiasts will enjoy discovering the unspoiled islets of Antique – the Nogas Island, Hurao-Hurao Island and Malalison Island. These islands have long stretches of white sand beaches and are ideal for shell hunting.

The communities, towns and barangays all over the Philippines must take the trouble to reconstruct their own history. Once they are compiled and validated, all the loose strands can be woven into that larger national narrative that is truly Philippine history.

Writing about Antique is incomplete without visiting the historic legends and folklorist stories that led it to be dubbed as the "Cradle of Philippine Civilization."

The history of pre-Hispanic time and the legends relative to Antique 800 years ago are simply fascinating. The Maragtas Legend was believed to be a document, which dated in between 1200 to 1250. It is about the ten datus, or chiefs, who escaped the tyranny of Datu Makatunaw of Borneo and immigrated to the island of Panay. According to the legend, in the middle of the thirteenth century (year 1250), ten Bornean Datus (led by Datu Puti) and their wives, children, warriors, servants and followers left Borneo due to the cruelty, oppression and tyranny of Sultan Makatunao. According to historians and folklorists, they landed in December at Malandog, three kilometers away from San Jose de Buenavista. The landing was also reported to be at Siriwagan, San Joaquin and the Province of Iloilo. Two fishing Negritos informed the datus their leader Chieftain Marikudo and his wife Maniwangtiwan were living nearby in Sinugbo. The datus went downstream and found the Ati ruler. Negotiations were made and the "Barter of Panay" took place. Panay was bought in exchange for a gold salokot (hat) for Marikudo and a long, golden necklace for Maniwangtiwan. The Atis relocated themselves in the hinterlands, the area high in mountains, and left the lowlands to the Borneans. The other three datus sailed northward to Luzon, leaving the seven datus under the leadership of Datu Sumakwel, the oldest and the wisest among them. The island was later divided into three "sakops" (areas): Hamtik, Aklan and Irong-Irong. In later times, Hamtik became Antique, Aklan became Capiz and Irong-Irong became Iloilo. Antique was where Sumakwel founded a system of laws, or the Code of Sumakwel. Datu Puti returned to Borneo to fight the tyranny.

These ten chiefs and their families were the ancestors of the entire Visayan population. The datus and their families were said to be responsible for populating the entire Visayan region and for forming a confederation of barangays (villages) called Madya-as under the leadership of Datu Sumakwel. For the last fifty years the Ati-atihan festival is celebrated in Pandan, as is the Ati-atihan Mardi Gras of the Santo Nino in Kalibo, Aklan.

MY KIND OF TOWN '(PANDAN IS)'
ECO-TOURISM DESTINATION

Dateline, June 16, 2012

ALMOST ALL OF us Filipino Americans are nostalgic about our hometown in the Philippines. It's hard to be nostalgic when you can't remember anything. Well, I do remember a multitude about my hometown.

At this very moment when Philippine Tourism is much promoted, the department's new slogan, "It's more fun in the Philippines" is going places. "More than 100,000 British tourists traveled to the Philippines in 2011 — an all-time high," the DOT said. Tourists from the United Kingdom lead the European visitor traffic to the Philippines and rank 10th overall. With the DOT-Manila who promoted the country worldwide through CNN International, and and in the UK, it is expected to jump-start the government's bid to draw 10 million tourist arrivals by 2016.

This is not my ad. Nostalgia is the right word.

The name of my town is Pandan. It used to be one of the impecunious towns in the province of Antique located in the island of Panay of the Philippine Archipelago (Visayan region).

The first time I visited my town was in 1978, eighteen years after I left for America. There was no electricity. The streets were pitch-dark after six pm. Now, it has changed to a progressive town with places of ecotourism's Paradise. Great water supply. The system was built through a joint undertaking of the Japan Asian Friendship Society and the Local Government of Pandan- draws water from a spring located in Malumpati. The Aklan Electric Cooperative (AKELCO) supplies electricity to the municipality. Pandan Beach Resort's computer and wireless Internet Services are in place- the Wonder of Cyberspace- cell phones are everywhere.

It is about 13 miles from the well renowned white beach Boracay Resort Island. Unique about the location of Pandan, it is geographically a "voca calle" (junction) to travelers, tourists and traders to and from Mindoro, Aklan, Capiz, Iloilo and Boracay Island. This geographical advantage plays a role in trade, commerce, industry and tourism.

In the 2000 census, it had a population of 27,647 people in 5,534 households with 34 *barangay*. A native of Pandan, I am proud of the beauty and nature's lavishness, the aura and ambience of a wonderful place for ecotourism. There is the creation of the Bugang River Nature, Cultural and Adventure Tour, a collaborative effort of the Tourism Office of Pandan with the barangays of Sto. Rosario, Guia, Candari and Zaldivar.

Pandan town is a mixture of flat and hilly terrain. The central and northwestern coastal area is level, the rest of the northern part from slightly to strongly rolling. The Northeastern part is hilly to mountainous. Innumerable creeks and seven major rivers criss-cross the land surface.

Every tourist will be amazed and impressed of Malumpati Spring, which leads to Bugang River, a favored place. I will brag - not like a braggadocio - that I feel proud of the beauty of the Bugang River of my hometown Pandan, Antique, Philippines. This river won in 2006 the President's Award for Environment "Gawad Pangulo sa Kapaligiran" as the cleanest inland body of water in the Philippines. In Latin, a *paradisiacus* rivulet of water in a desert of sand. It has been a Gold Winner in the International Green Apple Environment Awards for Environmental Best Practice, Local Authorities and Ecotourism category in London. The Bugang River, with its blue clear, tranquil flow of water that illuminates purity along the barrio Candari (my ancestry) and the barrio Zaldivar, the former governor and Associate Justice of the Supreme Court of the Philippines, cousin of my dad. The people of Pandan, Antique are very proud of the cleanest river in the Philippines. Add to this is the Malumpati Resort, again with a nature made swimming pool of fresh spring water with jumping board enjoyed by visitors who flock to the

Malumpati Health Resort. The place have an invigorating and overwhelming freshness, the blue waters from turquoise blue to sapphire blue are inviting and the surrounding milieu of lush green trees and other vegetations hugging the edge of the nature's swimming pool is a paradise to behold. It will energize your soul – rouse your senses. It is said the pool possesses a 'healing phenomenon'. Its depth remains a mysterious puzzle to everyone. There are headsprings and caves and are absolutely ideal place for those who would like to commune with nature and for adventure lovers. Trekking is a wondrous thing around Malumpati Spring, its height and beauty with endemic species of its flora and fauna.

For Ecotourism – the buzzword term applied to tourism and travel that pays special attention to environmental concerns, Pandan have it. This destination is the best in the province of Antique. This is enriching personal experiences and environmental awareness. This is the getaway body and soul experience at Malumpati Resort. A place to enjoy, to relax, unwind, relieve tension, bring balance to the entire body, compliment your health, and consequently create calming and healing responses for the body and soul. This is to provide a soothing, healing vacation care atmosphere on the cool water pool.

Here's a slogan, ""It's more fun in the Philippines". It has gone viral.

OTHER RESORTS IN PANDAN

Pandan Beach Resort with Marquessa's Bar in Dionela is only 5 minutes from town - a waterfront retreat and restaurant with a serene atmosphere owned and managed by a good friend Gigi. You will experience a heartfelt service where tropical living is at its finest. It is the ideal destination for guests whether it is for business or pleasure. Enjoy incredible sunsets, breathtaking nature, pristine waters, hear the sound of the sea as the waves lap against the shore and the tide rises; the beach is infinite, quiet, tranquil surroundings. The gourmet foods are fantastic- a cultural ideal associated with the culinary arts of fine food and drink a selection of cocktails, mixes and wines.

For accommodation, Pandan Beach Resort has eight air-conditioned rooms with toilet and bath with hot and cold shower, television and refrigerator. It has one dormitory-type fan room with toilet and bath, which could accommodate at least ten persons.

Pandan Resorts that meet international standard with first class facilities and amenities are:
- Pandan Beach Resort in Dionela
- Rosepoint Beach in Mag-Aba
- Le Palme Beach Resort in Zaldivar

Standard category resort and inn:
- Green Park Hotel in Centro Sur with Olympic-size swimming pool
- Bunny's Beach Resort in Mag-Aba
- Unterpertinger Place in Jinalinan
- Rovel's Inn in Dionela
- Mico's in Baybay
- Bulod de Saresan Farm Resort in Callan
- Sta Cruz Farm Resort and Family Retreat

If you like the Golden Beaches, visit Duyong and Tingib, excellent for beach lovers and sports enthusiasts.

How to get to Pandan: International visitors can reach Pandan through various international airports located in the country. Most accessible is the Ninoy Aquino International Airport in Manila. From there, anybody can choose to take air transportation going to either Iloilo City, Roxas City, Caticlan or Kalibo. Kalibo Airport is approximately fifty-five (55) km from Pandan and serves three (3) commercial flights daily.

From Caticlan town, Aklan, a jump-off point to Boracay is only about thirty (30) km to Pandan. Our town is a neighbor of Boracay. To those who will visit Boracay, stop over in Pandan to see its beauty- the ecotourism wonder.

REMINISCING THE PAST - MY TOWN

Dateline, June 2012

I REMEMBER MY visit home to Pandan in April 1978, my first in eighteen years. There was no electricity in town. Now, it is a progressively growing town.

I went home with my wife Cely and my father for a short vacation and attended the municipal and religious 'fiesta'of Pandan. My Tia (Aunt) Pasing and her husband Tio (Uncle) Dadong Sardina were thrilled to welcome us and were extremely hospitable as well. Tio Dadong, a member of the town council, and Mayor Plaridel Z. Sanchez invited me speak at one of the town fiesta's gatherings at the Town Park Pavilion. I spoke about my beloved high school Alma Mater, Pandan Bay Institute (PBI), across the street from the Park Pavilion. I expressed my sincere gratitude to the Mill Hill Mission under the Mill Hill fathers, stating my alma mater could be compared to my dear parents who had made me follow the guiding star. I conveyed my gratitude to Rev. Father Ignacio Dionela, the parish priest who had founded PBI in 1947, and to the president of the board of directors, Lolo (Grandfather) Mariano (Anoy) Dioso. Among the original teachers were Jose Rectra, assistant principal, my aunt Teodora D. Alojipan, and my godmother Maria Varon. I was reflecting the time I spent in high school where I graduated with high honors. This was one of the best days of my life. I continued to speak:

"Speaking to you this afternoon gives me the opportunity to represent the Pandananons abroad and the ability to share our jubilations and joy over the achievements we have accomplished as well as our dreams and shared values for the common good of our hometown Pandan. It also provides me the opportunity to inspire others to reaffirm their vision, loyalty and sense of duty; their commitment and dedication towards improving the socioeconomic conditions of the people of Pandan; joint celebration of our town and the religious fiesta. All this reflects the extraordinary and

genuine harmony under the leadership of your present mayor, Plaridel Z. Sanchez.

In terms of historical perspective, I remember our 'fiesta' many years ago when I was growing up in this town, 'nagatuhay-tuhay ang fetcha,' (the dates were different). I considered Pandan in those times a community of factions for both political and religious orientations. We were divided into enclaves of kin, the air of bitterness between the two religious groups were blatantly apparent. Do I see it now? No. That divisive atmosphere is all gone. The people of Pandan have eventually come to the point of realization that in order to move forward there must be unity and understanding. I have been informed that the Urihing tubo (young generation) led by Bobby Alojipan has something to contribute to this air of unity. The unification of the town and religious fiesta in 1974 is a legacy of the late Mayor Plaridel Sanchez---a milestone to remember. Now, the celebration of the town's Saint (San Vicente Ferrer), both the Catholic and the Philippines Independent Church, and the celebration of the town fiesta signify our harmonious and unified town. We celebrate in the spirit of what our elders termed the SANDUGO (traditional rites). It is significant in this celebration that we Pandananons bring to life the cultural riches of our heritage at the heart of which is our tradition of hospitality and graciousness of our kasimanwa (town mates). But beyond that, the 'fiesta' is a showcase of the faithful demonstration of Philippine life, giving us a sense of living history and a glorious history of the living past. I am proud to be a Pandananon and an Antiqueno."

After the town fiesta, my wife Cely and I flew via Philippine Airlines from Iloilo City to Manila. Ike Zaldivar provided us his jeep to take the road to San Jose. It was a joyful ride on the unpaved road, reminiscent of what I had experienced in my youth. In San Jose, Atty. Esdras Tayco invited us to have lunch with the members of the Rotary Club of Antique. He was a relative and a prominent practicing lawyer in the province. After speaking in the Rotary Club, we proceeded to Iloilo City by car provided by my friend and Antique Governor Evelio Javier.

ANTIQUE ASSOCIATION OF SOUTHERN CALIFORNIA

Dateline, 1984

THERE IS AN amusing story of being a vice president of the Antique Association of Southern California. I submitted my curriculum vitae to the members of the City Council of San Diego when I was vying for a commissioner position as board of governor of the San Diego Stadium Authority. Almost everyone was extremely interested and asked me if they could see my antique collection. Those who did not ask may have been impressed that I was so indulged in such an expensive hobby.

In 1973 the Antique Association of Southern California (AASC) was founded in Los Angeles. The late Dr. Ernesto de la Cruz, PhD., and Atty. Sofia L. Nietes were the primary brains and movers in establishing this non-profit social welfare organization. I was elected as vice president to represent San Diego County.

My love for Antique has never faded. Being the vice president of the Antique Association of Southern California for several years had given me the privilege to serve my community. Dr. Ernesto de la Cruz was a close friend who stayed in the home of my sister Eden in Santa Monica, California. Here was where we discussed how to pool the talents and energies of Antiquenos into a unified effort to establish closer ties among each other while engaging them in worthwhile activities to improve the standard of living in Antique. We recognized that Antiquenos were scattered all over southern California. We would meet once in a while at social gatherings and other functions, but these encounters were limited only to close friends and relatives. There was a need for involvement with our province mates in the area, some of whom we had not met. We felt a feeling of nostalgia for our old province, a common homesickness that made us want to know each other better and share our lives together.

In the preliminary meetings of some thirty Antiquenos, we unanimously agreed there was a need to help the needy people back home. These poor families remained poor and were unable to get education and healthcare. This situation became AASC's major rallying point. In our August 1973 meeting, the officers were elected, with Dr. de la Cruz as the president and Atty. Sofia Nietes as the executive vice president.

Everything went smoothly in the association and four projects were in place: scholarship, student loan funds, a hospital drive named as Operation *"Kasing-kasing"* (heart), and a book drive. Five students, five hospitals and eighteen rural health units were the recipients of our donations.

What did the AASC members attribute this success? It was the COMMITMENT AND UNITY by every member to share. Commitment stood on the strong foundation of self-sacrifice and cooperation.

For every smile, a tear must fall. Even as the AASC rejoiced over its successes in 1976, it also had its share of grief. My sister Eden Candari Baclig, a senior member of the AASC board of directors and one of the founding members, passed away in September 1976, leaving behind a remarkable record of service to the association. Despite a two-year lingering illness that could have otherwise totally incapacitated her, my sister was still very much involved with the AASC until her last breath. The Antiquenos in southern California will always emulate her altruism and spirit of cooperation.

FRIENDS LTD.

Dateline, 1993

THE ASSOCIATION OF Philippine Physicians in America (APPA) botched to adhere to the key elements of supportive value system: the virtues of concern, readiness to assist each other, mutual sharing and tolerance, self sacrifice, honesty and unity. With all that, I came to realize that my dreams, desires and aspirations were non-achievable.

General Douglas McArthur did return when he promised, "I shall return". Was I wrong not to return to APPA despite my promise? As I had confessed before, I am not overly ambitious politically. When Brutus murdered Julius Caesar because of his ambition, this time, I was not in AGONY despite having been a victim of a farcical election. With no sour grapes, I left the APPA with the hopes it would redeem itself and rediscover its compromised pride, honor and integrity, so that it would not perish from this earth. This is not to say that Filipino Americans usually leave an organization if they had succumbed to the likes of a ludicrous and fraudulent election.

FRIENDS are a group of individuals where friendship, camaraderie, unity and love pervade. Absolutely, nobody had a semblance of a **bête noire** of the oligarchic designs of the few remaining as senior officials of the APPA. But the most important and significant loss for the APPA was the departure of a group of high-caliber visionary leaders, honorable men and women with untarnished integrity and dedication. Dr. Daniel Fabito, initiated the formation of FRIENDS, acted as the first Chairman until Dr. Rolly Santos took over.

It was profoundly consoling to note that the Leadership Alliance was my ally in my decision not to return to the APPA. This was indeed a blessing in disguise. My involvement in the Far Eastern University DNRSM Alumni Foundation, and my beloved alma mater, FEU Institute of Medicine, was at hand for my full service dedication, which was also rightfully true for most members of the

Leadership Alliance.

We had a yearly get-together. If not a reunion of twice a year, we gathered on special occasions, especially at gala wedding celebrations of our sons and daughters. This gathering took place in different cities of the U.S. My daughter Marjorie's wedding was in Indianapolis, Indiana, thousands miles away from our home city of San Diego. And yes, the FRIENDS were there as in the following decade and a half, where we were in attendance at the ultra grandiose wedding celebrations of each other's families. So as not to miss or remember any of our wonderful reunions, I apologize for not mentioning all of them. For our reunions, no city was considered too far for us, no expense too great, and the time spent away from our medical practice was compensated by the precious opportunity to be together. I planned on drafting the goals and objectives of FRIENDS with the help of Dr. Art Basa and tried to define what FRIENDS are really for. This plan did not materialize. Enumerable articles are written about the subject of friendship and how they are defined; however, my research on Wikipedia has come up with some pragmatic points about the nature of friendship:

- "Friendship is the cooperative and supportive relationship between people. In this sense, the term connotes a bond that involves mutual respect, affection, and esteem along with a degree of rendering service to friends in times of need or crisis.
- Friends will welcome each other's company and exhibit unselfishness towards each other.
- Their likings will usually be similar and may converge, and they will share enjoyable togetherness.
- They will also engage in mutually helping manner, such as the exchange of advice and the sharing of hardship.
- A friend is someone who may often demonstrate reciprocating and reflective actions. Yet for some, the practical execution of friendship is little more than the confidence that someone will not harm them."

Humanitarian projects are included in our goals and objectives, and medical missions to the Philippines were part of our accomplishments. The Philippine Economic and Cultural Endowment (PEACE) on Artesian Wells Project and other humanitarian program are vigorously participated. Kudos goes to Dr. Sarie Laserna.

MEDICAL ALUMNUS CLASS '61

"History is a nightmare from which we
are trying to awaken"

- JAMES JOYCE

FAR EASTERN UNIVERSITY INSTITUTE OF MEDICINE

Dateline, April 2011

IN JULY 2002, I was elected as executive vice president of the Far Eastern University-Dr. Nicanor Reyes School of Medicine Alumni Foundation (DNRSM Alumni Foundation) that was established in America in 1971. I considered this position as a stepping-stone for the Presidency and Chairmanship of the board, which was the usual succession of leadership in the Alumni Foundation. The Foundation is a non-profit corporation that assists our beloved alma mater, Far Eastern University- FEU-NRMF Medical Center located at Fairview, Quezon City, Republic of the Philippines, to maintain and conduct a medical school and to administer donations. There are over 2,600 FEU alumni physicians practicing in the United States of America. The Foundation became a pre-eminent U.S.-based alumni foundation supporting a Philippine Medical School. In the last four decades of its existence, the assets of the Alumni Foundation have come close to $2 million.

From the time I started as a member of the Medical Alumni Foundation in 1978, Dr. Renato Ramos, chairman of the board of trustees for about seven years, has given me the inspiration, high energy and enthusiasm to serve our organization.

I consider him a friend, highly deserving of my profound respect and inspiration. His sterling leadership, compassion, integrity and intelligence are incredibly commendable. I became a member of the board of trustees in 1984. For nine years, I served as vice president of the Foundation. I will never forget when Dr. Ramos, as chairman emeritus, spoke to the board of trustees on my behalf to elect me as executive vice president: "Dr. Cesar Candari is the next person to be in the executive vice president position based upon the standard practice of succession. No other person is over Cesar's qualifications." I did not seek this position, yet somehow there was this person who recognized impartiality with a non-political intuition and a pure, genuine decision of selecting persons for senior positions in the Alumni Medical Foundation. It was a challenge, a prestige and a bigger chance to be at the highest leadership level of our Alma Mater's organization.

HOST OF BOARD MEETING

I cannot forget when I hosted the regular board of trustees meeting in San Diego California on March 14-15, 1997, at the Embassy Suites Hotel in San Diego Bay. A Continuing Medical Education (CME) speaker was a world-renowned physician, Dr. Elizabeth Barrett-Connor, professor and chairman of the department of Family Preventive Medicine at the University of California in San Diego. It was at the time when Dr. Daniel Fabito was the board chairman. He is one of the most outstanding alumni whose leadership ability is beyond reproach.

The meeting was well attended by the board of trustees. Part of the major agenda was the ground breaking of the new site for the FEU medical school campus and hospital from Morayta/Espana to Fairview, Quezon City. The blueprints showed a hospital and medical school that would have the distinction of being the only medical school in the Philippines to have modern and brand-new facilities. We discussed maintaining and supporting the vital needs of the medical school in the form of funded professional chairs, funded entrance students scholarships, and over $200,000 dollars in undesignated class funds.

After that meeting at the Embassy Suites, a dinner reception was held in our home in Del Cerro, replete with exquisite native foods, wining, dancing and singing. The late Dr. Romeo Abella of Los Angeles was on the piano all night. The late Dr. Beth Jimenez, the beautiful, friendly, and talented wife of Dr. Cesar Jimenez, was the leader in the impromptu 'line-dancing.'

My wife and I were very thankful and honored that nine members of the board accepted our offer of a two-night accommodation in our home.

Our reunions had been enjoyable and memorable festive events. Since 1992, I had been chosen as the master of ceremonies (emcee) of the Grand Ball that highlighted the celebration of Class '67 Silver Jubilarian. It was Dr. Ramos' idea to introduce me into public eye at the time when I was a candidate for President of the APPA. I will never forget the Silver Jubilarian celebration held at the downtown Marriott Hotel in San Francisco that coincided with the July 4th Independence Day celebration. Dr. Arsenio Martin, the class president, presented a grandiose jubilee celebration under his leadership. Dr. Renato Ramos, the chairman of the board, whispered that my emcee performance is   presidential. I was not sure what he meant. I was then running for president of the Association of Philippine Physicians in America (APPA). In our succeeding four reunions, I did the same task of being the emcee in the Filipiniana Night and the Grand Ball, helping keep the events moving smoothly.

FORTY-TWO MICROSCOPES: In 1998, during the chairmanship of Dr. Daniel Fabito of the Alumni Foundation, I was vice president of the board of trustees. Dr. Fabito, a man of superior intelligence, well-known for his role of emotions and vision, as well as leadership effectiveness and performance, assigned me to chair an ad-hoc committee to respond to the letter of Dr. Liberato C. de la Rosa, chairman of the department of microbiology and parasitology, FEU-NRMF, Institute of Medicine.

"We would like to request some help from you in improving our laboratory facilities being used by our students. We need about sixty binocular microscopes in the Department of Microbiology and Parasitology," de la Rosa's letter to Dr. Dan Fabito.

By then the new building and laboratory at Fairview, Quezon City, was about to be completed. Dr. de la Rosa quoted that the Philippine price for each "Norinco" microscope was 41,000 pesos each vs. an "Olympus microscope" of $1,025.00.

I was extremely happy to chair this committee. It has given me the inspiration and enthusiasm to be of service to our organization. This was a challenge, a prestige, and a bigger chance to fortify a dream to help my beloved alma mater. In 1999, in one of the meetings of the board, I presented with complete slide demonstrations of binocular microscopes and their prizes.

On May 15, 1999, I wrote a memo to Dr. Fabito stating the Olympus was a much better microscope, and I offered to negotiate the price. I strongly suggested that each class of alumni be asked to donate $2,000 immediately. I exchanged letters with Dr. de la Rosa and assured him that we were working hard to grant his request.

On July 12, 1999, I wrote a letter to each class president, from Class '57 to Class '89 and the jubilarians. This letter was also printed in the Ectopic Murmurs FEU-DNRSM newsletter to solicit the generous support by contributing two or three microscopes.

At the winter meeting of the Board in St. Louis, Missouri, in March 2000, I presented again the request for the microscopes and finally, it was unanimously approved. Dr. Emelie Ongcapin, the investment and financial coordinator, was instructed to release the funds for the purchase of CH20 Olympus microscopes with a quoted price of 28,000 pesos per scope.

Finally, Dr. de la Rosa wrote me a letter on October 30, 2000, stating that forty-two microscopes were purchased, and expressed his appreciation and thanks to the officers and members of the FEU -DNRSM Alumni Foundation (he later corrected it verbally to sixty microscopes when I met him last January 2011). This was one of my greatest and most memorable accomplishments under the Chairmanship of Dan Fabito.

DONATIONS TO OPHTHALMOLOGY DEPARTMENT

The late Dr. Eduardo Manaig, an alumnus of the FEU-DNR Medical School and I appealed to the Paradise Valley Lions Club of San Diego (we were both active officers of the club) for ophthalmology equipment to be donated to the FEU ophthalmology department.

On August 15, 2003, I received a letter of appreciation from Dr. Reynaldo B. De Vega, Acting Medical Director, and similarly from Dr. Azora B. Capuchino, chairman of the Ophthalmology Department. In its entirety, Dr. De Vega's letter stated:

Dr. Cesar Candari
Dr. Eduardo Manaig
Paradise Valley Rotary Club of San Diego, California USA District 5340

"Dear Dr. Candari and Dr. Manaig:

On behalf of the FEU – NRMF Medical Center, the undersigned would like to acknowledge with gratitude your donation of:

- 1 Unit SL, CSO, 990 Slit Lamp 2X Mag. Mounted to Table (Spring Set to Slit Lamp)
- 1 Unit TO, DIG, Applanation Tonometer R900, New

These will help us a lot and will be utilized in the Department of Ophthalmology where they are most needed. Here is hoping that more graces will come your way in days to come. Again we thank you most sincerely.

Signed: Dr. de Vega"

FEU MY ALMA MATER

Dateline, January 2011

MY ALMA MATER can be compared to my dear parents who made me to be what I am today. This statement could be true to anyone. It is not an exaggeration when I say that ninety percent are nostalgic about their time in the schools and universities from which they graduated in their chosen profession. Those days, the best in my life, gave me an evergreen impact in my mind, and I became a dreamer ready to embrace life with passion.

We gain a lot more than just an education from our medical schools, and it is imperative that we try to give back as much as we can. We must realize that we are giving back for the future and continued development of our institution. Our donations go a long way to sustain our alma maters' regular programs and initiatives to support deserving students. It will help improve the education and curriculum being offered by our alma mater. I have volunteered my time as service to give back, realizing that I am helping someone gain the valuable asset of a quality education in my medical school.

I wish to express my highest respect and deepest gratitude to the people who have inspired me to participate in the leadership of the Foundation for over twenty-five years. A number of people have inspired my tenure in the board of trustees and as an officer in this foundation for so many years. Dr. Renato Ramos, the former chairman of the board, was there to support me, as we have known one-another for a long time. I consider him a bright person, energetic, and an excellent leader. He is nothing less than a dreamer and a goal-oriented achiever, a man of effulgent vision and wisdom, honesty and integrity. Thank you to all past chairmen of the boards for their trust and confidence in appointing me as chairman of the constitution and bylaws. I am proud of my services.

I retired from practicing medicine eleven years ago, but I made a pledge that my loyalty and support of my alma mater will never fade. However, because of health reasons, I will not be able to run for president of the Foundation. It was a hard decision to make. Allow me to take this opportunity to thank you one and all. It was a privilege to work with all of you.

Above all, it was beyond my expectation to be acquainted with Dr. Josephine C. Reyes, chairman of the board of trustees, a venerable and pleasurable woman, a humble patrician. The first time I met her personally was in 1981 at the Anaheim convention.

In February 2011, I spoke to Dr. Arsenio Martin, immediate past chairman of the FEU -DNRSM Alumni Foundation. I have known him for a long time and consider him a bright person, an excellent leader, another dreamer. A goal oriented man, he very much deserves his many awards from his career and humanitarian endeavors.

Dr. Arsenio Martin's brilliant and outstanding capability as leader of the scholarship program of the Foundation produced a top notch in the recent medical board examination in the Philippines, i.e., in French, *fait accompli*.

Because there was a hiatus in my attendance to the annual reunion and scientific convention due to a major ailment, he wished me to attend the next reunion. I said I was looking forward to next year's convention in Las Vegas. Yes, it would be the United Class '61's Golden Jubilee. Dr. Martin was the very first person that informed me of his sincere desire for choosing me as a recipient of year 2011 FEU alumnus awardee. His word is trustworthy. With all humility, I wish to thank him for his kind heart, his trust, loyal friendship, respect, and a man who has dignity and grace, a paragon physician.

I am a member of the Golden Jubilarians. I have since recovered from my ailment, and I am now back on my journey with both feet forward.

I should also mention that I have been recognized as one of the longest-serving board trustee-at-large of the Alumni Foundation. The Ectopic Murmur in June 1992, Vol. 3 No. 2 Dr. Ramos stated: "With FEUDNRSM Alumni Foundation, Dr. Candari is one of the longest serving board trustees." This was at the time when I was vying for President of the Association of Philippine Physicians in America (APPA).

I became a member of the Alumni Foundation in 1978 and attended the very first reunion held at the Marriott in Lincolnshire, Illinois, in 1980. The succeeding years of annual reunions and scientific seminars in different cities of North America became my yearly schedule of attendance. Eventually I rose to the position of member of the Board of Trustees-at-Large of the Alumni Foundation during the 1984 convention at the Indian Lake Resort in Chicago, Illinois. I do remember that starting in year 1993, I was elected as vice president for a total term of nine years and two years as executive vice president.

UNITED CLASS '61 COVERAGE

IN THE CLASS '61 alumni, I took the liberty of writing the diary articles of every important event such as the 25th anniversary **(Silver)** 35th anniversary **(Coral)**, 40th anniversary **(Ruby)**, the 45th anniversary **(Sapphire)**, and the 50ᵗʰ **(Golden)** anniversary for posterity.

SILVER JUBILARIAN - 25th ANNIVERSARY JULY 27-30, 1986

Dateline, August 1986

I HAVE LONG BEEN relentlessly active in the class '61 reunions and social activities. There is no question the class fervently supported our alma mater. Our 25th Silver Jubilee was on July 27-30, 1986, held at the Cavalier Oceanfront Hotel in Virginia Beach, Virginia. Thirty-three jubilarians attended this festive anniversary celebration. This was followed by a silver jubilee celebration in Manila in December 1986; a grand ball held at the Silahis Hotel and on the second day, a dinner party at the beautiful home of Lilia Luna. It was an evening full of joy and happiness. We laughed, ate and reminisced during this most memorable evenings. I will never forget this reunion, seeing my classmates including my ex-fiancée after twenty-five years.

It was in 1994, the United Class '61 finally published the hardbound 33rd Anniversary Yearbook by Philip Chua. His energy, dedication, labor of love and patience made this possible. It took him seven years of gathering the materials to produce this awe-inspiring yearbook, which was beyond our imagination. He is a man worthy of our admiration. No one and no other class were able to duplicate it. It was Philip's own hard work and the envy of other classes. If I am feeling very proud, please indulge me and forgive me. My pride of the United Class of '61 is simply so great.

The New Orleans reunion in July 1994, reminded me of our first impromptu part in the program during the Filipiniana Night when Philip performed his talent *ala* Lance Burton. I was the emcee and was asked to sing a popular 'Visayan' folk song for United Class of '61 who danced in style and was highly appreciated.

Our class group luncheon was unbelievably full of contentment, joy and glee. Everyone wanted to be Letterman and Leno's comic style with rampage of *pinoy* jokes.

Every time that the class '61 has a reunion, my three buddies in medical school were foremost in my mind: Manuel Catalan, Gerardo Delfin and Bonifacio Gamo. Both Gerry and Boni had passed away. Manny has always kept in touch with me. He even visited me in San Diego several times with his pretty wife and our classmate Amelia (Pally) Levardo. At one time we traveled together on a carnival cruise and had a most memorable and wonderful time. Every time my wife and I are in Manila, they always entertained us. I admired his professional career, successes, opulence, public popularity and respect by the community of Carmona, Cavite. He owns a hospital in Carmona. He wrote lately and stated: "...but I do manage to stay young. I am still involved in activities like biking and dancing multiple times a week. At seventy-six, I am still active in my medical practice in Sto. Tomas, Batangas and running my hospital in Carmona, Cavite."

SHINING CORAL – 35th ANNIVERSARY CLASS '61 JULY 1996

Dateline, August 1996

BLOOMINGTON, MINNESOTA, WAS the chosen venue where one out of six people owned a boat, one out of three owned a fishing license, and nearly everyone spent at least some part of the year relaxing by the lake.

On a bright summer day, the six sparkling lakes in the heart of Minneapolis seemed as blue as lapis lazuli, their shimmering surfaces spangling with rowboats, canoes, and sailboats. Not far from Bloomington, where the Mississippi and Minnesota rivers join together, are the Twin Cities of Minneapolis and St Paul, the choice spot for our reunion.

The skies were hazy, the humidity fair, with rainfall at times; nonetheless, it did not matter much to the attendees. The host and local alumni chapter made good their promise of fun and festivities and a superb CME program. Altogether, it was a very successful reunion of friends, classmates, and our families.

Some twenty-five members of the United Class '61 alumni, the Coral Jubilarians, were there. Coral symbolizes a deep pink color, reminiscent of the showy pink-and-white lady's slipper, the official flower of Minnesota. At thirty-five years after graduation for United Class '61, pink was incredibly beautiful. It was majestic.

From the very first day of the festivities, with a welcome reception motif of "Back to the 50s," it was evident that the reunion was full of nostalgic moments from the Morayta/Azcaraga/Quezon Boulevard/Espana campus. The pomp and feast during the Filipiniana Night showed a musical extravaganza spotlighting the hidden talents of the Coral graduates of 1961. It was an outstanding performance on the stage, with a chorus of the *Kundiman* dedicated to our alma mater under the baton of Philip Chua.

The practice sessions were full of fun. We were no longer highly intellectual, serious, respectable doctors of sorts; we simply became our true selves, the boys and girls of the FEU days of yore. With all the laughter, the giggling, and the kidding, one had to marvel at this spontaneous transformation of happy human beings. It was as if we were at the FEU campus again.

At the luncheon's get-together with our spouses, we resolved to convince a classmate who missed the gathering to attend the next reunion in Dallas. Meanwhile, a cruise was being entertained to take place soon. Certainly the spirit of Class '61 was vibrant, alive, more reinvigorated, thanks to the super leadership of Philip. Philip's magic and the off-colored jokes of the boys - Pat Avila, Dick Chiu (hubby of Isabel Uy), and yours truly- also entertained us. If there were any punch lines in those jokes, Baby Espino De Leon missed them most of the time.

The grand dinner ball was resounding proof that the Class '61's spirit was high and well in the hearts of its members. Cameras were clicking as we posed here and there. I had a funny feeling that we had invented in our vernacular the absolute adjective of *katakot-takot na kodakan* (camera-induced pyrotechnic demonstration). The flash of lights from those cameras was the order of the night. In a strange way, it evoked a feeling that 'our existence was but a brief crack of light between two eternities of darkness.'

Lionel "Buddy" Foz's son, Lyle, was present. So was Fred Millan's son, Marc, Efren Barzaga's beautiful daughter, Cindy, an American Airline stewardess, flown in from Florida. Conrado Doce was at his daughter's wedding that evening, but with Roger Acosta around, he was able to join us later that night.

Furthermore, Pat Avila, a successful surgeon from Oklahoma, not only could belt a song *ala* Engelbert Humperdinck, but could also entertain one and all. "I'm poor, but I go in style," Pat joked. He was in the process of building a mansion in San Juan, Batangas, and the blueprint of the Moorish architectural design was something to behold. He promised to take care of me if I were to fly out there for vacation upon its completion. "Ot" De Leon still jogged every morning. Listen to Ot's barber. I was the barber when we were training at Edgewater Hospital, Chicago, Illinois. Amado "Jobo" Chanco still sported "white-white" hair. Bert Barreto was in excellent condition. Fred Lim looked very prosperous. Roger Acosta was fighting the allergies. The triumvirate of Vic Asanza, Buddy Foz and "Ming" Buzon were the same nice guys as ever. Marianito Chua played host to a sumptuous lunch at a Chinese restaurant. Lydia Aquino came solo because her husband, Rene, was in Manila. From Chicago, Luming Holgado Daza and Letty Subido Dacanay drove in their Carrera. As always, Ulysses and Fe Baje were present with their cameras. Everyone in attendance appeared to be in good health. Farida Chua commented she was retiring in two years. We missed the words of wisdom from "Mommy" Baldemor on the topic of retirement. She had indeed convinced me to change tires instead.

During this convention, two of the Class '61 members were elected to higher positions in the Alumni Foundation. Philip Chua was elected president and yours truly as one of the vice presidents.

In the midst of the increasing barrage of information regarding managed care, capitation, market focus, competition, buy-outs, and mergers of practices, the United Class '61 nonetheless took it all in stride and style. We came to this reunion to savor fond memories to have fun, for at this stage in our lives, we could not predict the Almighty's will. Those who did not make it were sorely missed.

During the years following our Class 61's 35thanniversary, my wife and I never missed the annual conventions and reunions in Manila. They were interspersed with medical missions to the Philippines. It was also during these times that I seriously planned for my early retirement. I had prepared for it and wrote articles relating to the right time to retire. Finally, in September 1998, I officially announced my retirement from my practice.

RUBY – 40th ANNIVERSARY CLASS '61 JULY 2001

Dateline, August 2001

UNITED CLASS OF '61 was there to MAMBO! It was our 40th (Ruby) jubilee. This time it was celebrated during the 22nd annual reunion and scientific convention held at the Monte Carlo Resort and Casino in Las Vegas, Nevada. This is a city of neon lights blazing around the clock, a metropolis that looks like an exotic jewel dropped into the middle of the vast Mojave Desert and where an estimated 4,000 people relocate every month.

The event took place on July 18-20, 2001. The summer heat in Vegas, with the temperature outside registering more than 100 degrees, did not matter much to the attendees of the reunion. Gambling was brisk and entertainment shows were aplenty. The host and local alumni chapter made good on their promise of fun and festivities and superb CME program. Altogether, we had a successful reunion of friends, classmates and families.

Some thirty-one members of the class came from all over the U.S. In our formal attires, deep red cummerbunds with red bow ties for the males and black long gowns for the female jubilations, the members, and spouses of United Class '61 were honored.

Ruby was beautiful and fantastically memorable! Oh yes, for the first time in forty long years, Ruby (no pun intended) Cureg was there too. Time went by so fast. *Nako ang bilis.* Obviously, we had been somewhat out of touch, but in this occasion we showed in our hearts our deep, true, unseen friendship and brotherhood that stayed forever green. We could see the yearning to see one another were never-ending within United Class '61 under the leadership of Philip Chua. He was our class president for life? Yes of course, we loved king Philip and Queen Farid.

From the very first day of the festivities, with a welcome reception motif of "Viva Las Vegas," it was evident that the reunion was to be more than nostalgia of our school days at Morayta. There was joviality, camaraderie, relaxation and fellowship and above all, deepened friendships. The Alumni Filipina night showcased impromptu but outstanding performances by Remedies Diasen-Sonson in a hula-hula solo dance and this writer serenaded his wife Cely with Ruben Tagalog's romantic kundiman, *"Ang Puso Ko"* (My Heart).

Lily Naguit and Abraham Sim were our dance instructors (DI). A Mambo #5 dance presentation was our number at the Grand Ball. It was a 2-minute salvo of distinctive hip movements plus the forward and backward footsteps- a dance that originated in Cuba. Mind you, we had been practicing this dance since July 2000 at our Bloomingdale, Illinois reunion. Then through cyberspace, Lily emailed the dance steps, and we finally practiced the dance as a group three hours a day for three consecutive days before the presentation. Practicing Mambo #5 in earnest at long hours was overkill, and it was never really perfected. Nevertheless, at the grand presentation, we turned out to be a colorful bunch, a magical production featuring dancers in a Copacabana-style of made-to-order costumes.

This reunion was as joyful as our previous reunion. We had our class luncheon meeting in the Market Place at the Monte Carlo. The planned cruise was resurrected. This time everybody was excited. It would be a cruise to Alaska either before or immediately after our July reunion in San Francisco the following year. We got everybody's email addresses, and King Philip was to use this medium whenever a decree was made. The United class '61 members had to obey it; otherwise, they would get beheaded. This was indeed super leadership. Seriously speaking, United Class '61 was vibrant as ever. Historically, we have many qualities. Our classmate, Vic Virzoza, topped the medical board examination; our class received eight out of the ten top places that year. We were the first to produce an alumnus who became the director of the FEU hospital, Lelia Pagtakhan Luna and we were always first in school spirit and participation. We topped the number of attendees in any jubilarian celebration and did so after forty years from graduation.

The grand finale was our recognition night - a repeat of the Coral reunion in Bloomington, Minnesota, where the Class '61 spirit was high and well in the hearts of its members. The flash of lights from our cameras was the order of the night. Then came the presentation of the jubilarians. We observed a minute of silence in honor of our departed classmates, about a dozen of them. The latest one was my very good friend Gerry Delfin. Thank God, all of us in attendance appeared to be in good health.

We danced the rest of the evening. We watched Zaida walk her walk at the Fashion Show of the convention and definitely, she did not appear the least bit nervous. Similarly, Candy Barzaga, daughter of Ephraim, Cely, Glicey and Estrella Tupaz were remarkably outstanding. Yours truly was part emcee of the program. All models were exquisitely beautiful, and I cautioned to the audience by saying, "Beautiful women are paradise to the eyes, hell to the soul, and purgatory to the purse." Those gowns were expensive. I could not afford any, especially now that I am retired.

I noticed Pat Avila was quiet and gentle. I loved it when we were jovial and festive in the reunion. That was what a jubilee is all about, to be giocoso and gleeful, is it not? He was not the Engelbert Humperdinck that I once knew. What a downer.

Pat, I am only kidding.

After the Grand Ball that evening, some of us stayed behind and sang our hearts out along with the band. Sam, Ted, Efren, Roger and I drank wine down to their dregs. No doubt the wine deepened our friendship, heart and soul. Guys, you are my friends. That was one of the most wonderful evenings in my whole life.

Together with Dick Chiu, we exchanged *dyoks na pang Pinoy lamang* (Filipino jokes), sometimes off-colored and with greener coverage. I wished Baby de Leon were present then. By the way, she usually didn't appreciate our punch lines. As a matter of fact, King Philip injected a joke in his masterful delivery at the 6th annual Dr.

Nicanor Reyes Jr. Memorial Lecture. His punch line was, "That was a hard one." Lovely.

We missed those classmates that attended the 40th wedding anniversary of Jobo and Ruby Chanco.

Those of us in the retirement circle are all at peace. To those of you still in practice part time or full time, don't change your 'tires' if you still enjoy working.

It was at this time that the United Class '61 had a lunch meeting at the posh residence of Philip and Farida to finalize the preparation for our 45th jubilee the following year. We considered many things for a big show. It was going to be epic.

SAPPHIRE 45th ANNIVERSARY JULY 5-9, 2006
UNITED '61 DANCE KIT A HIT

Dateline, August 2006

THE VENUE OF the 27th Annual Reunion-Convention of the FEU-DNR School of Medicine Alumni Foundation was Houston, Texas, known affectionately by its citizens as the "Bayou City." It is located in the southeast Texas coast of the Gulf of Mexico. Founded by the Allen brothers in 1836, Houston boasts of its interesting and extensive history, even serving as the temporary capital of the Republic of Texas after the war of Independence from Mexico. Today, Houston covers over 540 square miles and is the fourth largest city in the United States of America. Over 2 million people and 100 ethnic groups call the city home, spreading their unique heritage and influence out in every direction. It is a city of rich diversity. The residents speak more than ninety languages, which is what makes it a global city.

Held at the Westin Oak Hotel, the alumni reunion-convention was on July 5-9, 2006, our Sapphire anniversary. Ushering it was a reception dinner followed by the Scientific Seminar, a Filipiniana Night (where the United Class '61 presented its Hawaiian Dance-Skit), and concluding with a grand ball. The Silver and Sapphire Jubilarians were honored and decorated with a medal necklace for their respective year by Mrs. Josephine C. Reyes, chairman of the board of the FEU-NRMF (Philippines), assisted by Rolly Casis, outgoing alumni chairman, and Arsenio Martin, outgoing alumni president. The host and local alumni chapter made good their promise of fun and festivities, as it was a superb CME program and altogether a successful reunion of friends, classmates and their families.

Our United class of '61, the Sapphire (45th year) Jubilarians, had the greatest number of alumni attending. We are, indeed, the United Class of '61.

This year, there were twenty of us from all over the United States, with two of them flying halfway around the world, from the Philippines, to join our reunion. Together with the spouses, there were about forty of us. About half were now retired, but we were all looking good, strong and robust. The men are balding and have potbellies, the women a bit older but nonetheless still sexy.

During the grand ball we were in our formal attire similar to the previous Ruby Jubilee except for the change of color, deep blue cummerbunds and blue bowties for the males and sapphire blue long gowns for the females. Our Sapphire jubilee was indeed beautiful and fantastically memorable!

Our Sapphire Jubilee rekindled once again our friendships and camaraderie from deep in our hearts. This love we have for each other will stay forever green in our group. The yearning to see one another is never-ending in this United Class '61, with the leadership of Philip Chua and the sincere intimacy of our loyal members.

The Alumni Filipiniana Night showcased the FEU version of the "Academy Award-winning presentation" of the "Sapphire Jubilarians, who presented a Hawaiian dance-skit on July 7th. The tireless and talented couple, Abe and Lily Sim, choreographed the skit, and all the members of United Class '61 participated. The male members were topless and wore only a crown made of green leaves, grass skirt, beaded necklace and anklets. Philip narrated the story before the dance behind the scene:

"Once upon a time, in a tiny remote and secluded island in Hawaii, untouched by civilization, there lived a mighty king by the name of King Candarloko, who was very sad and depressed about his inability to father a son, a successor to the throne. His eight wives failed to give him a son. One day at dawn, he had a dream. In his dream, from out of the blue, he met a beautiful woman who bore him a son. His dream was so vivid, so real, he became so obsessed in finding this fertile maiden, but no one knew who or where she was. He believed that the gods would bless him, and find this fertile wife for him, if he made a special offering to them by the 7th sunset of the 7th moon. He then summoned his best chieftains and their wives from the various regions in the island to perform an ancient religious dance ritual to please the gods. After the offering, like in his dream, the future mother of his son would suddenly appear from nowhere, and dance her way to his heart."

I played King Candarloko. I was in my throne while my chieftains and their wives swayed to the rhythm of the famous music from the cartoon movie "Lilo and Stitch" as they performed the fertility dance to the gods. The women wore a long Hawaiian MuMu, a necklace and bracelet with large beads; the men were topless and wearing authentic grass skirts, necklace and anklets, exposing their potbellies. Notwithstanding arthritis, all of us danced with grace (albeit out of sequence sometimes) and gusto. The dance skit was met with a standing ovation, and paparazzi from various classes swarmed our class as we posed for a posterity souvenir shot.

Philip had coined my new name, King Candarloko, with his subjects of *lokos* and *lokas* (crazy men and women). As he had stated in a post reunion email to all of us, "Our ability as a class to make fun of ourselves make fools of ourselves when the right occasion comes, signifies our zest for life and our love to enjoy it. We are all game and good sports, even willing to dance practically naked in the name of friendship and fun and to entertain...all these qualities make united class '61 what it has been in our life and career and during our reunions."

Our Hawaiian dance-skit was only a five-minute presentation. We had three rehearsal sessions. Lilia attended the last one and did well. Absolutely amazing, at the grand presentation, we turned out to be a colorful bunch, a magical production turning into a big hit. As the story went, King Candarloko finally got his wish when a beautiful maiden (played by Remy D of Hawaii) came out from nowhere and made the king happy, and they walked down towards the sunset with his tribe and lived happily ever after.

GOLDEN 50th ANNIVERSARY JUNE 15-18, 2011 CLASS '61

Dateline, August 2011

THE GOLDEN JUBILEE of class '61 of the Far Eastern University-Dr. Nicanor Reyes Medical Alumni Foundation (FEUDNRS-MAF) was by far the ultimate celebration ever for our batch of successful medical doctors who migrated from the Philippines in search for the proverbial greener pastures. The good news is, most of us are still engaged in successful practices, while others are in gainful employment in various hospitals and medical centers. The majority, however, had retired and is now living comfortably in the United States and elsewhere.

And just like any historic occasion of this magnitude, 50 years of memories which started on the first day at the medical school continues to this day as great efforts and time were expended by the committee headed by our Class '61 president Dr. Chua to ensure the success of the four-day event.

As is common in any Class Reunion, old memories were re-lived, friendship were re-kindled, new ones were forged, and new memories were made. Indeed, this reunion will always be remembered as the most pleasing, wholesome and fabulous episode of our lives. It was nostalgic. It was the best of times.

Forty-six Golden Jubilarians, jetting in from all over the United States and the Philippines, showed up along with their respective spouses – the largest attendance ever since the FEUDNRS Medical Alumni foundation was founded 32 years ago. I will list those that were present. Ephraim B. Barzaga, Minerva Bruno-Racela, Amada G. Chanco, Jr., Elsa Cura, Remy Diasen –Sonson, Graciano Dichoso, Godofredo Lim, Ernesto Madarang, Rodolfo de Ocera, Zaida Padua- de Ocera, Leona Raymundo-Calderon, Emma Reyes-Carbonel Herminia Salvador, Nardo T. San Diego, Isabel Uy-Chiu. However, to highlight a few not listed above, the Board topnotch of our class Vic Virzosa displayed a grandfatherly physique, illustrious man, which surprised everyone and I. Virgilio Dumadag was all smile, Pat Avila, vociferous full of anecdotal wisdom, Prospero Jim Sendaydiego, (I call him Senday) the tallest and loudest of all can never be forgotten. Lydia Aquino and hubby Rene came from Bicol, Manuel Catalan and his lovely wife Amelia (Pally) Levardo Catalan from Carmona Cavite. Manolo was a former Vice Mayor, then Mayor of Carmona and finally a provincial board member in the province of Cavite. He could have been a governor and who knows, President of the Philippines. Bernardo T. Mora Jr., from Surigao City, former member of the board of directors of the PMA in the Philippines, a senior government health official, Consultant on Agriculture Sector, President Family Planning Organization of the Philippines was present. Lilia Pagtakhan Luna, from Manila, our former Medical Director of the FEU Hospital was always present in the past reunions and still looks beautiful. Ruby Cureg, (pardon me) I did not recognize you since you attended the Ruby Jubilarian. It was likely due to my 'dementiating' memory cells. Zeny Espino-Ostman was one classmate I could never forget. When we were in our internship at FEU hospital, she unremittingly wore a *contodo-plantsado* white uniform. No, I cannot recognize her now. She is as attractive as before. Bimbo Ceniza is still a heavyset man. The troika (Russian word- 3 horses pulling a cart), Ming Bozon, Vic Azansa and "Buddy" Foz were the same old horses, and in the cart ridden by Rose, Lucy and Inday Nora. 'Ot' de Leon, my client in my barbershop at Edgewater Hospital, Chicago, Illinois and spouse Rosemarie are tightly inseparable ever since we were in Medical school. Abraham Baccara and his attractive wife Zeny came for the second time. Letty Subido-Dacanay gave me a hug. Uley Baje, you are an avid photographer. Ted Teodoro remained young-looking as ever. Bert Baretto, Manuel Ramos, Emil Quilala, *kilala ko pa rin.* We missed those that were unable to attend.

Credit rightfully belongs to Class'61 president Dr. Chua, who left no stone unturned to secure the success of the event, with the help of various committee chairs. Once more, the venerable and inspiring Dr. Chua showed his enduring leadership as everyone agreed that the recently held 50th anniversary celebration was the most significant, and the grandest ever. Everyone went home with a happy heart and more memories to look back in years to come.

THE EVENTS

The welcome night: From the very first day of the festivities, beginning with a welcome reception motif of "Viva Las Vegas," it was evident the reunion was again more than nostalgia of our school days at Morayta. There were shows and entertainments. A professional singer of Las Vegas demonstrated – Elvis Presley look-alike, with the antics, singing modulations and bodily movements no different from the real Elvis. Yes, Elvis is still alive. Exhibitions of two showgirls, tall six-footer blond beauties, were attractions of burlesque-like sensations in the alumni of men. What we found significant was our Las Vegas style of attire in the ambiance of Viva Las Vegas. Prospero (I fondly call him Senday) Sendaydiego did a beautiful invocation, a master of prayers in all native lingo.

The grippingly nostalgic moments from the old days continued.

I was in my black suit wearing a hat, entertaining the alumni as a one-man-band in my keyboard synthesizer - dance music in the rhythm of cha-cha, bolero, rumba, and big band. Thereafter, the hotel manager approached me. He asked for my business card and wished to hire me as a one-man band for special occasions at the hotel. He was surprised when I told him I am a doctor and would do it for free (only kidding). Seriously, not to toot my own whistle, I can play this electrical musical instrument ensuring a talent no one can imagine--my performance repertoire.

Thursday, June 16: Three Class '61 members were participants on the first day of the CME program. At 8:00 o'clock that morning, Philip S. Chua was the moderator. I delivered my lecture and then followed Lily Naguit-Sim. My lecture touched some hearts of listeners about our country, the Philippines, reminiscing a story of how we all migrated to this land of Milk and Honey. Not only have we enjoyed the blessings of freedom, opportunities, and prosperity not available in our beloved homeland, but we were also blessed with an American Dream.

The first schedule of rehearsal of our 'dance troupe presentation' was planned on this day after our joint-lunch at a Filipino *Kapit Bahay* restaurant in the Strip. We walked our way from the hotel to the restaurant under the hot sunrays of Las Vegas, the temperature in the high 90s.

We were a happy bunch of humans renovated into young vibrant students of Morayta. One could imagine we were like the boys and girls in the far distant past at the FEU campus.

At 1:30 pm our rehearsal began. The producer and choreographer presented a complicated variety of marching, dancing, positioning, along with hip and hand movements from tribal styles to the current modern free-style dancing. Every five minutes the choreography changes. Philip ran around dictating tempos, timing, and the firing of cannons between two tribal warriors. It was a skirmish. He became a combination of a director, a choreographer/producer, and everything else, King Philip, the dictator... (*kidding lamang*). Everyone was obedient, serious, (afraid to be beheaded if you do not heed) and excited. Can you imagine professors, directors, hospital department chiefs, corporate presidents, Fellow Emeritus, and diplomates spontaneously acting like medical students of yore?

Pally and Lilia were interested in perfecting the precise movement of body and soul. First, the musical background was dull. I missed my meeting in the board of trustees due to the engrossing practice session. We were seemingly ridiculous, crazy and yet serious, obedient and calm followers. We expressed our intensity in our rehearsal in order to become Academy Award fame, another hit presentation.

The Filipinana Night: Friday Friday June 17, 2011. I was the MC with Dr. Ben Reyes '70 as my co-MC. For the Class '61 it was an evening of attractive Filipina doctors and their friends, spouses, and good-looking Filipino doctors in their seventies, with their balding heads, potbellies and knee weaknesses. The Kundiman, bolero, cha-cha music in the synthesizer I was playing, welcomed the alumni in their entrance to the ballroom; the Bohol Song Bird Band followed.

Yes, it was indeed Philippines. Barong Tagalog, Philippine Terno, Kimona with modern long gowns were the attires of the night. It was a nationalistic fervor. Cameras' flahes all over resembled pyrotechnics. Somehow, a strange feeling of the questionable last hurrah of our lives, our friendship, the fond memories, our camaraderie radiating from all these burst of lights that seemed to place us into the horizon of the moonlight. Were these examples of afterglows in the sunset of our lives?

Amelia (Pally) Levardo-Catalan sung *Saan Ka Man* with accompaniment in the piano by her husband Manuel Catalan. I introduced her the Doris Day of United Class '61, as she enthralled the audience with her magnetic performance, incredible voice, and beauty that was something to behold. Conrado Doce (Ado), the professor and a charismatic performer, sung his hearts out for a number of Kundiman songs. I belted one Ruben Tagalog song and someone described as a compelling voice - my contemporary approach to the Kundiman song. Dance, dance, dance 'til midnight showing off our terpsichorean prowess on the floor.

THE GRAND FINALE : The grand finale of the four-day event was a Dinner-and–Ball with the Golden Jubilarians Class '61 and the Silver Jubilarian Class '68 as honorees. It started with the male members stepping into the grand ballroom in their best tuxedoes with gold bowties and cummerbunds, while the women, not to be outshined, sashayed in long black gown highlighted by golden sash. One of the momentous highlights of the night was the distribution of commemorative medallions by no less than the late Mrs. Josephine Reyes, chairman of the FEU-NRMF Board of Trustees. FEUDNRS Medical School Dean Remedios Habacon, FEU-DNRSMAF chair Dr. Pepito Rivera, and FEU-DNRSMAF president Oscar Tuazon assisted her. Photos for posterity were taken in abundance.

Then the much awaited Golden Jubilee presentation began.

With all the preparation and rehearsals tightly kept from other alumni, the audience was in for a huge surprise. Where the United Class '61 "Hawaiian-motif presentation during the Sapphire

Anniversary in 20005 in Houston, Texas, was considered an Academy Award-winning presentation by most.

The special presentation delves on a bit of Philippine history. Legends has it that "On April 7, 1521, Portuguese explorer Ferdinand Magellan landed in Cebu. He was welcomed by Rajah Humabon, the King of Cebu, who together with his wife and about 700 native islanders, were converted into Catholicism on April 14,1521. Magellan, however, was killed by King Lapu-Lpu in the battle of Mactan, barely 20 days after the Portuguese set foot on Mactan."

However, the United Class '61 presentation actually trekked back to 50 years before the arrival of Ferdinand Magellan, where the two warring tribes dominated the southern Philippines. After Magellan landed, the Spanish friar (priest) convinced the two chiefs of the tribes to stop their fighting and unite. From these unified tribes was born a King, later to be known as Lapu-Lapu.

Participants who hastily changed from their formal attire to G-strings (*bahag*) for men, and *tapis* for women, wearing black tights, wigs, bracelets, necklaces, earings, leg trinkets, and whatever native accessories there were during those days, made dramatic entry in a darkened ballroom to the tune of staccato music and native sounds of the clanging cymbals and drums.

Led by Dr. Bernie Mora holding a Santo Nino, I followed him in friar's frock, and with my right and left hand movements of priestly blessings and **Signum Crucis**. Philip Chua and Abraham Sim acted as leaders of the warring tribes.

After performing the tribal war dances, I delivered a sermon for peace in Latin, Spanish, Visaya, Tagalog and Ilocano (which no one, including myself, understood) much to the delight of the audience.

Consequently, both members of the tribes laid down their Hawaiian torches, spears and daggers at the center of the ballroom, and everything ended with a resounding pronouncement from the priest, *"Mabuhay! Puri-in natin ang* United Class '61.

In our final special Tribal presentation lasting for about fifteen minutes, it was a hit, a trademark of an Oscar - it was a big show, an epic. The Class '61 presented a colorful full-costume tribal dance received a lot of applause and praises, a fitting electrifying conclusion of the reunion.

MOST OUSTANDING ALUMNUS OF 2011 + CLASS '61 PRESIDENTIAL AWARD

Our performance occupies a special place in our hearts. Written in Global Balita, Las Vegas Newspaper stated, "The highlight of the night belonged to Cesar D. Candari, M.D., FCAP Emeritus, who was honored with not one, but two exceptional awards: Most Outstanding Alumnus of 2011 from the FEUDNRSMAF, and the Dr. Philip S. Chua Class '61 Presidential Award. Also received the Presidential Award went to Dr. Lilia Pagtakhan-Luna, formerly Medical Director of FEU Hospital.

What a pleasant surprise for me, it was an honor to be chosen as an MOA. In receiving the award plaque, I said, "With all humility, I thank you all who supported me and I share my award with my dear wife. Without her, I would not have been where I am now..." My last seven words that I stated in receiving this award were, "I love my wife Cely very much." An applause was loud with a request heard distinctly, "Kiss! Kiss! And she did. The former Chairman of the Board, Dr. Arsenio Martin, was the very first person that expressed his sincere desire for choosing me as a recipient of year 2011 FEU alumnus awardee. His word is trustworthy. With all humbleness, I wish to thank him for his kind heart, his trust, loyal friendship, respect, and a man who has dignity and grace, a paragon physician.

In my presidential award, I took this opportunity to thank Dr. Philip S. Chua whom I praised as our president of United class '61 for half a century. I stated, "This great award is an unexpected and a surprise for me as a member of class '61. I'm very pleased and honored. I was living in the shadows during my medical school days. Somehow, things changed when I journeyed into the path of the American Dream."

Beyond these, there were joviality, camaraderie, relaxation and fellowship and, above all, deepened friendships between the FEU Alumni. It seems like only yesterday. Memories are the threads that hold together the patchwork of friendship. The 50th Jubilee Reunion was an excellent time to be reconnected with former classmates and friends, shared the fond memories of college days, and celebrated this once in a lifetime occasion.

CHAPTER THIRTEEN

READY TO RETIRE?

The trouble with retirement is that you never get a day off.

- ABE LEMONS

RETIREMENT ON TRACK?

Dateline, January 2012

THIS POSTING WILL mostly talk about the retirement of practicing doctors in America. The Filipino-American physicians are my primary interest on how they can prepare to retire early. I have written articles about early retirement that was published in the APPA quarterly magazine back in 1988 and 1989. These dates were about ten years before I decided to retire. Regardless of the time that I wrote my articles, it is still informative and worth considering in your plans for early retirement. Therefore, I spent about a decade to plan my early retirement, as it was my dream. Excerpted from my previous articles are in this chapter.

I retired in September 1998 at age sixty-five. I worked part time for two additional years. My two associates also retired ahead of me at the same age.

There were three retirement parties, one from the Hospital Medical Staff, secondly from San Diego Pathologist Medical Group Inc. and the third from Scripps Mercy Hospital Surgical Tumor Board done in separate dates. It was a tribute to honor me as I began my retirement. Indeed, I was extremely happy and felt honored by these displays of friendship and expression of goodwill.

With all the pressures in medicine these days, many doctors find themselves thinking about early retirement. While most just dream about it, many actually achieve it, often long before they're sixty-five. Unfortunately, many retirees haven't saved enough, or planned carefully enough, to finance their dream. For many of them, the stock market's recent decline has made their plans obsolete. It is therefore imperative that early planning is a necessity.

IS EARLY RETIREMENT FOR YOU? When does one start making retirement plans? A writer from Medical Economics stated: it is, "at the prime of life, the pinnacle of middle age. Middle age occurs at the end of rearing children. It occurs for a workingman before he reaches his level of incompetence. It occurs when the worker is still in power-making decisions." Some say retirement means when not having to say, "I owe". Indeed when the retirement funds have reached the mark you planned and the debt service obligations are gone, then you are working from the right blueprint. Physicians who have availed themselves of the tax deferred retirement plans as early as 20 years ago, particularly taking advantage of the Define Benefit Plan, could have easily accumulated enough in pension assets. If that describes you, it is certain that you have already reached your goal and you can retire anytime you want to. The typical young doctor in his 30s or 40s will still have ample time to catch on and for sure will have reasonable pension account before age 65.

In this year 2012, are times of economic uncertainty; especially the financial crisis brings a sad story to millions of people in this country. There is inflation, recession, and energy crisis, foreclosures of homes, home equity destroyed, company pension plans across America are woefully underfunded, 401ks are devastated when the stock market nose dive and planning for tomorrow is an extremely tricky business. The shrinking dollar is the number one problem facing anyone trying to guarantee himself a comfortable retirement in this country. The sad truth is that the vast majority of Baby Boomers have not adequately saved for retirement. For many, their home equity was destroyed by the recent financial crisis. The federal government has already begun to pay out more in Social Security benefits than they are taking in, and the years ahead look downright apocalyptic for the Social Security program.

Would you believe that 10,000 Americans retire everyday? It is stated that this is going to keep happening every single day for the next 19 years. It involves the baby boomers that turned 65 years old last January 2011. Sad to say, they are not happy with their retirement life.

For the Filipino Americans there is a different situation. There is an alternative to a "better life," and it should not be difficult for most Filipino professionals who worked similar length of time as the baby boomers. That alternative is retirement in the Philippines. The biggest allure that living in the Philippines can offer is money value. For one thing, the cost-of-living in the Philippines is advantageous for someone earning a pension in U.S. dollars; living in luxury on a small budget is easy. This is the reason why for many Filipino immigrants, the option to retire in the Philippines has become a serious consideration. Simple math answers many questions.

Earlier in 2010, it was a poll by Investor's Business Daily (IBD) and TechnoMetrica Market Intelligence (TIPP) that four of nine doctors, or 45%, said they "would consider leaving their practice or taking an early retirement" if Congress passes the plan the Democratic majority and White House have in mind. Finally, the Obamacare was approved. More than 800,000 doctors were practicing in 2006, the government says. Projecting the poll's finding onto that population, 360,000 doctors would consider quitting.

The Filipino-American doctors might be a part of this 360,000 considering quitting or retiring early.

While you are both still in the prime of life, you look forward to this momentous milestone, your retirement, as the next adventure in your lives to pursue the finer aspects of life, family and community as you put the troubles and pressures of the medical profession behind you. Now, you are getting older. Financially, you are likely ready and prepared to enjoy your dream for the rest of your life because you have that ace you will ever need to get the best things that money can buy.

After devoting so many years of your life in working, you will soon be able to devote more of your time to the interest, which you enjoy including service to the Philippine community and ongoing medical missions for the poor in the Philippines and around the world. Although you will be retired from your work, you will not be retired from the good things in life. 60-year olds like you don't trade in your health for wealth anymore because your money may not be able to buy your health. A Chinese advice – "Spend the money that should be spent, enjoy what should be enjoyed, donate what you are able to donate, but don't leave all to your children or grandchildren, for you don't want them to become 'parasites'."

Try to calculate what you need during retirement and do it right now. That figure is like a destination on a map, giving you direction as you save, invest and create your overall financial plan. You must have started making retirement plans at the prime of life, the pinnacle of middle age. Find the right pension plan, even if you have to fund it yourself.

The children are all grown and have graduated from college. You have sold your big house and moved to a smaller one like a condominium. Besides having the pension nest egg, the sale of your practice and other real estate assets can be another source of income. The sale of your home will probably produce a large chunk of money, including a large capital gain. The law allows you to exclude the first $500,000 of capital gains from tax, provided that you are fifty-five and have lived in the house for at least five years. The cash generated can possibly let you buy a home in one of the exclusive places in or around Manila. As an alternative, put the money in the bank and rent a vacation home in Manila with caution: rents are astronomically expensive in these fashionable places. You will have a home, fully furnished, a spectacular place of incomparable luxury. It will have all the amenities you can think of at your disposal. All of these at a cost you can easily afford.

Many have said they will never retire; nonetheless, the stress of work, Medicare and malpractice threats will eventually make them realize that enough is enough. Consequently, you should prepare for retirement. In addition to having a retirement timetable, you must also know where to spend it enjoyably.

A good number of doctors are afraid to retire at an earlier age because they think they will have nothing to do. They are worried of boredom; friends have told them that they will go crazy and die early. For as long as the pension pay is adequate, and they do not have to face a lot of adjustments, things will go smoothly. The question is when will they enjoy that money?

Have you planned what you will do when you retire? To some it is a dreadful situation to ponder; however, to others, they could not wait and are eagerly looking forward to it.

Have you thought of spending your retirement time in Manila, Philippines? Here is one retirement plan that you might consider. Do you realize that Manila speaks the merriest version of things that it can offer to individuals with reasonable retirement income? Think of the things you have been putting off for 20-30 years of working: golf, tennis, travel, fishing, and comfortable living.

The recreational and cultural amenities and outlets for your personal interests are all there. At your disposal, you will have a butler, house help, a gardener, and a driver all of these at a cost you can easily afford. Therefore, realistically at an earlier age, you can retire and enjoy it all. For one thing, you are at the prime of your life, as you are active and functioning both mentally and physically. Not only will you accomplish your wishes and desire to help your countrymen, but also you will have emotionally satisfying and very comfortable living conditions. This is not to say that you will retire for good in the Philippines.

The sentiments to go back home for Filipino Americans as they age are varied. At the point of retirement, a notable percentage of Filipino Americans return back to the Philippines. There is no doubt, like everything in life, there are pros and cons and retiring in the

Philippines is no different. It's far more complicated. According to the Filipino American Senior Health Assessment, a longitudinal study conducted by the Filipino American Community Health Initiative of Chicago, half of 35 immigrant seniors surveyed between 2008 and 2010 still plan to return to the Philippines, The other half don't, and a handful aren't sure. Reality check: "They want to return to their home country to derive maximum benefits from savings," says Leo Herrera-Lim, Consulate General for the Philippines.

A drawback: "The problem in going back to the Philippines is that when you get sick, you spend your own money. I prefer to stay in the United States because of health coverage," A friend says. "It's good that when my husband got sick this year, we were here in the United States. We have money from retirement, pensions, social security and health insurance." These problems echo those shared by other Filipino Americans.

Therefore, with my opinion of going home and enjoy your retirement, consider the following points to ponder:
- You and your spouse must be in good health.
- Are you welling to leave your children and grandchildren in the U.S?
- Those that came back to the US said relatives constantly having their hands out?
- Infrastructure problems, traffic, brownouts, outdoor humidity, and lots of rainy days. Public utilities like electricity and water, telephone, Internet and mobile phone Ipod reception and access and not to mention the postal service, things that you are not used to.

Here is an option: On a programmed basis, stay in the Philippines for a certain period of time and at anytime you are back to your condo in America. A popular slogan now is, "It's more fun in the Philippines."

MORE REASONS FOR DOCTORS TO RETIRE EARLY

Dateline, February 18, 2012

THIS YEAR 2012, a recent article in CnnMoney, published in New York stated: "Doctors in America are harboring an embarrassing secret: Many of them are going broke. With the recent steep 35% to 40% cuts in Medicare reimbursements for key cardiovascular services, such as stress tests and echocardiograms, have taken a substantial toll on revenue.

This quiet reality, which is spreading nationwide, is claiming a wide range of casualties, including family physicians, cardiologists and oncologists." Currently, a 27.4% Medicare pay cut for doctors started on March 1, 2012. This means primary care doctors particularly the Family practice and Internist is predestined. It is hopeless. Physicians will plummet to the bottom of doom.

Doctors cannot survive this cut due to the flawed estimated Sustainable Growth Rate (SGR) of Medicare. By 2014, 30 million people without insurance will be covered by the ObamaCare. Physician's services fee will undoubtedly be reduced. The impact to seniors in regards to their premium insurance are as follows:

"The per person Medicare insurance premium will increase from the present monthly fee of $96.40, rising to: $104.20 in 2012; $120.20 in 2013 and $247.00 in 2014." This is in ObamaCare Legislation.

Beau Donegan, senior executive with a hospital cancer center in Newport Beach, California, is well aware of physicians' financial woes."Many are too proud to admit that they are on the verge of bankruptcy," she said. "These physicians see no way out of the downward spiral of reimbursement, escalating costs of treating patients and insurance companies deciding when and how much they will pay them."

As the practice of medicine in this country becomes less and less exciting, less satisfying, and more non-rewarding, you will realize that it isn't fun anymore. Nearly one-in-three primary care physicians limit the number of Medicare patients they are able to see. It is a fact that $500 billion were cut from Medicare since 2010.

The crux of the matter is the need to resist this intolerant and regressive progressive liberal arrogance and its assumption of superiority on the rate-setting formula that has transformed into a budget-busting juggernaut that will hit doctors with a lower pay cut for their Medicare patients. We must address the whole health care delivery system, a system of coordinated care, and eliminate cost shifting that results from treating the uninsured. The disturbing problem is insurance industry will fight anything that threatens their profit. If the 30 million people can choose not to be insured and a mandate that providers treat them, which will undoubtedly push the costs onto the rest of us. Repeal of the ObamaCare might result changes - comprehensive resolution of the federal healthcare plan.

You might ask why I am not in the Philippines after my retirement when in fact I was recommending it in my early writings. Well, I followed all the plans I had mentioned above.

In year 2000, I added two master bedrooms suite in our home in my hometown and furnished it with full amenities you can imagine. During its construction I have to go home every three months to watch the progress of the architect who designed it for me. My need for security in our house is not necessary. Our home is the nearest house to the municipal building, across the Candari Street, a stone's throw away. Police guards are on duty twenty-four hours a day. The Candari compound was established ever since my grandfather was the *presidente municipal* of our town many years ago.

My wife and I went home for a short vacation in 2001. On our second trip in April 2002, my youngest daughter Arleen came with us, which coincided with the town fiesta. It was an enjoyable vacation, and my daughter participated in several water sports events at the pristine Pandan Bay seashore.

The Philippines no question, is beautiful, each island will mesmerize you. The beauty of the Philippines is infinite. It's a nice place to retire.

The 7100+ Islands in the archipelago is something to behold. The land surface is 115,800 square miles (300,000 square kilometers) across the warm, serene Pacific waters, a geographical landscape that we all love as Filipinos. We have displayed a Filipino Diaspora of who we are, our divine abilities to blend with all cultures, race or creed anywhere in the world. Our characters are unique, dispersed in the thousand of islands. The Philippines no question, is beautiful, each island will mesmerize you. The beauty of the Philippines is infinite.

CHAPTER FOURTEEN ★

THE ULTIMATE

Dateline, May 25, 2012

IN MY FIRST BOOK "SUCCESS IS A JOURNEY", is an autobiographical-diary of memories covering a specific period in my life up to the present time. I wrote the final word. What you have read today is the quintessence about general events in my journey and the makeup of this book – my writings for the omnibus.

My dear wife Cely has inspired my life in every instance. As my partner, she continually prayed for me and spiritually discerned all that is coming against me, and showed me those things that God's grace bestow. She helped me to stay focused in the spiritual areas of life, so that I will continually be a blessing to others and be blessed by God. She helped me fulfill my calling. A well-known proverb says, "Behind every good man is a good woman."

A brilliant quotation from William James. "These then are my last words to you. Be not afraid of life. Believe that life is worth living and your belief will help create the fact,"

Finally, we're conditioned to think that our lives revolve around great moments. But great moments often catch us unaware-beautifully wrapped in what others may consider a small one.

I've learned that people will forget what you said, people will forget what you did, but people will never forget how you made them feel.

Thelma Mantic Ramos made this statement: "Your readers will be impressed at how you have risen above the shackles of poverty in pursuit of your dream. Through your own resolve, grit, determination, and ingenuity, you have accomplished great things for yourself and for others…. recapture the many events in your life in vivid color and accuracy. The best part of it all is your finding the passion and making the time to put your life story in writing so that others will be inspired to follow their dream and seek their own niche in life."

To the growing youth of our time, there is something in you that you have to do. If you have noted the diverse subjects in this book, then all that is left to do is to do it.

MY INFIRMITIES

CHIEF OF PATHOLOGY DEPARTMENT, EL CENTRO
REGIONAL MEDICAL CENTER

Dateline, May 2012

FOUR MONTHS BEFORE the end of my second term as president of Paradise Valley Lions Club, in March 2002, I was offered a position as Chief of the Pathology Department of El Centro Regional Medical Center, in El Centro California. Of course this mean I would have to come out of retirement and head back to work. It presented more of a challenge.

El Centro Regional Medical Center is an acute-care medical center serving the healthcare needs of the Imperial Valley since 1956. It was a 107-bed hospital until a $44 million expansion let it grow to 165 beds. The expansion project allowed for a state of the art facility, including a new trauma center and rooftop heliport for superior trauma care.

In my first three months, the College of American Pathologist inspected the laboratory for accreditation under my directorship and passed without any problem. Unfortunately, I started to have double vision symptoms in my left eye.

I relinquished my position from El Centro Hospital before the end of the year. Four months later, in March 2003, I had brain surgery.

The following is my past clinical history. In 1981, I had been diagnosed with a small congenital benign epidermoid cyst in my left cerebello-pontine angle. It was discovered after I had a noise-induced hearing loss (NIHL) in my right ear due to electrical saw wood cutting machine I was using. The following CAT-Scan of my brain showed a small cyst that has nothing to do with my hearing loss to the right ear. Nothing was done and was followed closely by my neurosurgeon for more than twenty-five years. I continued to be healthy and functioned very well—a state of complete physical, mental and social well-being. After the surgery, my activities in civic, social, humanitarian, and community involvement had been curtailed. A second brain surgery was successfully performed in Las Vegas, Nevada, in April 2008 and thanks to God Almighty, I survived and recovered. Currently, I am legally blind in my left eye and my hearing is impaired.

Being blind in one eye, with bits of anxiety and depression, I continued to fight. I had to focus more on what I could do rather than on what I could not do. It is not what happens to us that matters most; it is how we respond to it.

Despite all these afflictions, I went back to be active in the FEU Medical Alumni Foundation and charitable projects in my hometown in the Philippines. I continued to write as contributor for Asian Journal San Diego, California, FEU newsletters and became a columnist for Philippine Times Las Vegas, Nevada. I still have the stamina, vigor, vitality, sanity and mental prowess to write my life story. I started writing my first book, my memoir in January 2011. This second book was recently written for publication in June 2012.

A man who strives to surpass himself and yearns for the impossible will always be equal to great challenges. That is what I am. I play that important string in life- attitude - surpassing my physical infirmities. All the time, my life has been like a dry leaf floating in the breeze. I have neither planned nor prepared anything; it's been a matter of total surrender to the Supreme One to guide me. Your life is a message in itself. Let your message be a message of hope to others.

Recently I received a forwarded email from my friend and classmate T.B. and here's what he said and I always have the same take; "In good spirit, sickness will cure; in good spirit, sickness will cure fast; in good spirit; sickness will never come. With good mood, music, suitable amount of exercise, always in the sun, variety of foods, reasonable amount of vitamin and mineral intake, hopefully you will live another 10 or 20 years of healthy life."

THE AUTHOR

CESAR D. CANDARI MD, FCAP EMERITUS is Board certified and Diplomate in Anatomic and Clinical Pathology; the first Filipino American pathologist Board certified in a sub-specialty - Immunohematology and Blood Banking. He is a Fellow of the College of American Pathologists and the American Society of Clinical Pathologists. In 1995, he became Fellow Emeritus.

Dr. Candari was Associate Pathologist of Mercy Hospital and Medical Center (now SCRIPPS MERCY) in San Diego, California for 30 years, a major teaching hospital of 500 hundred beds. He served as Medical Director of the Blood Bank and Transfusion Service. In his thirty years as partner of the San Diego Pathologist Medical Group Inc., that runs the Department of Pathology he served as Secretary and later as vice President of the corporation

Cesar was elected by the California Pathology Society as Alternate Delegate to the House of Delegates of the College of American Pathologists.

In 2002, he was Chief of the Department of Pathology, El Centro Regional Medical Center in El Centro, California. The author is past president of the Philippine Medical Association of San Diego in 1981 to 1982, and a second term in 1987 to 1989.

Dr. Candari graduated valedictorian in high school, was a well-recognized orator. He moved to the United States after graduation from the Far Eastern University Institute of Medicine, Manila Philippines in 1961. Cesar has held several major positions in the community civic Associations, medical and specialty organizations.

One outstanding position was an appointment of Dr. Candari as Field Commissioner (field examiner) of the Licensing Division of the State Medical Board of California in 1978 and stayed in this position for more than twelve years. This position involved conducting the oral and comprehensive clinical examination process to candidates applying for licensure in the State of California to both Foreign Medical Graduates and American doctors from other states.

In 1990, Dr. Candari has the distinction of being the first City Commissioner of Asian descent appointed to the Governing Board of the San Diego Stadium Authority, now known as Qualcomm Stadium with the main function of overseeing San Diego's famous athletic stadium for the San Diego Chargers His appointment was four years.

Cesar served for Congressman Jim Bates of the 44th congressional district of California from 1983–1991, a supporter of Foreign Medical Graduates (FMGs). In 1982, Cesar was appointed as his liaison for the Asian Community in San Diego and as a member of the Asian-American Advisory Committee. Dr. Candari was able to connect with Bates regarding the situation of discrimination on Foreign Medical Graduates (FMGs) that helped led to the passage of an anti-discrimination legislation signed into law in 1992- the Health Profession Reauthorization Act.

Dr. Candari was one of the three founding physicians of Operation Samahan Community Health Clinic where he volunteered his services mostly as chairman of the board for 17 years. He considers this as the highlight of his career. In 1975, the very first community service award was bestowed upon him and his two colleagues, Drs. Romeo Quini and Adelito Gale by the Association of Philippine Physicians in America.

A very good writer endowed with a pleasant disposition, Dr. Candari writes a column OPINION weekly in Philippine Times of Southern Nevada, a regular contributor for Asian Journal San Diego, California, FEU Ectopic Murmurs, FEUMAANI News and PMAC newsletter. In 1980s and 1990s, he was a contributor for Filipino Press newspaper of San Diego, California.

He authored his first book, "SUCCESS IS A JOURNEY" in 2011. He is married to the former Miss Cely M. Asprec, a pharmacist and they have 4 children and 6 grand children.